THEY CALLED HIM
THE "IRON MAN."

Standing five feet, ten inches tall and weighing 240 pounds, Craig Price pleaded guilty to mass murder. He told a Rhode Island judge that he broke into two homes in the summer of 1987 and murdered four neighbors: two adult women and two girls, ages ten and eight. The victims were beaten and brutalized—one woman was stabbed fifty-eight times.

After hearing Craig Price's plea, the judge sentenced him to the stiffest penalty allowed under Rhode Island law: incarceration for five years and seventeen days.

Craig was just seventeen days shy of his sixteenth birthday.

KIDS WHO KILL

CHARLES PATRICK EWING

AVON BOOKS ◆ NEW YORK

AVON BOOKS
A division of
The Hearst Corporation
1350 Avenue of the Americas
New York, New York 10019

Copyright © 1990 by Lexington Books
Published by arrangement with Lexington Books
Library of Congress Catalog Card Number: 90-34603
ISBN: 0-380-71525-2

The Lexington Books edition contains the following Library of Congress Cataloging in Publication Data:

Ewing, Charles Patrick, 1949–
 Kids who kill / Charles Patrick Ewing.
  p.   cm.
1. Juvenile homicide—United States.   I. Title.
HV9067.H6E954 1990
364.1'523'083—dc20   90-34603   CIP

First Avon Books Printing: July 1992

AVON TRADEMARK REG. U.S. PAT. OFF. AND IN OTHER COUNTRIES, MARCA REGISTRADA, HECHO EN U.S.A.

Printed in the U.S.A.

RA   10   9   8   7   6   5   4   3   2   1

To my Mom, Pauline Rogers Ewing,
with love and thanks.

Acknowledgments

Many people have contributed to this book, each in their own special and appreciated way. Margaret Zusky, my editor at Lexington Books, suggested that I write this book. Sharon Harris-Ewing, my wife, gave me the time to write it. Marv Gellman, my friend and advisor, encouraged me and helped me to decide to write the book. Roseann Perrin, my secretary, helped keep the book on schedule. And, as always, Elaine and Benjamin contributed by helping their Dad to remember what's really important in life. I thank them all.

Contents

1

Kids Who Kill:
An Overview

THEY CALLED HIM the "Iron Man." Standing five feet, ten inches tall and weighing 240 pounds, Craig Price pleaded guilty to mass murder. He told a Rhode Island judge that he broke into two homes in the summer of 1987 and murdered four neighbors: two adult women and two girls, ages ten and eight. The victims were beaten and stabbed— one woman was stabbed fifty-eight times. After hearing Craig Price's plea, the judge sentenced him to the stiffest sentence allowed under Rhode Island law: incarceration for five years and seventeen days.

Craig Price fell through one of the cracks in Rhode Island law. Already on probation for assault and burglary, he committed one murder when he was thirteen and three others just weeks later when he was fourteen. By the time he pleaded guilty to the four killings, Craig was just seventeen days shy of his sixteenth birthday. Under Rhode Island law, no one under the age of sixteen may be tried as an adult, even for murder, and no one tried as a juvenile may be locked up beyond his or her twenty-first birthday.

Craig Price will walk out of the Rhode Island Training

School a free man on October 11, 1994. Leaving the court-room after being sentenced, Craig seemed well aware that he had beaten the system. Greeted by a rowdy throng of his high school friends who had come to see him off, Craig told the crowd, "When I get out of here, I'm going to smoke a bomber (a marijuana cigarette)." Then, as the Training School van pulled away, he bid his friends a trite teenage goodbye: "Later."

For almost his entire life, seventeen-year-old Dale Whipple was physically, psychologically, and sexually abused by his parents. Dale often sought help from school guidance counselors but no one ever did anything to stop the abuse. Finally, Dale decided he could take no more. The Indiana youth lured his mother into the garage and hacked her to death with a rusty, double-edged ax. Dale then went back into the house and did the same to his sleeping father.

Charged with two counts of murder, Dale claimed self-defense, saying he killed his parents to protect himself from his father's increasingly severe beatings and his mother's recent sexual advances. Although the judge concluded that "fear of future physical abuse was a factor essential to these crimes," he refused to allow the jury to consider Dale's plea of self-defense.

After the jury found Dale guilty but mentally ill, the judge handed down two concurrent sentences of forty years in prison. Explaining why he made the sentences concurrent rather than consecutive, the judge said he was impressed by the evidence that Dale had, in fact, been severely abused by his parents for years. Dale Whipple must serve at least twenty years in prison before he is eligible for parole.

No one disputed the facts. Fourteen-year-old Johnny (a pseudonym) liked to load his father's .357 magnum revolver, put it to his friends' heads, and pull the trigger. One day in May 1989, Johnny decided again to play what he called "controlled Russian roulette." He loaded the revolver with five cartridges and asked several friends to play.

After taunting one playmate who was afraid to have the gun pointed at his head, Johnny turned to thirteen-year-old Gabriel and pointed the gun at him. When Gabriel seemed unafraid, Johnny told the other boys, "See, Gabriel isn't afraid." Johnny then pulled the trigger, the gun went off, and Gabriel was shot and killed.

Charged with second degree murder, Johnny was represented by a public defender who told the juvenile court judge that the killing was just "dangerous horseplay that got out of hand." The attorney went on to argue that Johnny was just showing off, trying to use the gun to make friends and become popular. The gun, he said, was a "pied piper" that brought the other boys back to Johnny's house time and time again despite their fears. Finally, the public defender argued that the killing was not murder but at most manslaughter because Johnny never intended to hurt anyone.

Not surprisingly, the district attorney saw things differently. From the prosecutor's perspective, Johnny was a bully who got a kick out of frightening his friends. He argued that the killing was cold-blooded and intentional. The judge accepted the district attorney's theory of the case and found Johnny guilty of second-degree murder.

On Christmas Day 1989, two couples were leaving the home of a relative in a drug-ridden New York City neighborhood. Suddenly a car pulled up alongside them, and one of the car's occupants sprayed the couples with machine gun fire, killing both women and seriously wounding one of the men. Police said none of the victims had any links to drug dealing. They added that in this particular neighborhood, random shootings were common, and drug gang members often shot at innocent people as a means of announcing their entry into the local drug market.

Several days later, police officers responded to a shooting call at a nearby fast-food restaurant. An eighteen-year-old youth was shot in the back. Two boys, ages seventeen and sixteen, were arrested, and police seized a machine gun from them. When ballistics tests showed that this gun was the same one used in the Christmas Day killings, both boys were charged with murder. A third youngster, age seventeen, was later charged as an accomplice to the killings. After wrapping up the investigation, police said the killings were "just random" and the victims were innocent people who "just happened to be in the wrong place at the wrong time."

"Something just snapped inside, or maybe he just has a mean streak." That is how the police chief of a small Texas town described sixteen-year-old Timothy Dwaine Brown.

Timothy, who had been expelled from high school for threatening another student with a switchblade knife, beat his eleven-year-old brother to death with a baseball bat and then shot and killed his grandmother and stepfather. According to the prosecutor, Timothy's parents refused to allow him to see or even call his girlfriend. Police officers said they believed that Timothy's brother caught him using the phone behind his parents' back and told on him. Enraged, Timothy bludgeoned the younger boy and then shot his grandmother and stepfather with a deer rifle.

After pleading guilty to killing his brother, Timothy was sentenced to life in prison.

On November 12, 1989, eleven-year-old Frederick Jones knocked on the door of a suspected crack house in Kansas City. Someone said, "Who is it?" The door opened and Frederick was shot. Taken to the hospital, he died an hour later. Police arrested a fourteen-year-old boy and charged him with the killing.

Although they would not say whether a drug deal was involved, investigators did say it is not unusual to see children as young as eight years old running and selling drugs on Kansas City streets. Police officers also noted that the killing occurred at a time when Kansas City was experiencing a sudden, acute shortage of crack cocaine. They said the shortage of crack was driving up the price of the drug and increasing drug-related violence in the city.

* * *

Every year at least 1,000 and often more than 1,500 American youngsters under the age of eighteen intentionally take the lives of others and are arrested for murder or manslaughter. Some of these killings are crimes of premeditated violence motivated by greed, lust, or a desire for revenge. Others are crimes of passion: impulsive overresponses to provocation by the victim or to some explosive drive within the killer. Still other cases seem utterly senseless.

Who are these kids who kill? To begin with, kids who kill are really a rare breed. While homicides committed by children and adolescents fascinate the public and generate a great deal of media attention, these killings are actually quite infrequent. People younger than eighteen constitute roughly one-quarter of the total resident population of the United States. Yet annually for the past decade or so, consistently fewer than 11 percent of all individuals arrested in the United States for murder or intentional manslaughter have been under the age of eighteen.

In 1988, the year for which the most recent data are available, there were 16,326 murder and intentional manslaughter arrests in the United States. Only 1,765—roughly 11 percent—of those arrested were under eighteen years of age. To put it another way, fewer than five juveniles in every 100,000 were arrested for intentionally killing someone—approximately half the adult arrest rate for these same crimes.

The homicide rate for younger juveniles is even lower. The vast majority (most years more than 85 percent) of juveniles who kill are fifteen, sixteen, or seventeen years old. Annually for the past decade or so, fewer than 1 percent of those arrested for murder or non-negligent manslaughter have been under the age of fifteen. And during this same time period, only a handful of those arrested for these homicide crimes have been younger than ten years old. For example, in 1988, only seven (.6 percent) of the 1,765 juveniles arrested for murder or manslaughter were nine years old or younger.

Arrest data undoubtedly underestimate the number of very young children who kill since at least some of these youngsters are probably never formally arrested. Indeed, in most jurisdictions, children under the age of seven are automatically deemed incapable of criminal conduct. Still, there is little doubt that extremely few homicides are committed by children under the age of ten.

Interestingly, although juveniles rarely kill, they often commit other crimes. In the United States, annually, youths under the age of eighteen consistently account for about 17 percent of all reported arrests, about one-third of arrests for serious property crimes (burglary, larceny-theft, motor vehicle theft, and arson), and 16 to 17 percent of arrests for all major violent crimes combined (murder, forcible rape, robbery, and aggravated assault).

Youths under the age of fifteen account for about 5 percent of all reported arrests, 13 to 14 percent of arrests for serious property crimes, and roughly 5 percent of arrests for all major violent crimes combined. Even children under the age of ten, who almost never kill, regularly account for about 1 percent of the annual number of arrests for all major crimes combined and just under half a percent of all arrests.

Like age, gender is also a factor in juvenile homicide. Juvenile homicide, like most crimes at all ages, is much more likely to be perpetrated by boys than girls. Just as younger juveniles rarely kill, girls of any age are extremely unlikely to kill. At all ages under eighteen, the vast majority of those arrested for murder or non-negligent manslaughter are boys.

In 1988, 93 percent of the juveniles arrested for intentional homicide crimes in the United States were boys. That figure, while striking, is consistent with statistics on homicides committed by adults. On an annual basis, men consistently comprise nearly 90 percent of *all* individuals arrested for murder or non-negligent homicide. In 1988, 87 percent of all adults arrested for these crimes were men.

Not only do girls kill much less frequently than boys, but their victims are different. FBI data on juvenile homicide indicate that while girls almost always kill family members or acquaintances, boys are more likely to kill acquaintances or strangers.

Race and ethnicity are also important variables in juvenile homicide. Black youths are vastly overrepresented among juveniles arrested for murder or non-negligent manslaughter. While roughly one-sixth of all Americans under the age of eighteen are black, in recent years approximately one-half the juveniles arrested for these homicide crimes have been black. Indeed, in 1988, over 57 percent of the juveniles arrested for these offenses were black. Hispanic youths are similarly overrepresented among juveniles arrested for murder and manslaughter. Although approximately 8 percent of the U.S. population is Hispanic, Hispanic youths account for almost one-quarter of all juvenile arrests for homicide crimes.

Undoubtedly, these racial and ethnic disparities reflect discrimination in the criminal justice system. It is widely acknowledged that blacks and Hispanics are more likely than whites to be arrested for the crimes they commit. Yet, even allowing for such discrimination, it is evident that black and Hispanic youths commit a vastly disproportionate share of juvenile homicides.

Available data also shed light on other characteristics of kids who kill, such as the extent to which these youngsters are emotionally disturbed, mentally ill, mentally retarded, learning disabled, neurologically impaired, behaviorally disturbed, or simply "normal" youths who commit extremely abnormal acts. Homicides committed by children and adolescents are so rare and often so apparently inexplicable that people tend to assume that any youngster who kills must be emotionally disturbed, if not mentally ill. Thus, it is not surprising that most juvenile killers are examined by psychologists, psychiatrists, or other mental health experts.

Nor is it surprising that, like most people referred for psychological or psychiatric evaluations, most juveniles who kill wind up with one diagnostic label or another applied to them. What may be surprising, however, is that most of these youths are diagnosed as suffering only relatively mild disorders.

Although some juvenile killers are psychotic, most are not. In the vast majority of reported studies, only a small fraction of the juvenile killers examined were said to be psychotic. As one expert observed, speaking of juvenile homicide, "The behavior [may have been] 'psychotic' but the youths were not." Most juvenile killers studied by researchers have been found to suffer only a "personality disorder," a diagnosis that encompasses a host of maladaptive "patterns of perceiving, relating to, and thinking about the environment and oneself."

If juveniles who kill are not generally mentally ill, are they often intellectually dull or mentally retarded? The answer seems to be "no." Most reports of IQ scores of children who kill place them at, near, and sometimes even above average in intelligence. One major exception is Dr. Dorothy Lewis and colleagues' recent study of fourteen juvenile killers sentenced to die and awaiting execution on death row. While only one of these convicts was determined to be mentally retarded, only two had IQs in the normal range.

Although juveniles who kill generally are not mentally retarded, a disproportionate number have learning difficulties and have experienced significant academic problems prior to killing. In Lewis' death row study, for example, ten of the fourteen juveniles had major learning problems, only three were reading at grade level, and three had never even learned to read until being incarcerated on death row. For the most part, these findings have been supported by other studies of more general groups of juvenile killers.

Both mental retardation and learning disabilities may or may not be associated with neurological impairment. It has long been theorized that there is an association between brain damage and juvenile homicide, and there is a striking prevalence of neurological impairment among juvenile killers. For example, among the fourteen death row inmates studied by Dr. Lewis, all of whom killed as juveniles, every one had a history or symptoms consistent with brain damage. In fact, eight had experienced head injuries "severe enough to result in hospitalization and/or indention of the cranium" and nine had "serious" documented neurological abnormalities, including focal brain injury, abnormal head circumference, abnormal reflexes, seizure disorders, and abnormal EEG findings.

On the other hand, many studies have reached more equivocal results regarding the relationship between neurological impairment and juvenile homicide. Several studies have documented juvenile killers with no apparent neurological impairment.

Juveniles who kill often seem to come from broken families in which one or both parents are disturbed, neglectful, or abusive. Although many youngsters may grow up in homes broken by parental separation or divorce, the percentage of broken homes is much greater among those who kill—at least among juvenile killers who have been the subjects of nearly half a century of published research.

Much of the research on juveniles who kill also indicates that many have parents who are alcoholic or mentally ill. The single most consistent finding regarding juvenile homicide, however, is that kids who kill, especially those who kill family members, generally have witnessed or have been directly victimized by domestic violence. The most common form of domestic violence witnessed by juveniles who kill is spouse abuse (one parent assaulting the other), but being directly victimized by child abuse is even more common.

The extremely high incidence of child abuse victimization among juveniles who kill has been widely documented. For example, among the fourteen juvenile death row inmates examined by Dr. Lewis and her associates, twelve had been "brutally" abused physically, and five had been sodomized by older family members. Similarly high rates of child abuse victimization have also been found in other multisubject studies of juvenile killers.

Even though most juveniles who kill are not seriously disturbed, given their family backgrounds, it should come as no surprise that many if not most of these youngsters have exhibited some form of noticeably deviant behavior prior to committing homicide—most commonly antisocial conduct, substance abuse, truancy, running away from home, enuresis, and problems getting along with peers.

Many juveniles who kill have histories of antisocial behavior, reflected in records of arrests and criminal convictions. In fact, many of those who have not been arrested or convicted have extensive histories of fighting and other antisocial behavior prior to killing. Overall, the research suggests that kids who kill strangers are more likely to have histories of antisocial behavior than those who kill family members and acquaintances.

Surprisingly few studies of juvenile killers have considered the relationship between substance abuse and juvenile homicide, but those that have provide rather striking results. Several studies have found that many if not most juvenile killers examined had histories of substance abuse or were under the influence of alcohol or other drugs when they killed.

Truancy and running away from home, two often-related behaviors, are frequently found among juveniles who kill. Not surprisingly, in this context, running away from home has been reported almost exclusively in juveniles who eventually killed one of their parents.

Childhood enuresis—repeated urination in bed or clothing after toilet training is or should be accomplished—has long been regarded as one of the more powerful predictors of later violence. Specifically, a great deal of scholarly, clinical, and empirical attention has been devoted to the so-called triad of enuresis, fire setting, and cruelty to animals—symptoms that often appear conjointly in children who later engage in violent behavior. Neither fire setting nor cruelty to animals have received much attention in the literature on juveniles who kill, but the same cannot be said about enuresis.

For nearly three decades, clinicians and researchers have been fascinated with the apparent correlation between enuresis and juvenile homicide. In a 1961 article entitled "Enuresis in Murderous Aggressive Children and Adolescents," Dr. Joseph Michaels set the theoretical stage for much of the later interest in this relationship. "Persistently enuretic" individuals, Dr. Michaels suggested, "cannot hold their tensions, are impatient, and are impelled to act. They feel the urgency of the moment psychologically, as at an earlier date they could not hold their urine." In numerous studies, substantial proportions of juvenile killers were suffering or had suffered from enuresis.

Who do kids kill? The bulk of the research dealing with juvenile homicide has looked primarily if not exclusively at youngsters who kill within the family. Many juvenile killers do kill their parents or siblings, but most kill acquaintances or strangers. In one recent study of seventy-two juvenile killers, for example, Dr. Dewey Cornell and his colleagues found that twenty-three killed strangers, thirty-four killed acquaintances or friends, and fifteen killed family members.

In 1984, the most recent year for which U.S. juvenile homicide arrest data have been analyzed with regard to victim-offender relationships, data were available on 787 cases. Roughly one-third of these juveniles killed strangers, almost one-half killed acquaintances, 8 percent killed parents or step-parents, and approximately 9 percent killed other family members.

How and under what circumstances do kids kill? Most of the killings described in the published literature on juvenile homicide were perpetrated with guns, knives, or the killer's bare hands, although occasionally other objects have been used. Perhaps the most consistent and striking finding is the extent to which juveniles kill with guns. Published studies indicate that between 33 and 100 percent of all juvenile killings are perpetrated with guns. Interestingly, though not surprisingly, gun use in juvenile homicides is lower in younger age groups and seems to increase steadily with increasing age.

Available data also indicate that many juvenile homicides are jointly committed by multiple perpetrators. In fact, these data also indicate that there is often an association between the number of perpetrators and the relationship of the victim to the perpetrator(s). For example, FBI data on victim-offender relationships indicate that while multiple perpetrator juvenile homicides are rather rare when the homicide victim is related to a perpetrator, a substantial percentage (42.1 percent) of juvenile acquaintance homicides are committed by more than one perpetrator, and the majority (68.6 percent) of juvenile stranger homicides are committed by two or more individuals acting together.

Other juvenile arrest data from New York City indicate that whether a homicide is committed individually or by a group is clearly correlated with the age of the offenders: younger perpetrators are more likely to kill in concert with others. From ages fourteen through sixteen, nearly half the homicides in this study were committed by groups of juveniles; by age seventeen, the percentage of group-perpetrated homicides fell to about 30 percent; and by age eighteen only approximately one-quarter of the killings were group-perpetrated.

Data covering all of New York State paint a similar picture. In 1987, for example, 60 percent of the killings committed by juveniles in the thirteen to fifteen year old range were perpetrated by multiple offenders. Fewer than 50 percent of the killings committed by youths sixteen to nineteen years of age were perpetrated by multiple offenders.

Why do kids kill? Many juvenile homicides appear motiveless or at least to have what one early researcher called "obscure motivation." In other cases, however, the juvenile killer's motive seems reasonably apparent, though not always understandable. For example, many if not most parricides (parent killings) seem rooted in the juvenile's desire for revenge against or escape from a parent who is (or at least is perceived by the youth to be) abusive. Some parricides also appear to be motivated by a desire to protect or please a parent. There are numerous published accounts of juveniles who killed their fathers or stepfathers during or after incidents in which these men abused the youths' mothers.

Killings of other family members, such as siblings, aunts, and uncles, are generally less clearly motivated and often seem rooted in the juvenile killer's own psychopathology.

Killings outside the family also have various motivations. Killings of acquaintances are most commonly related to some immediate interpersonal conflict, or they occur in connection with the commission of other crimes, such as burglary or rape. Killings of strangers generally occur in the course of committing other crimes, such as burglary, robbery, and rape, but often have no apparent motive.

Numerous data address the question of juvenile homicides committed in the course of or in furtherance of theft crimes. For example, FBI data indicate that roughly one-fifth of the juvenile killings in one recent year were associated with a theft offense. In only two of these theft-related killings did juveniles kill family members. Among the other victims of these theft-related killings, 6 percent were acquaintances and more than 57 percent were strangers.

While there are a variety of theft crimes (e.g., simple larceny, robbery, or burglary), for obvious reasons, robbery (theft by the use of force or threat of force against a person) is the theft offense most likely to result in homicide. The extent to which robberies committed by juveniles result in homicides seems to be almost a direct function of the juvenile perpetrator's age.

New York City arrest data, for example, demonstrate that the likelihood of a robbery resulting in a homicide is strikingly and positively correlated with the age of the youngest perpetrator in the robbery. When the youngest perpetrator was twelve or thirteen, fewer than two robberies in a thousand resulted in a homicide. In one study, when the youngest perpetrator was fourteen, the rate was just slightly more than two killings in every thousand robberies. But by age fifteen, the rate of killings per thousand robberies almost doubled; by ages sixteen and seventeen, the rate virtually tripled; and by age nineteen, the likelihood that a robbery victim would be killed was roughly seven times greater than when the youngest perpetrator was fourteen or younger.

2

Family Killings

ON NOVEMBER 16, 1982, Richard Jahnke and his wife Maria returned home from a dinner celebrating the twentieth anniversary of the day they met. As they emerged from their car in the driveway of their Wyoming home, the roar of shotgun blasts filled the air. Four slugs hit Mr. Jahnke and killed him instantly. Mrs. Jahnke was uninjured.

The shots that killed Richard Jahnke were fired by his sixteen-year-old son, Richard Jahnke, Jr., who had been hiding in the darkened garage awaiting his parents' return. Prosecutors charged that Richard and his seventeen-year-old sister, Deborah, plotted the killing in advance. Richard was charged with first-degree murder and conspiracy to commit murder. Deborah was charged with conspiracy.

At trial, Richard claimed self-defense, alleging that his father had abused him, his sister, and his mother for years. The evidence backed up Richard's claims. For some fourteen years, Mr. Jahnke had repeatedly and brutally beaten and psychologically abused his children and wife. He had also sexually abused his daughter. Although Richard sought help from both his mother and the authorities, nothing was ever done to stop his father's abuse. Richard testified that he thought about killing his father for years but "always chickened out."

In response to this evidence, the prosecutor claimed the killing was an act of revenge rather than self-defense. The jury compromised, rejecting Richard's claim of self-defense but convicting him of manslaughter rather than murder. Deborah Jahnke was convicted of aiding and abetting manslaughter. Richard was sentenced to five to fifteen years in prison; Deborah was sentenced to serve three to eight years in prison. Both sentences were eventually commuted by the governor. Deborah was released at age nineteen and Richard at age twenty-one.

In early August 1983, fifteen-year-old Jory Kidwell ran away from home and told Nevada juvenile authorities that he had been beaten and abused by his mother's common-law husband since he was four years old. When authorities investigated Jory's charges, Don Knautz admitted whipping Jory several days earlier but promised never to do it again. When the juvenile officer decided to return Jory to his home, Jory told her, "I know he won't beat me because I'll kill him."

Seventeen days later, on August 27, Jory Kidwell shot and killed Don Knautz as Knautz walked out the front door of the family's mobile home. After a judge set aside his second-degree murder conviction, Jory was allowed to plead guilty to a lesser offense. Though sentenced to serve twenty years in prison, he became eligible for parole in five years.

In March 1984, in an ambush similar to that staged by Richard Jahnke, Robert Lee Moody used three shotgun blasts to kill his father. Robert, an eighteen-year-old born-again Christian, told California authorities, "I thought God wanted me to do it."

Charged with murder, Robert opted for a non-jury trial. After hearing four days of evidence, the judge convicted

Robert of manslaughter but publicly denounced Robert's dead father as "the scum of the earth." What the judge learned was that Robert's father terrorized his family for years, raped his two older daughters, forced his wife into prostitution, and had recently started molesting his eleven-year-old daughter. Irritated by his son's religious interests, Robert's father had urged him to take drugs and watch pornographic movies rather than read the Bible.

The judge was also told that on the day of the killing Robert awoke to the sound of his father slamming his mother's head into a microwave oven. Robert called the police, but his mother refused to press charges, saying, "He'll only come back and kill us." Robert then grabbed his father's shotgun, hid in his father's boat, and shot him three times as he walked by.

Though facing a possible eight-year prison sentence, Robert was given a four-year suspended sentence, placed on probation for five years, and ordered to spend two years abroad working as a Christian missionary.

On February 6, 1986, at 6:00 in the morning, James Pierson, a forty-two-year-old widower from Long Island, New York, was gunned down in front of his home by seventeen-year-old Sean Pica. Sean was not related to Mr. Pierson, indeed he barely knew the man. Sean was a classmate of Mr. Pierson's sixteen-year-old daughter, Cheryl, a popular high school cheerleader.

Three months earlier Sean and Cheryl sat together in their high school homeroom and discussed a newspaper article about a battered woman who hired someone to kill her abusive husband. Cheryl asked who would agree to do such a thing. Sean replied that he would—for the right price. Eventually, Cheryl offered Sean $1,000 to kill her father. Sean accepted the offer and received a $400 downpayment from Cheryl's boyfriend before killing Mr. Pierson.

Sean Pica pleaded guilty to manslaughter and was sentenced to eight to twenty-four years in prison, after the prosecutor told the judge that Sean was a "cold-blooded

murderer" who killed James Pierson "out of sheer greed."
Cheryl Pierson, on the other hand, pleaded guilty to the
same offense but received a sentence that allowed her to
be released from jail after serving only 106 days.

Why? When Cheryl was about twelve, during what turned
out to be her mother's fatal illness, her father began sexually abusing her. Cheryl's mother died, and the sexual
abuse, including intercourse, continued on a regular basis,
occasionally coupled with physical abuse. At the time that
Cheryl turned to Sean Pica, her older brother had left the
home, and Cheryl feared that her father was about to begin
sexually abusing her younger sister as well.

Although the prosecutor asked for a minimum sentence
of two years in prison, the judge said he believed Cheryl's
detailed story of abuse and sentenced her to six months in
jail. With time off for good behavior, she was freed in less
than four months. Shortly after her release from jail, Cheryl
married her boyfriend, who had been sentenced to five years
probation for his part in the killing of her father.

The vast majority of juvenile killers kill outside their own
families. The best available data indicate that fewer than 20
percent of the victims of juvenile homicides are members
of the immediate family of the youthful killer. These
data also indicate that among intrafamilial homicides,
the percentage of parental victims is slightly lower than
the percentage of other family member victims. To put
it another way, juveniles who kill within the family are
somewhat more likely to kill relatives other than their
parents.

Intrafamilial homicides committed by juveniles are especially intriguing and troubling. Killing one's own kin, especially when the killer is a child or adolescent, seems the
most dreadful of crimes. Yet, juvenile intrafamilial homicides are perhaps the most understandable of all killings.

The actual incidence of parricide is unknown, but one
recent estimate suggests that approximately 2 percent of
all homicides in the United States are parricides. Annual

FBI data consistently indicate that among those arrested for murder or non-negligent manslaughter, fewer than 1 percent have killed their fathers and a slightly lower percentage have killed their mothers. Unfortunately, these data include those arrested at all ages, so there is no way to say just how many parricides are committed by juveniles. Also undetermined is how many of those arrested for murder have killed both mother and father.

What little systematic research there is on the subject of parricide suggests that both matricide and patricide are virtually always committed by sons. There are, however, a number of recent cases, like that of Cheryl Pierson, in which daughters have killed parents.

Those few professionals who have researched and written about juvenile parricide emphasize a common theme: youngsters who kill a parent have generally been severely victimized by that parent. For example, Dr. Emanuel Tanay, the nation's leading psychiatric authority on the subject, says that parricide may be adaptive and often "has a large element of self-preservation." As Dr. Tanay views parricide, it is generally a reaction to parental cruelty and abuse, "a last resort effort to protect the psychic integrity of the perpetrator threatened with psychic disintegration" by the behavior of a sadistic parent.

Similarly, Paul Mones, a California lawyer who specializes in defending juveniles who kill their parents, says: "The child who kills his/her abusive parent is taking that action which is most likely (in the child's perception) to prevent him/herself from being further abused. The act is one of self-preservation." Attorney Mones also emphasizes that youths who kill their parents tend to "fall into a rather unique category of delinquency"—they rarely have any history of delinquency and "do not present the characteristics of either the classic status offender or the classic violently aggressive delinquent."

Most patricides, like those committed by Richard Jahnke, Jory Kidwell, Robert Lee Moody, and Cheryl Pierson, fit the portrait painted by Dr. Tanay and Attorney Mones. Virtually all involve juveniles killing physically, psychologically, or sexually abusive fathers or stepfathers. And almost all the juvenile perpetrators have no significant history of delinquency. Indeed, many, like Richard, Jory, Robert, and Cheryl, appear to be exemplary youngsters.

Although most patricides are solely the work of the youthful killers (and their accomplices, if any), in many cases there is good reason to believe that these juveniles have been consciously or unconsciously prompted, if not encouraged, by other family members—especially their mothers—to kill their fathers.

Referring to juveniles who kill in what he calls a "family conspiracy," Dr. D. Sargent speculates that "sometimes the child who kills is acting as the unwitting lethal agent of an adult (usually a parent) who unconsciously prompts the child so that he can vicariously enjoy the benefits of the act." Dr. Sargent cites several cases in support of his hypothesis, including one in which an eight-year-old boy shot and killed his abusive father after the boy's mother repeatedly expressed the wish that the father would die.

Dr. Carl Malmquist describes a more blatant case of "family conspiracy" resulting in patricide. In this case, a fifteen-year-old boy had often seen his father beat his mother while the father was intoxicated. Finally, after one such beating, the father went to get a piece of wood to use on the mother. While the father was gone briefly, the mother sat down next to the boy, told him "I know you're big enough to protect me now," and handed him a pistol, which he promptly used to shoot and kill his father.

Richard Jahnke's shotgun slaying of his father provides another possible example in support of Dr. Sargent's hypothesis. Although Richard denies that his sister, Deborah, was involved in planning or carrying out the killing of Mr. Jahnke, Deborah was convicted of playing an active role in assisting her brother. And while there was never any charge that Mrs. Jahnke, their mother, was in any way involved in the killing or its planning, she had clearly been victimized by Mr. Jahnke for many years. After the killing, Mrs. Jahnke told reporters, "I'm going to live to the hilt. My son has freed me."

Several other recent cases also illustrate the "family conspiracy" patricide. In December 1981, Eric Witte, a sixteen-year-old Indiana boy, told police he tripped while carrying a gun and accidentally killed his father. Four years later, when Eric's mother was tried for murder in the killing, it was revealed that Eric had killed his father at her request. Testimony at the trial indicated that Eric's mother started asking him to kill his father several months before the shooting. Eric initially refused, but finally agreed after his mother threatened to kill herself if he did not kill his father. Eric then shot his father as the man lay sleeping on a sofa.

In 1985, James Brown, a seventeen-year-old New York youth, was charged as an accessory to the murder of his step-father, who had repeatedly abused James and James' mother. According to James, prior to the killing his mother told him she would give $50 to have her husband killed. James, who was of borderline intelligence, passed this "offer" on to a friend who told a second friend.

The second friend, a nineteen-year-old, immediately agreed to do the killing for the amount "offered." That night, the nineteen-year-old arrived at James' home, got the stepfather's loaded rifle, and then—with James by his side—ambushed, shot, and killed James' stepfather. James, his mother, and the nineteen-year-old shooter all pleaded guilty to homicide charges.

In February 1987, eleven-year-old Mary Bailey shot and killed her stepfather. Mary and her mother, Priscilla Wyers, were both charged in the killing. Testifying at her mother's trial, Mary told the jury that her stepfather physically abused her mother. Mary testified further that her mother asked her to kill her stepfather and "I told her yes. I told her right off the bat." On the morning of the killing, Mary's mother woke her up and directed her to the living room, where she found her stepfather asleep with a loaded rifle sitting nearby. Mary picked up the rifle and—after three tries—succeeded in killing her stepfather. Mary was placed in a state foster home; her mother was convicted of first degree murder.

Even where there is no conspiracy, explicit or implicit, between parent and child, the killing of one parent to protect the other parent is not an uncommon scenario in juvenile patricide. One example is the case of Robert Lee Moody, who shot and killed his father after his father beat his mother and his mother refused to press charges for fear that she and her children would be killed if she did.

In a more obvious case of patricide motivated by a youth's desire to protect his mother, a fifteen-year-old Los Angeles boy recently shot and killed his stepfather as the stepfather was beating the boy's mother. The stepfather, who had abused his wife for fourteen years, was slamming her against the metal security door outside the family's home when his fifteen-year-old stepson grabbed a gun from the man's bedroom and shot him once through the door. Wounded, the stepfather released his wife, but the boy chased him into the driveway and fired several more shots, killing him.

On October 13, 1984, sixteen-year-old Torran Lee Meier, with the help of two acquaintances, strangled his mother, thirty-four-year-old Shirley Rizk, put her body in a car along with Torran's eight-year-old half-brother, doused the car with gasoline, set it afire, and pushed it over a sixty-foot California cliff. Amazingly, the eight-year-old survived without injury.

After the killing, Torran's maternal grandmother said Torran was driven to kill by his mother who made his life "a living hell" through years of psychological abuse. According to Torran and more than a dozen friends, relatives, and neighbors who testified on his behalf, Mrs. Rizk constantly berated, belittled, and humiliated Torran. She called him a "faggot," told him he was "not man enough," and went out of her way to be sexually provocative with him—doing housework topless and swimming nude when he and his friends were around.

Charged with murder, Torran sought to show that as a result of his mental condition, he was guilty at most of manslaughter. Expert testimony from a psychiatrist-neurologist indicated that Torran was a youth with brain dysfunction and significantly impaired ability to cope with stress. The physician testified that Torran demonstrated an extremely rare brain wave abnormality and suffered from brain damage, severe allergies, and frequent headaches—all of which impaired his ability to deal with the accumulating stress created by his mother's abuse.

Although this testimony was disputed by experts testifying for the prosecution, the jury was convinced that Shirley Rizk's abuse caused an "emotional breakdown" that prevented Torran from acting with malice or premeditation. As a result, the jury accepted Torran's defense that when he killed his mother he was in a state of "diminished capacity" and thus guilty of manslaughter rather than first-degree or even second-degree murder. Torran was committed to the custody of the state Youth Authority until his twenty-fifth birthday. His adult accomplices were each sentenced to serve from fifteen years to life in prison.

On October 6, 1987, at about 8:30 in the morning, Alonzo Williams, a seventeen-year-old New Yorker, shot and killed his mother with a .22 caliber semiautomatic rifle. Alonzo then left for work. At noon, he returned to the house, opened all the gas jets on the stove, and left, expecting the house to burn down. His mother's body was found later that day and Alonzo was arrested that evening.

Initially, Alonzo told the police that he killed his mother "because she said bad things about me." Later Alonzo told authorities that his mother had been abusing him for years. As far back as he could recall, he said, his mother—an unmarried woman with several children—had beaten him and his siblings with sticks, belts, and extension cords, ostensibly as a form of discipline. County child abuse records corroborated this claim. Alonzo also claimed that for as long as he could remember, his mother had called him vile names and repeatedly told him that if she could turn back the hands of time, she would never have given birth to him.

Finally, according to Alonzo, his mother had been sexually abusing him since he was seven years old. What started out with her fondling his genitals in the bathtub, progressed to making him masturbate her, and ultimately led to sexual intercourse between mother and son. By Alonzo's account, the last episode of sexual abuse took place just minutes before he picked up a rifle and shot his mother five times.

Charged with murder, Alonzo raised what amounted to a claim of self-defense. Midway through his trial, however, he claimed that someone else—a relative—had killed his mother. A jury convicted Alonzo of murder, and he was sentenced to twenty years to life in prison.

At about 3:30 in the morning on June 25, 1988, the very day he was scheduled to speak as class valedictorian at his high school graduation in Niagara Falls, New York, seventeen-year-old William Shrubsall beat his mother to death with a baseball bat.

William had always excelled academically, but even being first in his class was not enough for his mother. From early childhood, she relentlessly pushed him to achieve—and achieve he did. First in his class throughout school and number one in his high school graduating class of 250, William had been admitted to one of the nation's leading universities with a full scholarship.

The killing, which occurred just two months before he was scheduled to leave for college, was the climax of several months in which his mother (a widow with no other children and few interests in life other than her son) selected the college he would attend, constantly berated his girlfriend, abused him psychologically, threatened him, and occasionally struck him.

On the night of the homicide, William's mother, who outweighed him by more than a hundred pounds, abused him verbally and physically, threatened to kill him, and backed him into a corner in his bedroom. Defending himself, he picked up a baseball bat and beat her to death. In a plea bargain to murder charges, William pleaded guilty to a lesser charge of manslaughter.

Like patricides, matricides also generally involve killings of abusive parents, but in cases of matricide the more severe abuse is usually psychological or sexual rather than physical.

Published accounts of matricide are relatively rare, but scientific and professional interest in the subject dates back at least half a century to Dr. Frederic Wertham's 1941 book, *Dark Legend: A Study in Murder*. Dr. Wertham reviewed the sparse literature on matricide, reported one case study, and concluded that juveniles who kill their mothers are generally intelligent males with no prior history of delinquency but excessively close attachments to their mothers. According to Dr. Wertham, the motive in most of these killings was the fusion of unconscious hatred and sexual desire for the mother.

Other mental health professionals who have treated boys charged with killing their mothers have emphasized that these killings often appear to be victim-precipitated homicides. Child psychiatrists, Drs. Donald Scherl and John Mack, for example, recount the story of fourteen-year-old "Richard," who shot and killed his mother as she lay sleeping.

Several hours earlier, Richard's mother had—as she often did—directed the boy's father to beat him with a belt. For years, Richard had been physically and psychologically abused by both his father and mother. Richard's father had beaten both Richard and his mother, but clearly the worst abuse was inflicted by his mother. She would often kick and slap Richard, call him a "fucking bastard," lock him in his room, and force him to kneel for hours at a time. On a number of occasions, she exposed her breasts and genitals to him. Two months before the homicide, Richard found her and her lover together in bed.

Psychological and medical evaluations revealed that although Richard had a history of running away and minor delinquency, he had an above-average IQ and suffered no major mental illness. He was diagnosed as suffering a personality disorder.

Why did Richard kill his mother? According to Drs. Scherl and Mack, his mother's "repeated gross seductions and brutal treatment of him, her highly eroticized, humiliating demands for absolute submission, unmitigated by tenderness, forced him into a position where to be free of her he felt he had no alternative but to kill her."

Undoubtedly many, perhaps most, matricides fit this pattern, but others clearly do not. Some matricides seem to result more from the juvenile perpetrator's psychological problems than any significant provocation on the part of the victim. Consider, for example, the following three recent cases.

Wesley Underwood, a fifteen-year-old Texan, shot his mother three times in the back after they argued about whether he had misplaced a knitting needle. Wesley, a "loner" addicted to heavy metal music, had been drinking whiskey and sniffing gasoline fumes shortly before he killed his mother as she sat watching television. Wesley pleaded guilty to murder and was sentenced to serve eighteen years in prison after the district attorney told the judge he was a "spoiled, lazy young man who got fed up with his mother and got rid of her."

A fifteen-year-old Colorado boy and his fourteen-year-old friend were charged with robbing, beating, and stabbing to death the fifteen-year-old's mother. Interviewed after the killing, people who knew the boy said he and his mother got along well, but that he was a "bully" who was "always smarting off." Another friend of the boy's said the robbery and killing were motivated by boredom: "All we want is something to do, somewhere to go."

Fifteen-year-old "Bob," recently described by Drs. Dewey Cornell and Elissa Benedek, stabbed his mother to death and afterwards was found in the basement of his home, reading a Bible and chanting, "Kill the Devil." When examined after the killing, Bob described his strong belief in witchcraft and said that rock music lyrics suggested that he kill his mother. Bob's mother had abused him, and he had twice run away from home before the killing. For two months prior to the killing, Bob had become increasingly withdrawn, seclusive, and apathetic—avoiding friends, skipping school, talking about witchcraft and demonic possession, refusing to eat, and complaining that his mother was poisoning his food.

At least some juvenile matricides appear to be drug-related. For example, four recent matricides, all in the New York City area, have been attributed to the effects of crack cocaine. A seventeen-year-old boy was charged with choking his mother to death after she confronted him about his obsession with so-called telephone "party lines," a fad among New York teens. Another New York boy was charged with stabbing his mother to death when she refused to give him $200—money he owed to a crack dealer. A fifteen-year-old girl from the suburbs stabbed her mother to death after the mother made a comment about the girl's poor grades. And a fifteen-year-old girl and her eighteen-year-old boyfriend hacked the girl's mother to death with a knife and a machete because she objected to their relationship.

On the night of February 18, 1988, sixteen-year-old David Brom talked with a friend on the phone and told her of his plan to take the family van and move from Minnesota to Florida. When she asked what his parents would think of that, David told her, "They won't be around to oppose it." Later that night, David used an ax to kill his mother, father, brother, and sister.

Tried on four counts of murder, David pleaded not guilty by reason of insanity. A psychiatrist testifying for the defense described David as "depressed, psychotic and suffering from evolving multiple personalities" when he killed his family. Even a psychiatrist testifying for the prosecution told the jury that David was mentally ill when he took an ax to his parents and siblings. According to the prosecution's expert, David killed his family because he thought doing so was "the only way to avoid killing himself."

After deliberating for twenty-one hours, the jury concluded that David Brom was not insane at the time of the killings. Convicted on all four murder counts, David was sentenced to three consecutive life terms, meaning he will spend at least fifty-two years in prison before becoming eligible for parole.

Ginger Turnmire was fifteen years old when, on April 26, 1986, she shot and killed her mother and father as they returned home from a church picnic in rural Tennessee. After the killings, Ginger drove to a local arcade, where she calmly told friends what she had done. Later, however, she testified in court that a "Charles Manson-type person" killed her parents. According to Ginger's testimony, a long-haired, bearded motorcycle gang leader known as "Papa Smurf" searched her home for drugs, shot and killed her parents, and told her he would kill her and everyone she loved if she did not confess to the slayings.

At a pretrial hearing, during which Ginger "chewed gum and winked at friends," a judge determined that Ginger should be tried as an adult after psychiatric testimony indicated that Ginger suffered from severe identity and behavioral problems, had previously attempted suicide, was suspended from school, and was, by her own admission, addicted to Valium. The judge said a major factor in his decision was the failure of previous efforts to treat Ginger: "All efforts of treatment have failed. Responses by Miss Turnmire have been negative." Tried as an adult, Ginger was convicted of first degree murder and sentenced to life in prison.

*   *   *

John Justice was a seventeen-year-old high school honor student in suburban Buffalo when, on September 16, 1985, within roughly two hours, he stabbed his mother, brother, and father to death, and then rammed his father's car into the back of another car, killing a neighbor who was driving.

After stabbing his brother and mother to death in the family home sometime between 2:45 and 3:30 in the afternoon, John cleaned up, picked his father up at work, drove him home, and then stabbed him to death in the living room shortly after 5:00. Over the next couple of hours, John tried unsuccessfully to slit his wrists with a razor blade and finally drove off in the family car in another attempt at suicide. After the crash that killed his neighbor, John told a police officer, "Check 308 Mang. I killed them all."

At John's trial on murder charges, psychiatrists testified that John hated his mother and that he was upset over his parents' refusal to help pay for his planned college expenses. The prosecution's psychiatrist testified that John was afflicted with a personality disorder, but the psychiatrist called by the defense, Dr. Emanuel Tanay, testified that John suffered from an undiagnosed psychosis.

The jury voted at least three times, eleven to one, to convict John Justice of all four killings, but one juror held out, arguing that John's mental illness precluded legal responsibility for any of the killings. In a compromise verdict, the jury ultimately found John not guilty by reason of insanity for the killings of his father and brother, but guilty of murder for killing his mother and neighbor.

On New Year's Day 1987, in the state of Washington, sixteen-year-old Sean Stevenson killed both his parents and raped and killed his eighteen-year-old sister. The killings apparently took place after Sean argued with his father over a party he wanted to attend. After the killings, Sean called his fifteen-year-old girlfriend, told her, "I think I just shot my family," and asked if she "wanted to go to Mexico" with him. Later that day, Sean walked into the town police station and confessed.

At trial, a jury found Sean guilty of two counts of first-degree murder for killing his parents and one count of aggravated murder in the killing of his sister, concluding that Sean killed her to cover up the rape. Arguing against the death penalty on the aggravated murder conviction, Sean's lawyer told the jury Sean had an "extremely high degree of emotional impairment." Even the prosecutor agreed, admitting to jurors that he had been wrong about Sean and that Sean "was and is severely mentally disturbed." After deliberating twenty-five minutes, the jury rejected the death penalty and recommended a sentence of life in prison. Sean was then sentenced to life in prison without hope of parole.

Less than a year later, in March of 1988, Sean and two other inmates escaped from a medium-security state prison, took three hostages, and robbed a family of their money and truck. Finally, cornered by police, the three escapees surrendered. After pleading guilty to escape and robbery charges, Sean was sentenced to 170 months in prison, to be served concurrently with his life sentence.

On September 8, 1984, in a suburb of Rochester, New York, fifteen-year-old Patrick DeGelleke set his adoptive parents' home on fire as they slept. His mother died in the fire; his father died eleven days later from burn complications. For years before the killing, Patrick had behavioral and emotional problems and had been in counseling. At school he could not seem to concentrate and often stared off into space for hours. At home he was quiet and withdrawn but would sometimes "erupt into violent, uncontrollable temper tantrums." Patrick's three natural brothers—also adopted by the DeGellekes—rarely played with him and sometimes beat him up.

After his parents took Patrick to court, claiming he was involved in truancy and theft and that they could not control him, Patrick feared that he was going to be institutionalized and abandoned. According to a psychologist who testified at Patrick's murder trial, the petition to the court "threw Patrick into a psychotic rage . . . during which he lost his sense of reality and set the fire." A psychiatrist—the same one who later testified that John Justice was sane when he wiped out his entire family—testified for the prosecution that Patrick's killing of his parents was simply a parent-child power struggle: a "straightforward case of 'We will see who's going to be the boss.' "

The jury apparently accepted that theory. Rejecting Patrick's insanity plea, they found him guilty of murder.

In addition to simple patricides and matricides, there are occasional cases, such as those of Patrick Degelleke and Ginger Turnmire, in which juveniles kill both their parents. Indeed, there are sometimes even cases, like those of David Brom, John Justice, and Sean Stevenson, in which juveniles kill not only their parents but their siblings as well.

In many ways, the forces behind mass killings of family members by juveniles are similar to those in simple parricides. Like those who kill one parent, juveniles who kill both parents or destroy their entire nuclear families are often abused youngsters, but many, probably most, of these young mass family killers are also psychologically disturbed and often seriously mentally ill.

In some instances, the bizarre circumstances of these multiple killings suggest that the juvenile perpetrator must have been psychologically disturbed. Witness, for example, David Brom, who ax-murdered his entire family. Consider also the more recent case of Jose Hernandez, a seventeen-year-old Philadelphia boy who killed his father, stepmother (who was three months pregnant), and two half brothers, one six years old and the other just eight months old. Both parents were shot, the older boy was strangled and the infant was beaten to death. The bodies of all four were found piled in a bathtub when Jose fled after an aunt demanded to be admitted to the family home four days after the killings.

Convicted of all four murders, Jose was sentenced to serve four life terms in prison.

Finally, consider the even more recent case of Brian Britton, a fourteen-year-old Poughkeepsie, New York boy charged with shooting and killing his parents and seriously wounding his seventeen-year-old sister after an argument over his school attendance. When taken into custody after the March 1989 killings, Brian was wearing military fatigues and identified himself as "Rambo."

In other multiple intrafamilial killings, evidence other than or in addition to the manner of death makes it clear that the juvenile perpetrator is seriously disturbed. Consider, for example, the cases of Ginger Turnmire, John Justice, and Patrick Degelleke. In each of these mass family murder cases, there was psychiatric testimony that the juvenile killers were mentally ill. Even in the case of Sean Stevenson, absent such evidence, the prosecutor conceded that the juvenile mass murderer was "severely mentally disturbed."

On July 8, 1986, a thirteen-year-old Colorado girl shot and wounded her mother and then shot and killed her younger sister because she wanted to leave no witnesses. In an early hearing in the case against her, the girl's attorney seriously argued that she was possessed by the devil and ought to be exorcised. After examining the girl for over nine months at a state hospital adolescent unit, psychiatrists testified that she "had an intense hatred for her mother . . . built up over a number of years." Tried as a juvenile, she was ordered confined for five years. In rendering that order, the judge recommended that the girl remain in the state psychiatric hospital for additional treatment.

On April 2, 1984, fourteen-year-old Michael Smalley kidnapped a five-year-old Ohio girl and slashed her throat. The girl's body was found in the attic of the family's rented home. Convicted of kidnapping and aggravated attempted murder in juvenile court, Michael was committed to the state Department of Youth Services for one year.

Three and a half years later, on September 20, 1987, at the age of seventeen, Michael Smalley shot and killed his fifteen-year-old sister, left her lying in a pool of blood, and hitchhiked from West Virginia to Arizona, where he was arrested. Although he pleaded guilty to first-degree murder and was sentenced to life in prison, Michael will be eligible for parole in 1998.

On January 23, 1989, a sixteen-year-old Chicago youth quarreled with his eight-year-old brother over a bicycle, pulled the younger boy off the bike by the throat, and then knocked him down a flight of stairs with a Karate-style kick to his chest, killing him. The sixteen-year-old, who had been released from a mental institution just one month earlier, had a five-year history of psychiatric hospitalizations and had earlier set fire to his family's home on three separate occasions. Charged with murder as an adult, he was ordered to undergo another psychiatric evaluation and was found incompetent to stand trial.

As these cases illustrate, some juveniles kill their siblings. Sometimes, as in the John Justice case, a sibling is killed along with a parent or parents. But in other cases, juveniles kill only a brother or sister. While it may be tempting to blame these killings on some extreme form of sibling rivalry, most cases of fratricide or sororicide defy such a simplistic explanation.

The rarity of juvenile sibling killings makes it difficult to generalize, but what little research has been done regarding fratricide and sororicide suggests that youngsters who kill their siblings have much in common with those who kill one or both parents. These youngsters have generally been abused by their parent(s), some are mentally ill, and a few appear to be budding psychopaths.

3

Theft-Related Killings

BETWEEN APRIL 25, 1987 and August 15 of the same year, Clinton Bankston, Jr., a Georgia high school dropout, robbed and killed five people. In April, Clinton was fifteen years old when he entered the home of two retired college professors, robbed the couple, and then killed them. According to the local police chief, the motive was robbery. The couple, he said, "gave the appearance that they kept money and valuables at their house, but they didn't."

Less than four months later, now sixteen, Clinton entered the home of three women intending to rob them. After robbing and stabbing the women, he used a hatchet to hack them beyond recognition. He was arrested the same day while driving a car belonging to one of his victims. After entering a plea of guilty but mentally ill to five charges of murder, Clinton was sentenced to five consecutive life terms, virtually guaranteeing that he will never be released from prison.

Between February 24 and March 27, 1987, two Catholic priests were found tortured and slain in their Buffalo, New York rectories. Both rectories were robbed and each priest was bound to a chair, gagged, stabbed, and bludgeoned. One was stabbed ten times, the other twenty. Within days of the second killing, police arrested two youths, seventeen-year-old Milton Jones and eighteen-year-old Theodore Simmons.

Tried on robbery and murder charges, both youngsters pleaded that their deprived and impoverished backgrounds led them to kill. Theodore Simmons, however, claimed that he acted under duress from Milton Jones, who was two inches taller and outweighed him by eighty pounds. Convicted, Theodore and Milton were each sentenced to serve from fifty years to life in prison. In announcing the sentence, the longest prison term possible under New York law, the judge told the youths he regretted that the law did not allow him to impose the death penalty.

Matthew Schrom and Anthony Holtorff were both sixteen years old when they broke into the home of an eighty-six-year-old Minnesota man on January 15, 1988. After stealing a sock filled with $40 worth of pennies, the boys attacked the elderly man with a hunting knife, left him for dead, and set fire to his house in an apparent effort to cover up the killing. The victim, who died from a stab wound to the heart, was found with multiple stab wounds and a slit throat.

At the time of the killing, Matthew was an altar boy and president of his high school class. According to his attorney, he was an impressionable youngster who followed the lead of his friend, Anthony—a boy described by a local pastor as being "in constant trouble." The defense attorney argued that Matthew "would never have done anything like that on his own." Echoing the attorney, Matthew's father added that he had done "everything" to keep his son away from Anthony.

Both boys ultimately pleaded guilty to murder. the court apparently accepted the theory that Anthony was the leader and Matthew the follower. Matthew was sentenced to nine years in prison. Anthony was sentenced to twenty-six years and must serve at least sixteen years and five months before becoming eligible for parole.

On February 8, 1988, two other sixteen-year-olds, Robert Demeritt and Jayson Moore, also killed an elderly victim. High on drugs and alcohol, Robert and Jayson broke into the home of an elderly neighbor in New Hampshire. Although the boys later claimed they intended only a burglary, the lights were on, the door was open, and the boys were armed with knives. Confronted by the woman's dog, Robert slit the animal's throat. Then confronted by the woman, Jayson attacked and stabbed her.

When Robert tried to flee, Jayson demanded that he remain and help kill the women because she had seen both their faces. Together, the boys stabbed the woman more than thirty times in the stomach, neck, and face. After the killing, they stole a large sum of money and numerous groceries from the woman's home and attached grocery store. Within hours, witnesses said the boys were partying with friends, bragging about the killing, and congratulating each other.

Even the prosecutor conceded that both boys had "deprived and dark backgrounds" and "dysfunctional families." Jayson Moore had begun drinking at age eight, was drug-dependent since age ten, and had a lengthy history of criminal violence. Robert Demeritt, described by psychologists as immature, passive, and dependent, had a history of burglaries and drug possession, but no record of any previous violence. After pleading guilty to murder, both boys were sentenced to terms of forty years to life in prison.

Fifteen-year-old Hillary Spruill, a suburban New York city boy, was walking a girl home from a basketball game on November 21, 1986, when he was shot and killed. Three youths accosted Hillary and demanded his leather "bomber" jacket. At first he resisted, and then he agreed to give up the jacket—but it was too late. The zipper jammed, and seventeen-year-old Austin Addison shot Hillary in the head with a sawed-off .22 caliber rifle. Hillary died three days later. Austin Addison was convicted of murder and sentenced to twenty-five years to life in prison. The other youths were convicted of felony murder and ordered jailed for five years.

Regardless of the age of the perpetrator, many homicides are committed in the course of theft crimes. Annually, nearly ten percent of cleared homicides in the United States (i.e., those resulting in arrests) occur in the course of a robbery. A large percentage of these homicides also occur in the course of other theft offenses, such as burglary (breaking and entering for purposes of theft) or simple larceny.

An even greater proportion of juvenile homicides—often 20 percent or more annually—are committed during the course of theft offenses. While these killings are often described as "motivated" by robbery or theft, this terminology is usually a gross oversimplification, if not a misnomer. Very rarely does one need to kill another person to steal from or rob that person. By far the vast majority of burglaries, larcenies, and even armed robberies are completed successfully without killing or even injuring anyone. Only a minute percentage of all theft crimes result in homicide.

For example, in 1987, according to FBI estimates, there were half a million robberies, over three million burglaries, and nearly seven and one-half million larcenies in the United States, but fewer than 21,000 cases of murder or manslaughter. FBI data for the same year indicate that while there were 25,779 juvenile arrests for robbery, 122,399 juvenile arrests for burglary, and 282,329 juvenile arrests for larceny, there were only 1,454 juvenile arrests for murder and non-negligent manslaughter. FBI data for preceding years paint a very similar picture.

Why then, and under what circumstances, do juveniles kill during the course of a robbery, burglary, or other larceny?

*   *   *

James McClure was twelve years old when, on May 7, 1985, he entered the home of his elderly next-door neighbor, planning to steal something. Unexpectedly confronted by the eighty-year-old California man, James panicked, pulled a kitchen knife from his pocket, and stabbed the man once in the chest, killing him. After pleading guilty to a reduced charge of voluntary manslaughter, James McClure was committed to the state Youth Authority until his twenty-first birthday.

Sixteen-year-old "Donald"—who was in the habit of mugging street people when he needed money—killed a vagrant while robbing him. The robbery victim resisted, calling Donald and his accomplice names and spitting at them. In response, Donald hit the man in the head with a brick and killed him. Later Donald claimed, plausibly, that he never intended to kill the man but hit him only to "get even" for the name-calling and spitting.

More recently, on October 18, 1988, two sixteen-year-olds, Brian Houchin and Joseph Hallock, and a nineteen-year-old, Larry Allen, robbed an Indiana bank. In the course of the robbery, Brian—described by his attorney as a "dope addict" seeking money to help his twenty-one-year-old pregnant girlfriend—shot and killed a sixty-year-old teller. Although Brian confessed to the robbery and shooting, he steadfastly maintained that he "didn't go there to kill anybody."

Many, perhaps even most, homicides committed by juveniles in the course of robberies, burglaries, and other theft crimes are unintentional if not accidental. A juvenile committing a robbery or burglary panics and overreacts when a burglary victim unexpectedly appears and confronts the juvenile burglar or when a robbery victim tries to use force to thwart the robbery.

Other theft-related killings undoubtedly result from the accidental overuse of force, as when the perpetrator means only to instill fear in the victim but misjudges the level of force used. In one case, a fourteen-year-old boy, short of money, stole a pistol and later used it to rob a cab driver. Although the boy planned only to scare the driver into giving him her money, the gun went off and the driver was shot and killed.

Still other "accidental" theft-related homicides seem to occur when a juvenile uses force that proves to be excessive for an especially vulnerable victim, such as an elderly person who is frail or in poor health. In a typical and all too common case of this sort, twelve-year-old Anthony grabbed an eighty-three-year-old New York City woman's handbag with such force that the woman was spun around, knocked to the sidewalk, and dragged a short distance. After surgery for a broken hip, the victim was recovering when she developed congestive heart failure and died two days later from a myocardial infarction.

At trial, the juvenile court judge found that Anthony "created a substantial and unjustifiable risk when he selected [the elderly woman] as the victim, that he was heedless of the peril created by his violence, and that his criminal act set in motion the sequence of events that led inexorably to her death." Finding Anthony guilty of manslaughter, the judge committed him to a state institution for delinquents.

When juveniles intentionally kill the victims of theft crimes, their motivation is rarely accomplishment of the theft. Indeed, most of the time, the theft has been accomplished before the killing. Instead, intentional theft-related homicides are usually motivated by one or more of three factors: (1) sexual impulses; (2) abuse or sale of drugs; and (3) a peculiar kind of peer influence that occasionally occurs when two or more juveniles jointly commit a theft crime.

Two reform school inmates, seventeen-year-old Terry Losicco and sixteen-year-old David Hollis, broke into the home of an elderly couple late at night, intending to steal money they thought was hidden there. Unexpectedly confronted by one of the occupants, a sixty-seven-year-old woman, the older youth sodomized her, kicked her in the mouth, and then beat her to death with a stick while the younger boy watched. After the killing, the two boys fled with $25 in cash, returned to the reform school, and bragged to their fellow inmates.

Both youths were convicted of murder. Terry Losicco was sentenced to twenty-five years to life in prison; David Hollis received a term of 20 years to life.

In a remarkably similar case, two New Jersey boys, ages fifteen and sixteen, were charged with raping and killing an elderly woman and assaulting her husband. The two boys broke into the couple's home on the night of December 3, 1986. First they beat the ninety-four-year-old bedridden husband when he failed to tell them where the couple's money was hidden. Then they confronted the ninety-one-year-old woman, who walked only with the aid of a walker. They knocked her to the floor, stripped her of her clothing, raped her, and beat her to death. Before leaving, they set fire to the house in an attempt to cover up the rape and killing.

Theft-related sexual impulse killings generally occur when juveniles set out only to rob or burglarize but, when confronted by a vulnerable female victim, impulsively rape and then kill her to avoid being identified. Usually these killings are the work of two or more juveniles acting in concert, but occasionally they are committed by juveniles acting alone.

Paul Magill's rape and murder of a convenience store clerk is typical of this sort of homicide when committed by a single juvenile. Looking for money to help him run away from home, seventeen-year-old Paul went into the store, pulled a gun, and ordered the clerk to hand over all the cash in the till. When the clerk did as he demanded, Paul realized that she would call the police as soon as he left.

To keep the clerk away from a phone, Paul forced her out of the store and drove her to a wooded area, where he planned to abandon her. But once they reached the woods, Paul changed his mind, raped the woman, and then shot and killed her to avoid being identified. He was arrested and confessed the same day. Psychologists who examined him later saw no evidence that Paul was seriously mentally ill, but concluded that he had "no capacity to handle his sexual drives and very little control over his aggression." Convicted of murder, Paul Magill was sentenced to die.

After swallowing six tabs of LSD and drinking three cups of grain alcohol mixed with Kool-Aid, seventeen-year-old Ralph Deer, Jr., and another juvenile set out to rob a convenience store to get money for fishing bait and cigarettes. Ralph pointed a loaded and cocked shotgun at the store's cashier, who handed over $11. As Ralph turned, the gun discharged, shooting and killing the cashier. Although Ralph pleaded insanity, based upon his drug and alcohol intoxication, he was convicted of first-degree murder and sentenced to life in prison when the jury could not agree whether he should be sentenced to die.

Many juveniles who kill are under the influence of alcohol or other mind-altering drugs. One recent study of thirty-seven juvenile killers, all of whom killed "during the course of another crime, such as robbery or rape" found that nearly 73 percent were intoxicated on alcohol or other drugs at the time they killed.

In most cases of this sort drugs appear to be a key factor in turning what would otherwise be just a robbery into a homicide. In other theft-related homicides, drug intoxication interacts with the juvenile killer's already disturbed psychological makeup. For example, seventeen-year-old Heath Wilkins and a friend, "both tripping on LSD," planned to rob a liquor store. After forcing the clerk to hand over the money, Heath killed her out of fear that she could identify him.

While drugs were clearly implicated in this case, so too was Heath Wilkins' background and psychological makeup. Abandoned by his father, a mental patient, at age three, and left with his mother, a drug abuser who frequently beat him, Heath was smoking marijuana by the time he reached kindergarten. By age seven he was setting fires and committing house burglaries. From the age of ten until just months before the murder, Heath was a ward of the state and lived in various detention facilities, mental institutions, and foster homes. At the time of the killing, he was living in an outdoor children's park.

Psychologists who examined Heath after the killing described him as an extremely impulsive, depressed, and alienated youth with little capacity to control his anger and aggression. As one doctor put it: "He is vulnerable to massive infusions of intense rage which leads to spasms of destructive action. His rage co-mingles with a profound depressive experience generated by an excruciating sense of lonely alienation whereby he experiences both himself and other people as being lifeless and empty." Convicted of capital murder, Heath Wilkins was sentenced to die.

Not only are many theft-related juvenile killings committed by youths under the influence of drugs, but many of these killings happen in the course of burglaries or robberies motivated by a desire to obtain money to buy drugs. Moreover, at least some juvenile homicides result from turf wars—territorial disputes over the right to sell drugs in a certain locale. In these cases, juveniles kill rival drug dealers to insure their own markets or those of their drug-dealing employers.

John Charles Smith is one such juvenile. A fifteen-year-old New York youth, John ran away to Dallas after several Jamaican drug dealers told him he could make easy money there in the drug trade. John was sentenced to eighteen years in prison after being convicted of three drug-related, execution-style killings. John shot the three victims a total of twenty-seven times—including three shots through the soles of one victim's feet and ten shots fired at another as he tried to telephone for aid. Interviewed after sentencing, John said he expected to receive $5,000 from his drug-dealing employers when he is eventually paroled. Similar cases involving the use of juveniles as "enforcers" in drug trafficking have been reported in Detroit, New York City, and New England.

Finally, some drug-related juvenile homicides result from drug deals gone sour—cases in which juveniles kill while trying to collect money owed for drugs. Consider, for example, sixteen-year-old Eugene Turley, a District of Columbia junior high dropout who used a .357 magnum to shoot and kill a thirty-year-old mother of four in a Virginia convenience store parking lot. Eugene told police he shot the woman because she refused to pay the $75 cocaine debt he had been sent to collect for a drug dealer. Convicted of first degree murder by a jury that deliberated only twenty-four minutes, Eugene Turley was sentenced to life in prison.

Two young burglars, sixteen-year-old Michael Boettlin and twenty-two-year-old John Calvaresi, broke into a Pennsylvania apartment looking for "lots of money and a nice stereo." Surprised by one of the occupants of the apartment, John Calvaresi beheaded the forty-two-year-old man with a kitchen knife. The two then left the man's head and body lying on the floor of the apartment near a wall on which they used his blood to scrawl "redrum"—murder spelled backwards—an idea they got from Stephen King's horror novel, *The Shining*.

John Calvaresi pleaded guilty and was sentenced to life in prison. Michael Boettlin went to trial and was convicted of murder, after his attorney argued that the sixteen-year-old accomplice had "mistakenly tagged along with . . . a madman . . . a maniac who killed without reason."

Fifteen-year-old John Morris and fourteen-year-old Alton Smith frequently ran errands for their neighbors, eighty-eight-year-old Boykin Gibson and his eighty-four-year-old wife, Sarah. On January 15, 1985, John Morris picked up an over-the-counter antihistamine for the Gibsons and delivered it to their Pittsburgh home. When the Gibsons opened the door, they were rushed by John, Alton, and three older youths: Christopher Caldwell, eighteen, Eric Anderson, nineteen, and Alan Williams, twenty-one. After ransacking the Gibsons' home and stealing $500 in cash and rare coins, the youths tied the elderly couple to chairs and then stood by as Christopher Caldwell slashed their throats.

Police investigations revealed that the three older youths—two of whom had criminal records—planned the robbery and used the younger boys to gain access to the Gibsons' home. Eric Anderson, John Morris, and Alton Smith all plea-bargained and were allowed to plead guilty to third-degree murder, robbery, burglary, and conspiracy. Eric and John were each sentenced to serve from five to twenty years in prison. Alton was sentenced to a maximum term of six years in prison. Alan Williams was convicted of first-degree murder and sentenced to two consecutive life terms. Christopher Caldwell was convicted of capital murder and sentenced to die. His death sentence was later vacated by the Pennsylvania Supreme Court, and he was ordered imprisoned for life.

These two Pennsylvania cases have much in common with several cases described earlier—those of Robert Demeritt and Jayson Moore, Terry Losicco and David Hollis, Matthew Schrom and Anthony Holtorff, and Theodore Simmons and Milton Jones. First, all started out as theft offenses, either robberies or burglaries. Second, all resulted not only in killings, but especially brutal and heinous killings, violent acts well beyond anything needed to complete the underlying theft crime. Third, all involved two or more youngsters acting together. Finally, in all there was reason to believe that some perpetrators were leaders and others followers.

Michael Boettlin was sixteen and John Calvaresi was six years older. John Morris and Alton Smith were juveniles, obviously used by their adult accomplices who planned the crime. Theodore Simmons claimed he was coerced by Milton Jones, who was two inches taller and eighty pounds heavier. Anthony Holtorff was a known trouble-maker while Matthew Schrom was a model youth with no history of being a discipline problem. Jayson Moore had a long history of serious crime while Robert Demeritt, a passive-dependent youth, had only a relatively minor criminal record. Terry Losicco, who sodomized and beat an elderly woman to death, recruited David Hollis for the crime only after failing to enlist two other youths. As the judge pointed out at sentencing, though equally guilty in the eyes of the law, David did not arm himself, did not strike the victim, and did not attack her sexually: "The only crime was his failure to take corrective action to stop it."

Taken together, these common features suggest a pattern of peer-influenced theft-related juvenile homicide in which one perpetrator, generally the older, larger, or more violent one, initiates the violence against the victim. The atrocious nature of these crimes further suggests that the joint involvement of the perpetrators works to create a situation in which the juvenile killers are unable to stop at simply killing the victim, but instead go on to inflict gratuitous and especially heinous violence. In at least some of these cases, it seems clear that one juvenile's violence feeds upon—or is somehow stimulated by—that of the other youth until the attack escalates to the point of atrocity.

On February 6, 1986, seventeen-year-old Sean Pica shot and killed James Pierson, the father of his high school classmate, Cheryl Pierson. Sean, a burglar with a $200-a-week cocaine habit, agreed to do the killing for $1,000, and was eventually paid $400 by Cheryl's boyfriend. On the night of James Pierson's funeral, Sean demanded additional money, a rent-free apartment, and motorcycles for himself and a friend.

Though he pleaded guilty to manslaughter, Sean claimed that he was only trying to help Cheryl, that money played no role in his decision to kill her father. Two psychologists and a psychiatrist examined Sean and supported his claim. One psychologist said Sean was a concrete thinker who saw the world "in black and white," would "go to any lengths to help a friend," and "refus[ed] to back out of commitment once he made one." As this doctor saw Sean's motivation: "His primary focus was on the notion that this girl needed help and that he, as a 'friend' and as a 'man' was 'duty bound' to help her."

A second psychologist theorized that Sean was a boy with "a Robin Hood complex, someone who had been searching for a cause, a test of his manhood, a rite of passage to enter the world of adult males." The psychiatrist suggested that in killing Cheryl's father, Sean may have been acting out "negative feelings" he "most probably had been harboring toward" his own father and stepfather.

Rejecting the experts' views, the judge found Sean Pica a "cold-blooded murderer" motivated by "sheer greed" and sentenced him to serve from eight to twenty-four years in prison.

Killings committed by juvenile "hit men" or hired killers are quite rare, but they do occur. Interestingly, though, when they do, there is often something more than just money behind them. Consider, for example, the brutal hired killing of Robert Pearce.

Just before 6:00 in the morning on January 31, 1989, two young men attacked Robert Pearce outside his apartment as he left for work. Using a hatchet and a kitchen knife, the assailants slashed and stabbed the forty-year-old construction worker fifty times before fleeing. Cut, bleeding, and carrying the knife in his back, Pearce managed to get back to his apartment. After his roommates called the police, Pearce was rushed by helicopter to a hospital, where he died before 7:30 A.M.

Within days of the killing, police arrested Robert Pearce's estranged wife, Roberta, a popular high school teacher's aide. They also arrested Anthony Pilato and Isaac Hill, both fifteen-year-old freshmen at the school where Roberta Pearce worked with learning disabled students. Anthony, an average student and star running back of the freshman football team, had no apparent history of trouble. Isaac, on the other hand, had a criminal record and multiple problems at school, including fighting, tardiness, and truancy.

Prosecutors charged that Roberta Pearce hired the two fifteen-year-olds, promising each a used car and a large sum of cash if they killed her husband. The boys admitted their guilt and claimed that Mrs. Pearce offered them two cars and $100,000—half the proceeds from a $200,000 life insurance policy—to kill her husband. After pleading guilty, both were sentenced to prison terms of twenty-five years to life.

Meanwhile, Mrs. Pearce was charged with murder as well as supplying drugs and sex to teenagers who hung out at her home. Although she maintained her innocence, she was convicted of first-degree murder and sentenced to life in prison.

4

Sexual Killings

ON THE EVENING of October 26, 1979, David Lawrence called his wife at 9:30 to say he would not be home until around 11:00 P.M. When he arrived home at 11:30 that night, he found his wife Sarah's body lying face up between the sofa and coffee table. Blood ran from a gaping hole in her throat, she was nude from the waist down, her legs were spread apart, and her panties hung from the bottom of her right leg. Mrs. Lawrence's three young children were sound asleep in their bedrooms. At first, because of the proximity to Halloween, Mr. Lawrence thought his wife was playing some kind of vampire joke.

It was no joke. Mrs. Lawrence was dead, stabbed more than thirty times. Autopsy evidence indicated that in addition to stabbing her to death, her killer had "cut open her abdomen and ejaculated into it before slitting her throat." The autopsy further revealed that after killing Mrs. Lawrence, the perpetrator probably had sexual intercourse with her.

Footprints in the alley outside the Lawrence's Amarillo, Texas apartment led police almost directly to the home of seventeen-year-old Jay Kelly Pinkerton. After being arrested and jailed pending trial on murder charges, Jay bragged to a fellow inmate about the rape and killing. According to John Alley, who heard Jay's boasts, "He cut her stomach open and fucked her in the wound until he come and he slashed her throat and cut her breasts off."

Charged with killing Mrs. Lawrence in the course of a burglary with intent to commit rape, Jay Kelly Pinkerton was found guilty and sentenced to die. Jay was later tried again on rape and murder charges in another Texas sex slaying that took place after he killed Mrs. Lawrence but before he was arrested. The outcome was a replay of the first trial: the verdict was guilty and the sentence was death. On May 15, 1986, Jay Kelly Pinkerton was executed by lethal injection.

In May 1981, two twelve-year-old sixth graders, Meghan and Melissa, took a shortcut through the woods in their hometown in Vermont. As Meghan would later tell it, "We were walking along and two men jumped out and grabbed us and dragged us off." The two "men" were fifteen-year-old Jamie Savage and sixteen-year-old Louis Hamlin.

After pulling the girls off the path, the two teens dragged them into the woods, forced them to disrobe, tied them up, tortured, raped, and stabbed them both, and then killed Melissa. For two weeks prior to the killing, the boys had egged each other on with talk of finding and raping "some girls." On the day of the killing, they had been hunting squirrels with BB guns when they saw the two victims and impulsively decided to ambush them.

Questioned after his arrest, Jamie claimed that he and Louis had no advance plan to kill the girls, "only to rape them, tie them up, and flee." But once the attack began, the two boys seemed to lose control. Jamie choked Melissa and told Meghan to look away or he would shoot her. Then Louis told her, "Now you're going to know what it feels like to be shot five times—to be killed—to be slaughtered like a pig." The violence escalated until ultimately the youths shot and stabbed both girls.

Louis Hamlin—who had also allegedly sexually abused his sister and accosted another girl with a knife—was sentenced to serve from forty-five years to life in prison. Because Jamie Savage was not quite sixteen at the time of the rapes and killing, he could not be tried as an adult. He was committed to the state juvenile authority and locked up only until his eighteenth birthday.

Marko Bey, a New Jersey boy, was ten days short of his eighteenth birthday when, on April 2, 1983, he sexually assaulted a nineteen-year-old woman and beat her to death with a two-by-four. Marko confessed to the killing but said the sex had been consensual. He told police he smoked six or seven marijuana cigarettes and consumed a forty ounce bottle of beer, had sexual intercourse with the victim, and then killed her when she refused to have sex with him again. In his words, "I got my nut and I wanted to start again and she didn't . . . I know I beat her but I don't remember how I did it."

Marko Bey's confession came as police questioned him about yet another sex killing, the April 26 rape and strangling of a forty-six-year-old woman. Eventually, Marko confessed to that homicide as well, telling police he accosted the woman in front of her home, demanded money, and then dragged her into a shed, where he beat, stomped, strangled, and sexually abused her. After the rape and killing, he took off in the victim's car, which he later wrecked and abandoned.

Marko Bey was convicted of sexually assaulting and murdering both women and was twice sentenced to die. His death sentence in the first killing was later overturned by the New Jersey Supreme Court because he was a minor at the time of the killing. The court also ordered a new trial in the second case because police violated Marko's constitutional rights in questioning him after he told them he wanted to remain silent. In ordering a new trial, however, the court did not rule out the possibility that a conviction might result in yet another death sentence, since the second killing took place two weeks after Marko turned eighteen.

*   *   *

Thirteen-year-old Barbara was also walking near a wooded area when she was sodomized and murdered. Her attacker was fifteen-year-old Shawn Milne, a neighbor boy who claimed the girl had constantly harassed and threatened him. Shawn admitted attacking Barbara on November 12, 1985, dragging her face down through several hundred feet of woods, and dropping her a number of times on her head before throwing her into a creek and leaving her.

Initial reports indicated that Barbara, whose body was found naked from the waist down, had been beaten to death. While she had indeed been brutally bludgeoned with a blunt instrument, the autopsy revealed that she was still alive when Shawn Milne dumped her into the New Jersey creek and left her for dead.

Shawn Milne was arrested the day after the killing. He told police that after dumping Barbara into the creek, he went home, cleaned up, and went to his girlfriend's birthday party. Interviewed later by a psychiatrist, Shawn said "voices commanded him to do things."

Tried as an adult, Shawn claimed he killed the girl in self-defense after she pulled a knife on him. A jury rejected that claim and convicted him of aggravated sexual assault and murder.

By the time Matthew Rosenberg turned fourteen in 1983, he had already sexually molested twenty young boys. In October of that year, the Massachusetts teen sexually molested five-year-old Kenny Claudio, beat and drowned the child, stuffed his naked body into a trash bag, and then hid the bag in his bedroom closet. Convicted of murder and remanded to a state juvenile facility, Matthew was accused of assaulting younger inmates. In 1989, when he turned twenty, he was transferred to an adult facility for sexual offenders, where he is expected to remain until he is twenty-two.

In their recent book, *Sexual Homicide*, Robert Ressler, Ann Burgess, and John Douglas define a sexual homicide as one in which there is evidence or observations indicating that the killing was sexual in nature. According to Ressler and his colleagues:

> These include: victim attire or lack of attire; exposure of sexual parts of the victim's body; sexual positioning of the victim's body; insertion of foreign objects into the victim's body cavities; evidence of sexual intercourse (oral, anal, vaginal); and evidence of substitute sexual activity, interest, or sadistic fantasy.

At least some juvenile homicides fit that definition. The actual percentage of juvenile killings that are sexual in nature is unknown and difficult to estimate. Most crime statistics do not differentiate sexual and nonsexual homicides, and even obvious cases of rape-homicide are most often reported as homicides, not rapes. Thus, many rape-murders end up being catalogued as murders with no mention of rape.

The difficulty determining whether a homicide is sex-related is well illustrated in one of the earliest works dealing with juvenile sex killings, Dr. Warren Stearns' article, "Murder by Adolescents with Obscure Motivation." Dr. Stearns described five adolescent boys who killed girls or women under conditions suggesting but not clearly establishing a sexual motivation.

The first boy, a fifteen-year-old, was giving a "scantily clad" fourteen-year-old girl a ride on his bike. With the girl sitting on the handlebars facing him, he stopped, pulled out a gun and shot her four times. The second youth, age thirteen, entered the home of a forty-one-year-old woman "clad in white shorts and a halter only," knocked her unconscious with a milk bottle, put a laundry bag over head, strangled her, and then plunged a knife into her abdomen.

The third youngster, eighteen years old, was leaving the home of a dressmaker who had just mended his jacket. On his way out, he grabbed the woman, strangled her, tied a pair of cloth panties around her neck, hit her in the head several times with a rolling pin, plunged a butcher knife into her heart, and tied her feet together with a piece of cloth. The fourth boy, also eighteen, went to a home where his girlfriend was babysitting, greeted her at the door with a bayonet, and then stabbed her forty-six times. The final youth, a boy thirteen, lured a thirteen-year-old girl into the woods and then plunged a knife into her back because he "wanted to see her breasts."

On the other hand, what seem to be juvenile sexual homicides may not be. For example, in a 1989 New York City killing, a sixteen-year-old boy stabbed his mother to death after she refused to give him $200 to pay off a debt to a crack dealer. After plunging a knife into her heart, the boy opened his mother's shirt, disrobed her from the waist down, tied her hands with a telephone cord, and then went to school. After school, he came home, "discovered" his mother's body and telephoned the police. When the police arrived, the youth told them he had come home and found his mother dead. After further questioning, he admitted killing her and arranging her body to make it look like she had been raped.

While it is often difficult to say with certainty whether a juvenile homicide is or is not sex-related, it is clear that juveniles do commit a significant proportion of all sex crimes. For example, in 1987, youths under the age of eighteen accounted for roughly 16 percent of all reported arrests for forcible rape. During the same year, according to FBI data, about 16 percent of all other sex crimes (crimes other than forcible rape or prostitution) were committed by individuals seventeen years of age or younger.

While difficult to categorize precisely, juvenile sex killings seem to fall into four sometimes overlapping categories: (1) sexual homicides committed by seriously disturbed juveniles; (2) killings apparently committed to cover up a sex crime or avoid being identified as the perpetrator of such a crime; (3) group rapes that end in homicide; and (4) individual and group robberies that lead to impulsive rape and homicide.

*   *   *

In many cases, both the nature of the crime and the juvenile perpetrator's mental state suggest that the crime is the product of serious psychological disturbance. Consider, for example, fifteen-year-old "Steve," who "killed his middle-aged cousin after she nagged him about his dirty shirt." Steve repeatedly beat the woman in the head with a pipe, choked her, and finally used a knife to mutilate her genitals. After the killing, he revealed that during the past two years he had often peeped into women's windows, had fantasized about rape and murder, and twice actually attacked women. Describing one of these attacks, Steve said,

> It's like the devil inside saying go ahead and grab her, stab her, choke her, kill her . . . . Like a magnet pulling you . . . . I feel hot and excited and the sex feelings are very strong. I had to hit her with a rock over and over. I wanted to choke her to death and then rape her.

After the killing, Steve was committed to a psychiatric hospital and diagnosed as suffering from chronic schizophrenia.

More recently, a seven-year-old California girl was strangled while being sexually assaulted by an emotionally disturbed fifteen-year-old boy. Sara Hodges disappeared and was reported missing on March 23, 1989. One of the first people to volunteer to help look for Sara was fifteen-year-old Curtis Cooper, who lived just five doors away. Curtis had recently moved to Southern California from Florida, where he had been arrested for a series of burglaries and petty thefts.

Three days after Sara disappeared, Curtis' landlady went looking for the source of a foul odor in the house. What she found was Sara Hodges' decaying body, stuffed behind the headboard of Curtis' waterbed. After molesting the child, strangling her with a dog leash, and hiding her body, Curtis had rigged up a fan to blow the odor out the window so he could continue to sleep in the room.

Described by his attorney as a "kid with real problems," Curtis Cooper was examined by several psychiatrists who determined that he suffered mild brain damage but was not so seriously disturbed as to qualify for an insanity defense. In a plea bargain that could eventually lead to his placement in a mental hospital, Curtis Cooper pleaded guilty to first-degree murder. Under California law, he could be locked up for life, but given his mental condition and age at the time of the crime, he will probably be released from custody when he turns twenty-five.

In some instances, psychological disturbances suffered by juveniles who commit sex-related homicides are clearly drug-induced. An example is the case of sixteen-year-old "Charlie," who looked into the window of an elderly woman's home and "thought I might have sex with her if I went in." In Charlie's own words, "I went in and said, 'Are you going to give me what I want?' And she said, 'No, get out of my house.' And then I took a stick and I hit her." The woman's partially nude body was later found in her home; she had a fractured skull and wounds on her legs, arms, and vaginal area.

Later examined by a psychologist, Charlie reported that he had spent the afternoon of the killing drinking beer and smoking marijuana and was intoxicated when he sexually abused and killed the elderly woman: "I remember I had a buzz on. A pretty strong buzz." Further evaluation revealed that Charlie had been abusing alcohol since the fourth grade. Found competent to stand trial and criminally responsible, Charlie was ordered to stand trial as an adult. In a plea bargain, he pleaded guilty to second-degree murder and was sent to prison.

Although it is often difficult to determine why a juvenile rapist kills his victim, in many cases the young killer fears that if the victim is left alive, she will identify him as a rapist. Perhaps the classic example is the case of the fifteen-year-old boy who tried to rape his thirteen-year-old sister, shot her to death several hours later, and then told authorities: "I had to kill her or my mother would have found out that I had done something bad."

In several more recent cases of this sort, a sixteen-year-old Missouri boy sodomized and strangled an eleven-year-old boy, a thirteen-year-old Illinois boy sexually abused and killed an infant, a thirteen-year-old New Mexico boy sexually molested and suffocated a five-year-old girl, and a sixteen-year-old Ohio boy raped a thirteen-year-old neighbor girl and then stabbed her to death.

In the Missouri case, which took almost two and a half years to solve, the teenager dumped the eleven-year-old's body beside a set of railroad tracks and was not apprehended until years later, when police received an anonymous tip linking him to the crime. In the Illinois case, the youth, who was babysitting, tried to have sex with an eleven-month-old baby and then beat her and held her head under water when she would not stop crying. In the New Mexico case, the teenage boy, who was also babysitting, got drunk, sexually penetrated the child, and then suffocated her.

Most recently, in the Ohio case, the partially nude body of a thirteen-year-old girl was found in a motel room where she lived with her parents. She had been raped, stabbed seven times, and had a broken neck. Sixteen-year-old Donald Shedrick was charged with the September 15, 1988 crime.

Donald, who lived in the same motel, was tried on rape and murder charges. His first trial ended in a mistrial when a jury split six to six over whether there was sufficient evidence to tie him to the rape and killing. In a second trial—after hearing the testimony of another girl Donald had allegedly raped and tried to kill—a jury convicted him of aggravated murder, rape, and burglary. Although Donald's attorney argued that his client was denied a fair trial by the earlier victim's testimony, the trial judge affirmed Donald Shedrick's conviction and sentenced him to life plus seventy-five years in prison.

*   *   *

Fourteen-year-old Wayne, twelve-year-old Billy, and sixteen-year-old Frankie spotted a fifty-year-old woman sleeping on a bench in a New York City park one night. As Frankie later explained,

> [W]e saw this lady sleeping on the bench. Billy said, "Let's drag her behind the house." I smacked her . . . Billy put his hand over her mouth . . . then we all dragged her behind the [boat] house . . . .We started taking her clothes off [and] feeling on her body. . . . She was fighting us back so I smacked her and Billy smacked her twice and Wayne smacked her once. Then she stopped fighting.

Then, according to Frankie, the boys took turns holding the woman down, raping, and sodomizing her. Afterwards, when she tried to get up, they beat her to death with a golf club, sticks, and their hands.

On the night of October 17, 1986, four Chicago teenagers—Marcellus Bradford, seventeen, Omar Saunders, seventeen, Larry Ollins, sixteen, and Calvin Ollins, fourteen—were partying and smoking marijuana. Around midnight, they decided to commit a fast robbery to get bus fare home. Looking for a victim, the four were walking down the street when a car started to cross their path. One of the boys stepped in front of the car. When the driver stopped, all four youths quickly forced their way in.

The youths grabbed the driver, a twenty-two-year-old medical student, and pushed her into the back seat. One of the teens then drove the car to a secluded area, where the woman pleaded for mercy before being forced into the trunk and raped. After being raped by one youth, she tried to get away but fell. Trying to get up, she was kicked and then struck in the head with a piece of concrete. Lifeless, she was then carried back into the car and raped again by two other youths.

Marcellus Bradford turned state's evidence and testified against his accomplices in exchange for a twelve-year sentence on aggravated kidnapping charges. The three others were all convicted of murder and sentenced to life in prison without hope of parole. Sentencing Omar Saunders, the judge called him an "evil person" and a "strange being," adding: "Note that I avoid the word human . . . ." Turning to Calvin Ollins, a mildly retarded fourteen-year-old and the youngest member of the quartet, the judge likened the boy to a wild animal and described the crime as "a bestial, barbaric, horrifying, senseless massacre of a human being."

Six-year-old Willie disappeared on February 27, 1987. Four days later, his body was found at the bottom of a swimming pool in an apartment complex near his home. Autopsy revealed that Willie had been gang raped and beaten before he drowned in the dirty water left in the pool.

Shortly after recovering Willie's body, police arrested four teenage boys—two sixteen, one fourteen, and the other thirteen years old. All four boys had significant behavioral problems. The oldest boys and the thirteen-year-old were all in special education classes for youths with behavior disorders. The fourteen-year-old had just been expelled from school for hitting two teachers as they tried to break up a fight.

According to the investigating officers, the boys took turns sodomizing Willie, threw him into the pool, pulled him out, attacked him again, threw him back into the water, and then threw a deck chair in on top of him. The youngest boy confessed to the gang rape and killing and agreed to testify against the others. While there are no definitive data, it appears that most adults who commit sexual homicides do so individually. But among juveniles, sexual homicides seem much more likely to be committed by two or more youths acting together. Many of these cases are strikingly similar to the peer-influenced theft-related homicides described earlier.

Generally there is nothing to indicate that these youths are seriously disturbed, but their crimes are among the most vicious and senseless of all juvenile homicides. As in the cases described above, what begins as an impulsive act of sexual violence gets out of hand, the youths are spurred on by each other's violence, and they lose control. The result is a particularly vicious killing.

Sometime after midnight on August 31, 1986, two college students, Wendy and Dawn, left the restaurant where both worked as waitresses and headed down an interstate highway toward a local bar. At about the same time, three teenagers—Richard Cooey, nineteen, Kenneth Horonetz, eighteen, and Clint Dickens, seventeen—were throwing things off a bridge over the same highway. Just as Wendy and Dawn's car approached the bridge, Clint threw a large piece of concrete over the bridge. The concrete hit the women's car and forced them to pull over.

The three teens offered help and eventually drove Wendy and Dawn to a nearby shopping mall, where Wendy used a pay telephone to call her mother. At one point in the conversation, Richard took the phone to give directions to Wendy's mother. While Wendy was on the phone, Clint saw some cash in her purse and suggested that he and his friends rob the two women. After agreeing to the robbery, the boys offered Wendy and Dawn a ride back to their car.

But instead of driving back to the car, they drove the women to a secluded spot and robbed them at knifepoint. After the robbery, Kenneth left the car. Richard then drove the women to another spot where he and Clint raped and sodomized both of them.

After sexually abusing the women, Richard and Clint beat them both with a billy club, strangled and repeatedly stabbed them, and then stripped them of their jewelry and left them to die. Afterwards, the two drove to a car wash to clean the women's blood off the car and themselves. The next day, Richard tried to sell the jewelry they stole from the women. He also bragged to an acquaintance about killing a woman and showed him the bloody billy club.

Clint Dickins was tried as an adult, convicted of murder, and sentenced to life in prison—escaping the possibility of a death sentence because of his age. Richard Cooey was convicted and sentenced to die. Kenneth Horonetz was allowed to plead guilty to felonious assault and obstruction of justice. He was ordered imprisoned for fifty-one months.

These cases illustrate a common pattern in which what starts out as an economically motivated crime progresses to rape and ultimately homicide: in the process of robbing a female, juvenile perpetrators impulsively rape and then kill the robbery victim. These kinds of crimes are committed individually and by groups of juveniles acting together, but most seem to be group endeavors.

In at least some of these group-perpetrated robberies-turned-rape/killings, it appears that more immature, less assertive, and sometimes disturbed youths impulsively become involved in the rape and killing by following the direction or lead of another youngster. One example is David Buchanan, a Kentucky teenager, who planned a robbery that resulted in the rape and murder of a twenty-year-old female gas station attendant.

Sixteen-year-old David enlisted two other boys to help him rob the gas station. David asked fifteen-year-old Troy Johnson to wait in the car while he and eighteen-year-old Kevin Stanford robbed the attendant. While David tried to locate and then open the safe, Kevin took the attendant into a restroom and raped her. When David could not open the safe, he joined Kevin in the restroom and both youths took turns raping and sodomizing the young woman. A short while later, Kevin abducted the woman and drove off with her in her car. Ultimately, David and Troy caught up to them and then stood by and watched while Kevin gave the woman a last cigarette and then shot and killed her.

After the killing, the trio fled with 300 cartons of cigarettes and $143 in cash. Within a week, all three youths were arrested after police learned they were selling cigarettes in their neighborhood.

Less than a year before this incident, a psychologist, who evaluated David Buchanan after a burglary arrest, reported that:

[David] presents as a quiet, rather withdrawn and at least moderately depressed sixteen-year-old black youth. . . . His thinking . . . is extremely simplistic and very concrete. Impulse controls even under minimal stress are felt to be very poor. He is not seen as sophisticated but rather as a very dependent, immature, probably pretty severely emotionally disturbed, and very easily confused youth. . . . He will be easily led by other more sophisticated delinquents or youths. He has very limited interpersonal skills and is likely to be seen by other youths as a pawn to be used.

David Buchanan and Kevin Stanford were charged with murder and tried together. Not being the triggerman, David never faced the possibility of the death penalty. He was convicted as charged and sentenced to life in prison. Kevin, who led the attack and actually pulled the trigger, was convicted of murder and sentenced to die after prison guards testified that he often bragged to his cellmates about the rape and killing. Troy Johnson, who testified against David and Kevin, was tried as an accessory in juvenile court.

5

Senseless Killings

As THE RESULT of several days of torture, James Thimm died on or about April 30, 1985. Thimm was a member of a communal group living on a farm in southeastern Nebraska. The group, a survivalist cult headed by Michael Ryan, consisted of twenty adults and children, including Ryan, Thimm, and Ryan's fifteen-year-old son, Dennis. For months, members of the cult had been stealing machinery and cattle and stockpiling guns and ammunition to prepare for "Armageddon." The farm commune was an armed and heavily guarded encampment.

Michael Ryan, who claimed to be able to speak to God and gave orders in the name of "Yahweh," ran the group like an army and assigned ranks to his armed followers, including Dennis. While the others held military ranks, Michael Ryan was "king" and Dennis Ryan was "prince." The "prince" had authority over the other followers and relayed messages to them from the "king."

A month or so before Thimm's death, Michael Ryan decided that Thimm was to be demoted to the rank of "slave." Thereafter, Thimm was allowed to work around the farm during the day but kept chained to a post at night. Not long before his death, Thimm was shot in the face by Dennis Ryan. Although Thimm survived and recovered from the wound without medical attention, he was not allowed to live for long.

On the day before Thimm's death, Michael Ryan, Dennis Ryan, and three other followers took turns torturing Thimm. Each man inserted a greased shovel handle into Thimm's rectum and then administered fifteen lashes with a bullwhip and a livestock whip. The next day, just before Thimm died, the same group, including Dennis Ryan, took turns giving Thimm fifteen lashes and shooting off his fingers. Later that evening, one of the cult members found Thimm's body. Both of the man's legs had been broken, and one leg was skinned.

After the killing, according to the testimony of one cult member, fifteen-year-old Dennis Ryan bragged about the killing and showed no remorse. According to the witness, Dennis told him "he thought it was kind of neat that he had helped kill somebody."

Prior to his trial on murder charges, Dennis Ryan was given a complete psychological evaluation, including a battery of psychological tests. The evaluation revealed that Dennis was average or above average in intelligence and was in good contact with reality but had the overall maturity of a twelve- or thirteen-year-old. The evaluation further revealed that Dennis "strongly and uncritically" accepted his father's "religion."

Michael Ryan was convicted of first-degree murder and sentenced to die. Dennis Ryan was convicted of second-degree murder and received the maximum sentence allowed by law: ten years to life in prison.

Rod Matthews was fourteen years old when, after school on November 20, 1986, he lured another fourteen-year-old boy into a wooded area with a promise of fireworks and then beat him to death with a baseball bat. Prior to the killing, Rod told friends of his plan to kill. After the killing, he showed them the body twice. One friend said Rod told him he killed the boy because "he wanted to know what it was like to kill somebody."

Charged with murder and tried as an adult, Rod Matthews pleaded innocent by reason of insanity. Although Rod claimed the killing was caused by Ritalin, a hyperactivity medication he had taken since the third grade, a psychiatrist testified that Rod was not psychotic at the time of the killing and suffered only a personality disorder. The jury rejected Rod's insanity plea and convicted him of second-degree murder. The judge sentenced him to life in prison.

On November 8, 1988, seventeen-year-old Kenneth Kovzelove and eighteen-year-old Dennis Bencivenga went hunting in an old pickup truck. Dennis was driving. Kenneth, dressed in Army fatigues, hid himself in the back of the truck, armed with a semi-automatic assault rifle. After driving around for awhile, Kenneth spotted his quarry, took aim, and fired repeatedly. Laughing out loud, he shouted "Die!"

Kenneth was a good shot. The spray of bullets struck and killed two Mexican laborers. Together the men were hit with a total of eleven shots. Dennis and Kenneth drove off, leaving the two dead men lying in the dirt.

In January 1989, while trying to enlist in the Army, Dennis confessed his role in the killing to a recruiter, who called the police. Meanwhile Kenneth Kovzelove had succeeded in joining the Army and was training to become a paratrooper. Arrested and charged with murder, he admitted killing the laborers and told authorities that he selected his victims simply because they were Mexicans—an ethnic group he hated. Kenneth went on to describe the killing as a "thrill" and said he joined the Army in the hope that he would have the opportunity to kill again—legally.

On October 13, 1989, Kenneth Kovzelove pleaded guilty to two counts of first-degree murder. He will serve from fifty years to life in prison. Dennis Bencivenga pleaded not guilty and awaits trial.

*   *   *

Steve Lofton was fifteen years old and Chris White sixteen when they killed fourteen-year-old Amber Matlock and dumped her body into an Oklahoma ditch known as "Dead Man's Cave." Their motive? The boys were angry with Amber because she repeatedly broke up with one of them and then started going steady with the other.

Testimony at a pretrial hearing revealed that Steve ambushed Amber in his garage and tried to break her neck. When that failed, he stabbed her with a homemade *kama*, a martial arts weapon consisting of a knife attached to a four-foot pole. Then Steve, Chris, and a younger boy wrapped Amber's body in a tent and pulled it in a wagon to Dead Man's Cave. On the way home from the "Cave," Steve and Chris stopped off at a public library to write songs.

Steve and Chris were both scheduled to be tried for first-degree murder when they agreed to plead guilty to second-degree murder. Steve Lofton was sentenced to life in prison. Chris White was ordered to serve forty years. The younger boy who helped dispose of the body was charged and tried in juvenile court.

Undoubtedly the most troubling, if not most terrifying, juvenile homicides are those committed for no rational reason whatsoever. Killings such as those committed by Dennis Ryan, Rod Matthews, Kenneth Kovzelove, and Steve Lofton can only be described as utterly senseless. But while these senseless killings are extremely deviant acts, it does not necessarily follow that youths who commit these acts are seriously disturbed. Indeed, many senseless, even brutal and bizarre, killings are committed by relatively normal juveniles acting on impulse—often in conjunction with or under the influence of other juveniles. Some of these youths are disturbed, some even appear to be sociopathic, but very few are psychotic or even show signs of gross psychological or psychiatric disturbance.

Most senseless juvenile killings fall into one or more of half a dozen categories: thrill killings; hate killings;

revenge killings; murder-suicides; cult-related killings; and killings committed by mentally disturbed juveniles. Cult-related killings and killings committed by severely disturbed juveniles are discussed separately in two later chapters.

Asked why she kept guns and ammunition in her California apartment, Carolyn Shelton explained that she needed protection: "I'm a single parent, and this is a bad neighborhood." Shelton added that she always kept the guns and ammunition hidden separately and constantly told her sons, who were fourteen and five, never to play with guns.

On April 2, 1987, just a couple of days before Shelton talked about her guns, she was babysitting in another apartment in the building where she lived. She heard a knock on the door. Her fourteen-year-old son walked in and told her he was afraid. When she asked why, the boy explained that he and a friend had just used one of her guns to shoot a man.

Minutes earlier, a truck driver was unhitching a trailer in the parking lot two stories below Shelton's apartment. Shelton's son and another fourteen-year-old found Shelton's .22 caliber rifle and ammunition. As the boys watched the man from a window in the apartment, Shelton's son loaded the rifle, handed it to the other boy, and dared him to shoot the man. While the boy tracked the driver through the telescopic sight for about two minutes, Shelton's son repeatedly urged him to shoot. Finally the boy pulled the trigger. Within seconds, the truck driver slumped to the ground, dead.

Both boys were arrested almost immediately. Police investigation quickly established that this had not been Shelton's son's first use of the rifle. Just a day before the killing, the fourteen-year-old had used the same gun to fire into a public transit bus. The slug ripped through a window and a fragment hit the upper lip of a thirteen-year-old passenger on her way home from school.

Both fourteen-year-olds were charged with murder, convicted, and sentenced to indeterminate terms in the custody of the state Youth Authority. Each boy may be held until his twenty-fifth birthday, or released earlier as the Youth Authority sees fit.

Perhaps the most common impulsive homicide committed by a relatively normal juvenile is the "thrill" or "dare" killing of a total stranger selected at random. These killings are generally but not always committed by two or more youths acting together. They also vary in the degree to which they are intended: some are clearly deliberate and premeditated efforts to kill, while others are clearly unintentional, often almost accidental.

Many of these unintentional thrill killings are committed by juveniles who risk the lives of others for "kicks" but really do not mean to kill anyone. For example, on November 5, 1987, seventeen-year-old Jimmy Iriel, with help from seventeen-year-old Robert McIlvain, dropped a 187 pound boulder from a highway overpass onto oncoming traffic below. The boulder struck a car and crushed to death a three-year-old child who was asleep in the front seat.

Jimmy Iriel was convicted of murder and sentenced to life in prison by a judge who called his crime "the most heinous thing imaginable." Robert McIlvain pleaded guilty to being an accessory to a felony. The judge said he intended to sentence Robert to the maximum of ten years but instead remanded him to the custody of the state Youth Authority after the father of the three-year-old victim pleaded that the seventeen-year-old not be imprisoned with adults.

Another all too common scenario for unintentional teenage thrill killings is one or another fatal version of "Russian roulette." In one recent case, for example, fifteen-year-old Stephen was in his bedroom showing two thirteen-year-old friends his collection of weapons: a sawed-off shotgun, Chuka sticks, and a gravity knife. After showing off, Stephen led his friends to his parents' bedroom, where he took out his father's shotgun and five shells.

Knowing that three of the shells were live and two were dummies, Stephen randomly loaded four of the shells into the gun's magazine. He then pumped the shotgun and—without knowing whether the shell he chambered was live or a dummy—pointed the gun directly at one thirteen-year-old and said, "Let's play Polish roulette. Who is first?" Stephen then pulled the trigger and fired a live round, which tore through the boy's chest, lung and shoulder, killing him. Although Stephen claimed the killing was an accident, he was convicted of "depraved indifference murder."

On the evening of December 19, 1986, three black men were driving through a predominantly white neighborhood of New York City called Howard Beach. Their car broke down and they took off on foot looking for help. As they walked, they passed a group of white youths who shouted racial slurs at them. Eventually the trio reached a pizzeria, entered, and had a pizza.

While the three black men ate their pizza, a white youth called to a gang of his friends, "There's some niggers in the pizza parlor—let's go kill them." As the black men stepped from the pizzeria, they were confronted by a mob of white youths shouting, "Niggers, you don't belong here." The three men tried to run but were caught by the mob. One escaped after being struck once with a baseball bat. Another was severely beaten with fists, bats, and a tree limb. The third man was severely beaten and then chased into the path of an oncoming car, which struck and killed him.

Three of the white youths—eighteen-year-olds John Lester and Scott Kern and seventeen-year-old Jason Ladone—were convicted of manslaughter. Several others were convicted on riot charges, and the rest were acquitted. Lester was sentenced to serve from ten to thirty years in prison, Kern received a sentence of six to eighteen years, and Ladone was ordered imprisoned for five to fifteen years. Ladone received the most lenient sentence of the three after publicly apologizing to the dead man's mother for what he termed "your senseless loss." Later at an appellate argument in the case, lawyers for the convicted youths conceded that, contrary to the youths' repeated assertions, the attack and killing had been "racially motivated."

In a similar though apparently less premeditated incident, four New Jersey youths—members of a much larger, self-proclaimed group of "Dotbusters"—beat a thirty-year-old Indian man to death on a city street. According to the police, these "Dotbusters"—who took their name from the red bindi mark worn on the foreheads of many married Indian women—were responsible for numerous violent attacks against Indian and Pakistani immigrants. The youths in this particular case, who ranged in age from fifteen to seventeen, denied any racial motive in their brutal attack. Instead, they insisted that they attacked the Indian man because he was bald. Though charged with murder, they were convicted only of assault.

The Howard Beach and the Dotbuster killings are just two of the many recent cases in which victims of juvenile homicide have been targeted for lethal violence solely on the basis of their race or ethnicity. Victims of similar "hate" or "bias" crimes have included not only members of racial and ethnic minorities but also homeless people and homosexuals.

The homeless are often the targets of juvenile violence—and sometimes that violence proves lethal. In California, for example, two sixteen-year-old boys were walking in a Burbank park on July 14, 1987, when they decided "to rid the park of bums." With no provocation at all, the boys viciously attacked two homeless men, killed one with karate kicks and beat the other into a coma.

The prosecutor described the assault and killing as "totally a straight-out attack, with no provocation but the status of the victims in society." Timothy Cargle, who was charged as an adult, pleaded guilty to murder and assault and was committed to the California Youth Authority until he turns twenty-five. His accomplice, whose name was withheld because he was charged as a juvenile, also pleaded guilty to similar charges and was committed to the Youth Authority for an indeterminate term.

Across the country, on September 18, 1988, three Massachusetts boys—two seventeen-year-olds and a sixteen-year-old—beat, stabbed, mutilated, and disemboweled a seventy-three-year-old homeless man who lived out of two shopping carts and slept in a downtown alleyway. According to police, for no apparent reason, the sixteen-year-old stabbed the man fourteen times and gutted him with a butcher knife. All three boys have been charged with murder and are awaiting trial.

In a similar incident in Florida on May 23, 1986, four high school classmates—two eighteen-year-olds, a seventeen-year-old, and a sixteen-year-old—beat to death a thirty-three-year-old Native American transient who had been living for days under an expressway overpass. Police said the sixteen-year-old struck the fatal blow. He was charged with murder. His seventeen-year-old companion was charged with conspiracy, and both eighteen-year-olds were charged as accessories after the fact.

The boys told the police they had attacked homeless people in the past and enjoyed it. According to Captain James Diggs, who investigated the killing, "They liked to beat up vagrants. It was sort of sport to them."

Whether any of these youths harbored actual bias against their homeless victims or simply found them convenient and vulnerable targets is not entirely clear. But, in any event, it seems obvious that being homeless caused all of these victims to be targeted for death.

Homosexuals have also become targets of juvenile violence, including homicide. While some juvenile killings of homosexuals seem motivated by a desire for "revenge," at least some homosexuals have been slain by juveniles just because of their sexual orientation. For example, on September 5, 1987, police in Albany, Georgia recovered the body of a twenty-nine-year-old homosexual who had been beaten, shot in the head, and run over with a car. Police said two boys, seventeen and fourteen, killed the man and then "went around town bragging about it." As for motive, one officer explained that "these boys just don't like gays."

On October 8, 1985, Edwin Dyer, a fifty-year-old Boy Scout leader, pleaded guilty to sexually abusing two Boy Scouts, seventeen-year-old Louis Conner and another youth. On January 17, 1986, Dyer was sentenced to serve only fifteen days in jail for the abuse. Five days later, Dyer and his wife confronted Louis Conner in Louis' driveway. In his coat pocket, Louis carried a shotgun. Earlier he had sawed off the barrel and removed the stock to make the weapon easy to conceal.

As Dyer and his wife approached, Louis pulled the gun from his pocket and aimed it at Dyer. Dyer yelled, "No, Louis" and started to run, but the teenager shot and killed him before he could flee. Louis Conner was later convicted of the equivalent of manslaughter in juvenile court and sentenced to serve six months in a residential treatment center for adolescents. After his release from the center, he was placed on probation until the age of twenty-one on the condition that he live with his mother and continue to receive counseling.

Avenging past sexual abuse is a common motive in juvenile "revenge" killings. In some of these cases, however, the motive is not nearly as clear as it was in the case of Louis Conner. Consider, for example, two cases in Texas and California. In the Texas case, on September 20, 1986, two seventeen-year-olds and a twenty-year-old lured Alvin Goode into the woods and then shot him with four different guns. According to the police, twenty-year-old Alvin was shot in the head and body with two shotguns, a revolver, and a semiautomatic pistol, as he ran from his assailants. The police also said that the boys were proud of the killing and bragged about it.

William Owens, one of the seventeen-year-olds, was convicted of murder. Facing a possible sentence of thirty-five to ninety-nine years in prison, William told a psychologist that he killed Alvin Goode because he thought Goode was a homosexual and because Goode had earlier tried to sexually assault him. At the sentencing hearing, William's father testified that his son killed Goode because "Alvin Goode raped him." At the close of the hearing, William Owens was sentenced to fifteen years in prison.

In another juvenile killing purportedly motivated by vengeance for past sexual abuse, a seventeen-year-old California boy killed a fifty-two-year-old homosexual. On November 18, 1987, George Smoot was found stabbed to death in his San Francisco home. In his defense, the youth claimed that Smoot made sexual overtures to him several hours before the killing and tried to force his way into the youth's home the day of the killing. The boy's sister testified that her brother, armed with a kitchen knife and a metal pipe, chased Smoot from their door. According to her testimony, he returned five minutes later and told her he had stabbed Smoot.

In convicting the youth of the equivalent of manslaughter, a Superior Court judge concluded that the boy stabbed Smoot in the "honest but unreasonable belief" that Smoot was about to kill or seriously injure him. Other evidence, however, suggested that the killing may have been motivated, at least in part, by an incident that occurred well before Smoot's death.

Roughly two months before he killed George Smoot, the youth was victimized in a locker room game called "Violation." After he made a number of mistakes during football practice, the boy was held down by four of his teammates while a fifth teammate poked him in the buttocks with a broomstick. The broomstick slipped, tore open the boy's scrotum, and caused a painful injury that required medical care, including fifty stitches. The youth's family and teachers minimized the significance of this trauma and any relation it may have had to Smoot's killing, but others who knew of the incident saw it as "tantamount to homosexual rape" and suggested that it could have been part of the motive for the later killing of George Smoot, a homosexual who may or may not have made advances to the youth.

Occasionally juveniles kill to avenge perceived wrongs other than sexual abuse. Interestingly, though, even these cases often have a sexual element. For example, in one particularly senseless and bizarre juvenile killing apparently motivated by a desire for revenge, three teenage male prostitutes killed Dr. Howard Appledorf, a university professor and nationally known nutrition expert.

Dr. Appledorf met nineteen-year-old Gary Bown in San Francisco and reportedly hired the teenager for sex. A couple of months later, Gary showed up at Appledorf's Florida condominium accompanied by two acquaintances, eighteen-year-old Paul Everson and fifteen-year-old Shane Kennedy. After spending two nights with Dr. Appledorf, the boys were arrested on charges that they forged Appledorf's signature on a $900 check. When Appledorf refused to drop the charges, the teens threatened him with countercharges of child molestation. Appledorf finally dropped the charges, but just a few days later, sometime during Labor Day weekend 1982, the three youths broke into his condominium and attacked him after he came home unexpectedly and took them by surprise.

Shane first stood by and watched but later became sick to his stomach and fled as Gary and Paul knocked Dr. Appledorf unconscious with a frying pan and then bound, gagged, blindfolded and suffocated the forty-one-year-old professor on his living room couch. Before leaving the condo, the boys also put out a cigarette on Appledorf's abdomen, covered his head with a tote bag, tossed food around the room, and scrawled "redrum" (murder spelled backwards) on a wall.

Convicted of murder, both Gary Bown and Paul Everson were sentenced to life in prison. Shane Kennedy pleaded guilty to reduced charges of burglary, robbery, and auto theft and was sentenced to four years in prison.

More recently, seventeen-year-old Robert Rosenkrantz became something of a *cause celebre* in the California gay community when he killed Steven Redman, a classmate, who told Robert's parents about their son's homosexuality. Steven was a close friend of Joey Rosenkrantz, Robert's younger brother. Together the two boys spied on Robert, looking for evidence that Robert was gay. After finally catching Robert in a homosexual act, they chose the night of Robert's high school graduation to tell his parents what they had seen.

Robert confronted Steven and begged him to recant his accusation, but Steven refused. Finally, on June 28, 1985, Robert went to Steven's home and waited outside for four hours, planning to bomb Steven's car. When Steven emerged from the house, Robert again confronted him about the accusation. When Steven responded by calling Robert a "faggot," Robert shot him ten times with an Uzi semiautomatic rifle. Six shots struck Steven in the head.

Immediately after the killing, Robert fled and hid for almost a month before surrendering to the police. Charged with first-degree murder, Robert Rosenkrantz was convicted of second-degree murder and sentenced to serve seventeen years to life in prison. Interviewed in jail, Robert said he has received and responded to hundreds of letters from youths seeking guidance regarding their homosexuality.

In another "revenge" homicide, in June 1989, a fourteen-year-old Detroit boy admitted killing a reputed crack dealer. The boy told police he shot the woman because she gave his mother drugs, and the drugs caused his mother to humiliate him. The boy said that after taking the drugs, his mother stripped naked and offered to have sex with several of his friends. After getting his mother dressed and taking her home, the boy returned to the dealer's house, lured her into an alleyway, and killed her.

Election Day 1988 was a school holiday for Marsha Urevich and Nicole Eisel, two thirteen-year-old Maryland girls who had smoked cigarettes, skipped classes, talked about Satanism, and listened to hard rock music together since they first met three months earlier. Marsha, the daughter of Soviet emigrants, had recently turned to drugs and was enrolled in a school for emotionally disturbed teens. Nicole, who lived with her divorced father, had low grades and poor attendance and was repeating the seventh grade.

On the morning of November 8, one of the girls used a hidden key to open the safe where Marsha's father kept a .32 caliber automatic pistol and an eight-round ammunition clip. At 11:30, the girls said goodbye to Marsha's grandmother and left for a walk in the woods. Less than twenty-four hours later, after being reported missing, Marsha and Nicole were found in a nearby picnic area facing each other, with legs crossed and knees almost touching. Both girls had been shot to death with the automatic pistol, which was still in Marsha's hand. Piecing the facts together, authorities concluded that Marsha and Nicole entered a murder-suicide pact and that Marsha shot Nicole and then herself.

More juveniles kill themselves than kill others. The juvenile suicide rate in the United States is low but still more than twice the juvenile homicide rate. More than 5,000 juveniles kill themselves each year. A small percentage of these suicides are committed as part of what might be called murder-suicides—cases in which a relationship between two juveniles ends in the death of both.

Most juvenile murder-suicides are the result of an agreement or suicide pact between two youngsters who are romantically involved. In New York City, for example, on April 30, 1986, the mother of sixteen-year-old Christina Ittermann returned home from work at 6:45 P.M. to find her daughter and eighteen-year-old Paul Gibbons lying in a bloody heap in the living room. Paul, who was Christina's boyfriend, was dead from a stab wound to his abdomen. Christina lay nearby, suffering from slashed wrists and an overdose of sixty to one hundred assorted pills. Three different suicide notes were strewn about the room, indicating that Paul and Christina intended to die together and wanted to be buried side by side. No motive could be determined from the notes.

Not all "romantic" teenage murder-suicides are so clearly a joint venture. For example, eighteen-year-old Daniel Yarbrough and sixteen-year-old Holly Dvorak had dated for six months and were to become engaged at Christmas 1988. The youngsters were, by all accounts, a happy young couple. Yet on November 28, 1988, at about 1:30 in the morning, Daniel shot and killed Holly and then turned the gun on himself. Both died from single bullet wounds to the head. Although the evidence was uncertain, police effectively ruled out a suicide pact and labeled the deaths a "homicide-suicide" of unknown motive.

Whether this particular murder-suicide was a joint venture is unclear, but at least some juvenile murder-suicides are not. In some cases, frustrated juveniles kill their erstwhile lovers and then take their own lives. For example, on June 16, 1989, in a small New Hampshire town, seventeen-year-old Steven Porell stabbed his father, killed two people, including his former girlfriend, and then committed suicide when cornered by the police.

It was a Friday evening in late spring, the day before his high school graduation, when Steven quarreled with and then stabbed and seriously wounded his father. Steven then left home and headed for a nearby ice cream parlor. Bursting into the store, he shot and killed the owner and then did the same to a seventeen-year-old employee—a girl who had recently ended their two-year relationship. When police surrounded the store, Steven shot and killed himself.

A short time before the killing, when the young couple was still together, Steven had written this message in the girl's high school yearbook: "Every rose has a thorn. But I don't mind the thorn if you're my rose."

6

Cult-Related Killings

"WHY ME, YOU guys?" cried nineteen-year-old Steve Newberry as three of his teenage "friends" beat him to death with baseball bats. Before Steve died, he may or may not have heard their answer to his question: "Because it's fun, Steve." Once Steve was dead, his assailants tied a two-hundred-pound boulder to his body and dumped it into a well.

Less than a day later, on December 9, 1987, police in Missouri followed a trail of rumors that led directly to three seventeen-year-olds: Jim Hardy, Pete Roland, and Ron Clements. After casually admitting their guilt, the boys told the police that for months they had been fascinated with Satanism and that the killing had been a human sacrifice to Satan. Police officers also learned that the boys earlier made several aborted attempts to kill Steve Newberry.

Jim Hardy, who struck the first of the roughly seventy blows that killed Steve Newberry, was an honor student and altar boy until age eleven. From eleven on, he had a long history of drug abuse, temper outbursts, academic problems, and extreme cruelty to animals. According to his friends,

Jim once drove screws into a Barbie doll's head, burned the doll's plastic face, and then said he wished the doll were human. With his friends, occasionally including Steve Newberry, Jim often tortured animals, sometimes killing as many as three or four a day. Still, at the time of the killing, Jim Hardy was president of his senior class.

Like Jim, Ron Clements was also a drug abuser and had been seen briefly at the local mental health center. Some time before the killing, Ron told a psychotherapist he was obsessed with morbid and violent fantasies of hurting others, interested in satanic worship, and feared that he was possessed by demons. The psychotherapist, who assured Ron's mother that this was simply a normal phase of adolescence, later testified in court that he did not find Ron's fantasies, interests, and fears "atypical" among adolescents.

At Ron's trial for murder, a psychiatrist testified that when Ron took part in the killing, he lacked the capacity to tell reality from fantasy. The psychiatrist added that Ron simply followed along when his friends suggested making a human sacrifice to Satan.

Pete Roland claimed to be an abused child and said he often heard voices in his head telling him to commit evil acts. At trial, the same psychiatrist who testified for Ron told the jury that at the time of the killing, Pete was suffering from a psychosis induced by drugs, heavy metal music, and the influence of Jim Hardy.

The jury rejected both Ron and Pete's insanity pleas and convicted them of murder. Jim pleaded guilty to murder. All three boys were sentenced to life in prison without parole.

Sean Sellers was a bright, likable, and high-achieving youngster until he reached his midteens. First, Sean's grades took a nose dive, and he dropped off the high school honor roll. Then he lost interest in sports and seemed to stop caring about his appearance. At the same time, he began conducting satanic worship services in an abandoned farmhouse with eight other youths who joined his self-styled cult.

Eventually their mutual commitment to Satanism led Sean and one of his fellow teenage devil worshipers to carry out what they called a "sacrificial ritual." On September 8, 1985, Sean and Jim Mathis stole a .357 Magnum pistol and drove to a convenience store, looking for a clerk who had once refused to sell them beer. Finding the clerk in the store, Sean shot and killed him. After the killing, Sean was upset—not because of what he had done but because it had taken so much effort. Speeding away from the store, Sean told Jim, "I fucked up. How could I have fucked that up so bad? He took three bullets, man. Three! I can't believe I missed him on that first one. I can't believe it."

For several months after the killing, Sean went about his life as always: conducting candlelight satanic services, working part-time at a pizza parlor, and dating a fifteen-year-old girl named Angel. But when his parents ordered him to stop seeing Angel, he ran away. They brought him back home and tried to work things out, but in March 1986, Sean shot and killed both his parents as they slept.

On the night of the killing, Sean returned home from his job at the pizza parlor, dressed in black ritual attire, lit candles, conducted a satanic service, and then went to sleep. A short while later he woke up, picked up a revolver, tiptoed into his parents' room, and shot and killed both his mother and stepfather.

Jim Mathis struck a deal with the prosecutors. He agreed to turn state's evidence regarding all three killings and received a deferred prison sentence of five years. Charged with three counts of murder, Sean Sellers pleaded not guilty by reason of insanity, claiming he could not recall any of the killings. A psychologist who examined Sean concluded that he was not psychotic but suffered from an antisocial personality disorder. In other words, Sean was what mental health professionals used to call a "psychopath." The jury rejected Sean's insanity plea, found him criminally responsible, and convicted him of capital murder. Sean Sellers was then sentenced to die.

*   *   *

Only relatively recently, law enforcement authorities, criminologists, and others have begun to recognize that many senseless or bizarre killings are somehow related to the occult. The extent to which cult activities are implicated in homicide is not known, but it surely cannot be as great as some have claimed. Recently, for example, one self-proclaimed expert on cult killings estimated that there are 50,000 such killings each year in the United States. Given the number of homicides in the United States each year, that estimate is clearly a gross exaggeration. For that figure to be anywhere near correct, every one of the 20,000 or so of each year's known homicides—plus an additional 30,000 undiscovered homicides—would have to be cult-related.

Still, from various reports, it is clear that at least a small number of homicides, including some senseless killings committed by juveniles, are motivated by or related to the killers' involvement in cults or cult-like rituals. The clearest cult-related homicides involve juvenile killers who are actually members of cults. Other cult-related killings are committed by youths who, while perhaps not formally members of any cult, fancy themselves as cultists. Finally, a number of juvenile killings occur in the course of acting out fantasy games that border upon cult rituals.

On June 15, 1984, seventeen-year-old Gary Lauwers was found stabbed to death in a wooded area about forty miles from New York City. Gary had also been beaten, kicked, and bitten, his eyes were gouged out, and pieces of his hair and clothing had been cut and burned.

Less than three weeks later, seventeen-year-old Richard Kasso confessed that he repeatedly stabbed and tortured Gary and forced him to chant "I love Satan." Richard told the police he initially attacked Gary because Gary had stolen ten bags of a drug known as Angel Dust. But he also said that as he and his companions were leaving the scene of the stabbing, Gary cried out and a crow cawed. Richard told the authorities he interpreted these sounds as an order from the devil to kill Gary. According to Richard's signed confession, he then went back, stabbed Gary in the face, and cut his eyes out.

For three years prior to the killing, Richard Kasso had belonged to the Knights of the Black Circle, a loosely organized satanic cult of some twenty teenagers. According to his parents, Richard was a "gifted pupil and athlete" until he reached the seventh grade, started becoming "insubordinate" at school, and took part in a burglary. In the three years leading up to the killing, Richard abused and sold drugs, threatened his sisters, threatened and attempted suicide, and was arrested for digging up a grave to obtain bones for a satanic ritual.

Just one day after being arraigned on murder charges, Richard Kasso committed suicide, using a bedsheet to hang himself in his jail cell.

Several other more recent cases illustrate the variety of killings committed by juveniles actually involved in cults. In Florida, for example, without apparent reason, eighteen-year-old Scott McKee and his sixteen-year-old brother Dean beat, kicked, and stabbed to death a forty-one-year-old black drifter they encountered at a downtown art museum in December 1987. After the killing, the boys' father described how he had watched them "change from happy children to sullen, depressed teenagers who hung swastikas on their bedroom walls" and joined the violent, neo-Nazi "skinhead" cult. Lowell McKee said Scott joined the skinheads two years earlier and Dean quickly followed his older brother into the youth cult, known for its Nazi symbolism and hatred of blacks and homosexuals.

Dean McKee was convicted of first-degree murder and sentenced to life in prison. His brother Scott pleaded no contest to a charge of attempted murder and was sentenced to five years in prison. In a plea bargain, both Scott and Lowell McKee testified against Dean. In the wake of the two sentences, leaders of the local "skinheads" said they were "motivated" by the McKee case. As one put it, "We're standing strong and beginning to organize."

On March 22, 1987, three Minnesota teenagers—all members of a recently formed, self-styled "vampire cult"—killed a thirty-year-old drifter and then licked the dead man's blood from their fingers. Tim Erickson, a nineteen-year-old Minnesota youth, told police that he and two other boys, seventeen and thirteen, agreed to form a "vampire cult," kill someone, and suck the victim's blood. They licked the victim's blood, Tim said, "because of a cult we believed in."

Authorities said the trio got the idea for the cult from watching a video movie called "Lost Boys," the story of a teenage vampire. After watching the film, Tim told his younger accomplices he wanted to tie someone up, "cut his wrist and drink his blood." A jury rejected Tim's plea of not guilty by reason of mental illness. Convicted of murder, Tim Erickson was sentenced to life in prison.

In another cult-related killing, a fifteen-year-old California boy confessed to his role in an October 1988 killing, the "sacrifice" of twenty-two-year-old Joseph Bradsberry in a satanic "initiation ritual." The boy told authorities he and four young adults, all members of a "satanic coven," were present at what the victim was told would be his initiation. Instead of initiating Bradsberry into the "coven," several of the cult's dozen members handcuffed him, listened as he pleaded for his life, then slashed his throat and threw his body into a nearby drainage ditch.

According to Bradsberry's girlfriend, a self-proclaimed "white witch," the killing was committed as part of her own initiation into the coven. She told authorities that an earlier initiation, which included sacrificing a dog, was interrupted by the police and therefore declared only a "partial initiation." Her "full initiation" into the "dark side," she said, required sacrificing Bradsberry.

Attorneys for the adults involved in the sacrifice claimed their clients were under the influence of hallucinogenic drugs at the time of the killing. Bradsberry's girlfriend and three adult males were charged with murder. The fifteen-year-old boy admitted being an accessory to murder and was committed to a state juvenile facility for up to three years.

For most people, February 2 is Groundhog Day. But for a small minority of devil worshipers, it is the day to celebrate the "Witches Sabbath." In 1986, it was the day Lloyd Gamble, a seventeen-year-old Michigan youth, was shot and killed by his fifteen-year-old brother. Police said the fifteen-year-old was "acting out a satanic sacrifice" when he shot his sleeping brother and then telephoned the police and threatened to kill his parents, who were due home at any minute. When the police arrived ahead of the boy's parents, the teenager led them to his brother's body in the basement.

Three days after the killing, the boy's parents called police back to their home to show them what they had found hidden in the boy's closet: "a hood, a long black robe, silver chalice, dark blue candle, glass bottle containing red liquid, piece of white parchment paper . . . a paper pentagram . . . a sword, and an upside-down cross"—according to the police, all "objects used in satanic rites." The closet also contained a book, *The Power of Satan*, which gave "step-by-step instructions on how to perform a Satanic ritual." Questioned after the killing, the boy confirmed that he was "into Satanism."

A police detective, consulted for his expertise in cult-related crimes, had this to say about the killing:

I think this kid crossed over from the dabbler stage to the self-styled Satanist stage . . . . Here's a kid who's a loner, not doing great in school, into drugs and so on. . . . This wasn't a spur-of-the-moment murder. It was cold and calculated. I believe he felt he was doing his brother a favor by killing him. He was elevating him to a higher level of consciousness. He mentioned those exact words to the police dispatcher.

In some cases where juveniles have committed what might be called cult-related homicides or attempted homicides, there is no evidence of actual cult involvement in the sense of belonging to some organized or even self-styled group, but rather only an individual fascination with Satanism and satanic rituals. That was the case, for example, with George Geider, a fourteen-year-old Illinois boy charged with attempted murder in December 1988 after stabbing three classmates who relentlessly teased him about his interest in Satanism and the satanic symbols he wore.

George was described by those who knew him as a "good boy" with a strong religious background, who was never known to be in any trouble. His pastor later described him as a lonely outcast whose interest in Satanism was a "superficial attempt to find acceptance among classmates who had constantly spurned him." In a plea agreement, George Geider admitted stabbing his classmates and was sentenced to five years probation, but only after both the judge and prosecutor complained about his lack of remorse.

The prosecutor pointed out that the injuries sustained by the victims were "very close to fatal." "What concerns me," he added, "is [George's] attitude; he is still not very remorseful." In ordering George committed to a residential treatment facility as a condition of his probation, the judge added that he, too, hoped George would eventually come to appreciate the wrongfulness of his acts.

When a juvenile becomes obsessed with Satanism and then kills someone as a result of that obsession, authorities usually question his or her mental health. As a result, most of these youngsters are examined by psychologists or psychiatrists after they kill. While most juveniles involved in satanic killings are probably disturbed, only rarely are they found to be psychotic. One exception is a case recently reported by Drs. Elissa Benedek and Dewey Cornell, two leading authorities on juvenile homicide.

Fifteen-year-old "Bob" stabbed his mother to death and then retreated to the basement of the family home, where he was later found reading the Bible and chanting, "Kill the Devil." Seen for psychological evaluation after the killing, Bob expressed a strong interest in witchcraft and said that on the day of the killing he heard special messages directed to him on phonograph records he was playing. These messages suggested that he kill his mother. Bob also demonstrated little understanding of the charges against him and said that he would be saved by Satan. He was diagnosed as psychotic and found not competent to stand trial.

In some cases, juveniles fascinated with Satanism kill or attempt to kill others and then kill themselves. Consider, for example, Thomas Sullivan, Jr., a fourteen-year-old New Jersey paperboy, Boy Scout, and "model son and student," who stabbed his mother twelve times with his Boy Scout knife, set a fire in the living room while the rest of the family slept nearby, and then went to a neighbor's yard and slashed his wrists and throat.

In the month or so before the killing, Thomas had become obsessed with satanic literature and heavy metal music. Just weeks before the killing, he told a friend that Satan appeared to him in a vision and urged him to kill his family and begin preaching Satanism. The fire Thomas set the morning he killed himself was fueled with his books on Satanism.

In a somewhat similar tragic case mentioned in Chapter 5, two thirteen-year-old Maryland girls, Marsha Urevich and Nicole Eisel, acted out a suicide pact on Election Day 1988. Marsha shot Nicole and then herself. Although both girls had troubled backgrounds, their deaths were at least partially the product of their mutual fascination with Satanism. Both girls were known to be obsessed with the occult. In the weeks before they died, they spoke to close friends not only of a suicide pact but also of their desire to "meet Satan."

In November 1985, fifteen-year-old David Ventiquattro and his eleven-year-old neighbor, Martin Howland, were in David's bedroom playing the occult fantasy game, *Dungeons and Dragons*. Suddenly fantasy and reality blurred. David was convinced that Martin was "evil." Since his own role in the game was to "extinguish evil," David grabbed a shotgun, held it just inches from Martin's head, and pulled the trigger. David first told authorities that Martin's death was an accident or a suicide. Later, he confessed that he killed his playmate as part of the game. David told state police officers he had "wanted to kill Martin, but not in real life."

Two other teenagers who occasionally played *Dungeons and Dragons* with David testified that he also pointed the gun at them during earlier games. A psychologist who examined David testified that although the boy was fifteen years old, he had the maturity of a twelve- or thirteen-year-old. Tried as an adult, David Ventiquattro was convicted of murder and sentenced to five and a half years to life in prison.

As this case illustrates, some cult-related juvenile killings stem not from any genuine devotion to Satanism or the occult but rather from an obsession with occult fantasy games, such as *Dungeons and Dragons*, which involves themes of satanic sacrifice, witchcraft, demonology, monsters, and killing.

As early as 1985, two public interest groups asked the Federal Trade Commission (FTC) to consider requiring warnings before a television show based upon the popular youth fantasy game, *Dungeons and Dragons*. The National Coalition on Television Violence (NCTV) and Bothered About Dungeons and Dragons (BADD) told the FTC that *Dungeons and Dragons* "has caused a number of suicides and murders."

Dr. Thomas Radecki, a psychiatrist who was then President of NCTV, said in 1988 that more than fifty criminal defendants had been convicted after using what he called the *"Dungeons and Dragons* defense," an insanity defense based upon involvement with the fantasy game. Dr. Radecki also reported that as of June 1988, he had been able to "link 116 deaths, cases of suicides and homicides, to these antisocial games."

Although the statement that *Dungeons and Dragons* has caused many murders is an exaggeration, there certainly have been juvenile killings related to the perpetrator's interest or involvement in fantasy games, including *Dungeons and Dragons.* In California in 1983, for example, sixteen-year-old Ronald Lampasi killed his stepfather and tried to kill his mother. Ronald shot both parents in the back of the head as they sat watching television. At Ronald's trial on charges of murder and attempted murder, the prosecutor claimed that Ronald fabricated claims that his stepfather had molested him. Instead, the prosecutor argued, the shootings were "a result of Lampasi's acting out a game of *Dungeons and Dragons.*" After Ronald was convicted, the judge questioned the significance of *Dungeons and Dragons* in the killing, but sentenced Ronald to serve from twenty-five years to life in prison.

In Alabama, in a May 1985 killing related to another fantasy game, three boys—two seventeen-year-olds and a fourteen-year-old—were charged with murder in the killing of a convenience store clerk. All three, described by teachers and others as "bright, popular, all-American youths," were heavily involved in fantasy games, including *Dungeons and Dragons, Secret Agent, and Top Secret.* On the day of the killing, two of the boys agreed to play out their respective roles in a fantasy game and then commit suicide. In playing out their roles, they stole guns, drove to the convenience store, shot and killed the clerk, and then took $700 in cash. The third youth alerted the police of the impending suicide. When police captured the two boys, they were both holding cocked guns to their heads.

Seventeen-year-old Cayce Moore, who fired the gun that killed the clerk, pleaded not guilty by reason of insanity. A jury rejected his plea and convicted him of capital murder. The Judge, however, rejected the prosecutor's demand for the death penalty and sentenced Cayce to life in prison with no hope for parole.

In other cult-related homicides not directly tied to *Dungeons and Dragons*, juvenile killers have been fascinated if not obsessed with the fantasy game. Sean Sellers, for example, the sixteen-year-old Oklahoma Satanist who murdered his mother, father, and a convenience store clerk, started playing *Dungeons and Dragons* when he was twelve. The game sparked his interest in the occult. In Sean's words, "*Dungeons and Dragons* got me started. I wanted to learn more about it, so I went to the library and stole some books about dragons, witches, wizards and Satanism."

7

Crazy Killings

FOURTEEN-YEAR-OLD Shirley Wolf and fifteen-year-old Cindy Collier met for the first time on the morning of June 14, 1983. Cindy, a delinquent with a history of arrests for assault, burglary, drug possession, and theft dating back to age twelve, had just been released from a juvenile detention center and was visiting a friend in the group home where Shirley was living.

By afternoon, the two girls had teamed up and were knocking randomly on doors in a nearby condominium development, asking for directions, a phone, a glass of water, whatever might gain them admission to one of the condos. Two people let the girls into their homes. The first, a seventy-year-old man, gave Shirley and Cindy a drink of water and let them use the telephone before they left.

The second homeowner, eighty-five-year-old Anna Brackett, invited the girls into her condominium unit and chatted with them for over an hour before her son called to say he was coming by to take her to a bingo game. Having already decided to steal the woman's car, Shirley and Cindy attacked Mrs. Brackett. Shirley grabbed her by the throat and knocked her to the floor. Meanwhile, Cindy got a butcher knife from the kitchen and threw it to Shirley, who used it to stab Mrs. Brackett some twenty-eight times as the elderly woman begged for her life.

Shirley and Cindy tried unsuccessfully to start Mrs. Brackett's car, then took off on foot. Mrs. Brackett's son passed the two hitchhikers as he drove to his mother's condominium. Early the next morning, acting on descriptions given by neighbors, police arrested both girls after finding them asleep at Cindy's house. Shirley confessed within minutes, and Cindy quickly followed suit.

Shirley told the police that she and Cindy killed Mrs. Brackett to get the woman's car. "Perfect car. Just a set-up. We figured we'd kill her," Shirley told one deputy sheriff. Later, investigators seized Shirley's diary and found her entry for the day of the killing: "We killed an old lady today. It was fun."

Confronted with Shirley's confession, Cindy also confessed to her role in the killing. Laughing, Cindy told the authorities that the killing was "just for fun" and that afterwards, she and Shirley "wanted to do another one."

Prior to being tried on murder charges, both girls revealed something of their troubled backgrounds. Shirley told a grim tale of sexual abuse. From infancy until age fourteen, she was sexually abused by her father, uncle, and grandfather. Her father raped her when she was nine, sexually assaulted her daily thereafter—sometimes as often as three times a day—and even obtained birth control pills for her once she reached puberty.

Finally, Shirley's father was arrested and convicted of child molestation. After serving one hundred days in jail, he was released on probation—on the condition that he have no contact with Shirley. He then returned to live with Shirley's mother and two brothers. To meet this condition of probation, Shirley was placed in foster care and then a group home—the home where she met Cindy just a few hours before the killing.

Cindy Collier told authorities that she and Shirley had "the same childhood"—a childhood she described as "rotten." Cindy said she had been beaten "since I was born" and raped several times as a child, including once by a relative. She added that she had unsuccessfully tried both suicide and homicide in the past.

A psychiatric evaluation revealed that as early as kindergarten, Shirley was identified as a child in need of psychiatric care. After receiving no treatment and suffering a lifetime of abuse, Shirley was, according to psychiatric evidence presented in court, "thoroughly comfortable with her role as a cold-blooded killer." Although she initially pleaded not guilty by reason of insanity, Shirley tried to withdraw that plea when she learned that an insanity verdict carried the possibility of lifetime institutionalization, while a juvenile court murder conviction would, at worst, result in incarceration until age twenty-five.

After hearing all the evidence, it took a judge just fifteen minutes to find that while Shirley suffered from "aberrant thinking," she was not insane but guilty of murder and should be remanded to the California Youth Authority until her twenty-fifth birthday. In an earlier trial, Cindy Collier was also convicted of murder and remanded to the Youth Authority for a similar term.

Four years into her sentence, Shirley Wolf was charged with stabbing a Youth Authority worker in the face and head and then breaking the hand of a deputy at the jail where she was transferred after the stabbing.

In the early morning light, a husky teenage boy sits alongside the river, drinking beer and staring into space. Next to him lies the nude, bruised, and apparently dead body of a teenage girl. So begins the 1987 movie, "River's Edge." The boy portrayed in this Hollywood docudrama is Anthony Broussard. Anthony, a sixteen-year-old Californian, raped and strangled his fourteen-year-old girlfriend, dumped her body near a river, and then reportedly laughed and told friends, "I raped and murdered this chick." Anthony also took at least seven and possibly as many as twelve teenagers to look at the body and throw rocks at it over a period of two days before two youths finally reported the killing to the police. Earlier, Anthony allegedly had tried to rape two other girls, aged thirteen and fourteen.

Charged with murder, Anthony was subjected to numerous psychological and psychiatric examinations and was diagnosed as a chronic paranoid schizophrenic with organic brain disease caused by drug abuse. The psychiatrist who made that diagnosis testified that Anthony had been devastated when, at the age of eight, he came home one day and found his mother dead. The psychiatrist told the jury that after his mother's death, Anthony's maturation stopped, and he developed a pathological fantasy life. Another psychiatrist testified that Anthony appeared to be without feelings or emotion, "as if nothing touched him."

Despite his obvious and severe psychological disturbance, Anthony Broussard pleaded guilty to murder and was sentenced to serve twenty-five years in prison, after the court determined that he was not amenable to treatment in the juvenile justice system. As part of the plea arrangement, the prior attempted rape charges were dropped.

In January 1988, seventeen-year-old Leslie Torres, a homeless New York City youth, went on a seven day "cocaine-inspired rampage"—a spree of armed robberies in which he killed five people and wounded six others. When arrested, Leslie told police that he committed numerous killings and robberies to support his $500-a-day addiction to the street drug, crack. Charged with murder, he pleaded not guilty by reason of insanity.

Testifying on his own behalf, Leslie told jurors that crack caused him to feel like God, but that he saw the Devil whenever he looked into a mirror. After examining Leslie, a psychiatrist testified that the teenager suffered from "cocaine induced psychosis" at the time of the robberies and killings. The jury rejected Leslie's insanity defense and convicted him of murder. Finding that the seventeen-year-old "showed utter and total disregard for the sanctity of life" and "would kill again" if ever released, a judge sentenced Leslie Torres to sixty years to life in prison.

On December 1, 1987, William Gustafson tried to call his wife at home all day but got no answer. When he got home from work that night, he was surprised, and more than a little concerned to find the house dark. He turned on the lights, went upstairs, and found his wife, who was three months pregnant, lying on the bed, face down, dead. Afraid to search the house for his two young children, he called the police, who came and found their bodies in separate bathtubs. Nursery school teacher Priscilla Gustafson had been stripped, tied to her bed, raped, sodomized and shot twice through a pillow placed over her head. Her five-year-old son and seven-year-old daughter were both either strangled or drowned.

The day after the killings, police were led by tracking dogs from the Gustafson house through the woods to another home half a mile away. Police questioned one of the occupants of that home, seventeen-year-old Daniel LaPlante. Daniel, described by neighbors as "always a little scary," was out on bail on charges that a year earlier he made himself up as an Indian, broke into a former girlfriend's home, chased the girl and her family around the house with a hatchet, and then hid in the house until found by police two days later.

When police returned to Daniel's house that afternoon to question him again, Daniel fled on foot through the woods, commandeered a van, and briefly held the driver hostage. Meanwhile, police searched Daniel's home and found a series of "disorderly and dirty" rooms littered with "hard-core pornographic pictures." A day later, responding to a tip regarding the stolen van, police found Daniel hiding in a dumpster.

Following his arrest, Daniel was charged with three counts of murder and subjected to a series of psychological and psychiatric examinations. Declared competent to stand trial, his attempt to have the jury consider an insanity verdict was over-ruled by the judge, who rejected the defense attorney's reasoning that "Whoever was involved in this is totally crazy." Daniel LaPlante was convicted by the jury and sentenced to three consecutive life terms with "no parole, no commutation, and no furloughs" by a Massachusetts judge who told him some people felt he should "receive the same sentence that [he] imposed on the Gustafson family."

Only a very small percentage of juveniles who kill are psychotic or otherwise severely disturbed. In fact, even some of those relatively few juvenile killers diagnosed as psychotic are probably not psychotic. Homicidal youths who demonstrate no psychotic symptoms are sometimes diagnosed as psychotic either because they claim amnesia for their crimes or because of the brutal and senseless nature of those crimes. The thinking among both mental health and legal professionals sometimes seems to be that since the crime was "crazy," the juvenile perpetrator must also be "crazy." It is also worth noting that a small percentage of youngsters charged with homicide—mainly those who have had prior contacts with the legal or mental health system—try to fake symptoms of psychosis when examined after killing.

Still, there are many cases in which apparently senseless killings are committed by juveniles diagnosed as psychotic or otherwise seriously disturbed. These "crazy" killings run the gamut of juvenile homicides, but the most frequent victims in these cases are members of the juvenile's own family. For example, Patrick DeGelleke and John Justice, whose cases were described in chapter 2, both killed their parents and were later diagnosed as psychotic.

Early in the morning on September 8, 1984, fifteen-year-old Patrick DeGelleke splashed lantern fuel outside the door to the bedroom where his adoptive parents were sleeping. He then set the room ablaze, and the fire killed them both. Testimony at his murder trial indicated that Patrick, who had been in counseling for the preceding five years, was a quiet, withdrawn boy who stole, skipped school, had frequent violent temper tantrums, and was scapegoated by peers. A psychologist testified that Patrick's fear that his parents would institutionalize him recalled past rejections and triggered a psychotic rage in which he "lost touch with reality and started the fire."

On September 16, 1985, in a span of about two hours, seventeen-year-old John Justice stabbed his mother, brother, and father to death, and then rammed his father's car into the back of another car, killing the driver. At John's trial on murder charges, psychiatrists testified that John hated his mother and was upset over his parents' refusal to help pay for his planned college expenses. Dr. Emanuel Tanay, one of the nation's leading authorities on juvenile parricide, testified that John suffered from an undiagnosed psychosis.

Convicted of two counts of murder and acquitted by reason of insanity on two others, John Justice was subjected to additional psychiatric and psychological examinations prior to sentencing. John told a psychologist that he was "already dead" but would someday "control the world." John also told the doctor that the killings occurred because he had been "cursed" by a "Satan worshipper."

Occasionally non-familial homicides are also committed by juveniles diagnosed as psychotic. For example, Anthony Broussard and Leslie Torres both committed apparently senseless killings and then presented evidence at trial that they suffered from psychosis. Interestingly, while all of these youths—Anthony Broussard, Leslie Torres, Patrick DeGelleke, and John Justice—were diagnosed by at least one psychiatrist or psychologist as psychotic, none of them was fully acquitted by reason of insanity and none presented the classic symptoms of psychosis: "delusions, hallucinations, formal thought disorder, or grossly bizarre behavior." In these cases and undoubtedly others, the diagnosis of "psychosis" was probably stretched somewhat to explain otherwise inexplicable, senseless, and horrible killings.

As an example of "a genuine case of psychosis" in a juvenile who killed, Drs. Dewey Cornell and Elissa Benedek recently described seventeen-year-old "Alan," who stabbed a sixteen-year-old friend to death. When arrested, Alan told the police that he had been "under lots of pressure" and that "radio and TV [were] giving me ideas . . . that I had to kill . . . like Baretta."

When examined, Alan admitted killing the other youth and explained that "Jesus died on the cross for me so I wouldn't have to die, but I could kill somebody else so we both could die." Alan also told the examiner that he was "Jesus Christ Superstar," that "music on the radio was directed specifically to him and referred to him as 'the Lord,'" and that a "violent voice" told him to kill.

Prior to the killing, Alan had a three-year history of serious mental illness and had been hospitalized three times—most recently after he tried to drown his two younger brothers. After each hospitalization, Alan had been discharged on antipsychotic medications, but his condition deteriorated when he stopped taking them. The results of psychological testing helped confirm a diagnosis of paranoid schizophrenia.

It may well be that Patrick DeGelleke, John Justice, Anthony Broussard and Leslie Torres were not psychotic, but it seems clear that all four were seriously disturbed when they killed. Whatever we choose to call these serious psychological impairments, there is certainly good reason to believe that such disturbances are implicated in many juvenile killings. It would seem, for example, that many if not most of the senseless and cult-related killings described in the two preceding chapters have to be attributed, at least in part, to serious psychological impairment.

Other examples of killings committed by seriously disturbed though perhaps not psychotic youths include—in addition to the case of Daniel LaPlante whose killings were described earlier—the cases of Joseph Aulisio, who brutally murdered two young children; Torran Lee Meier, who killed his mother and tried to kill his younger brother; Brenda Spencer, who sprayed gunfire into a crowded schoolyard; Robert Ward, who shot and killed two preschoolers he was babysitting; and Nicholas Elliott, who opened fire on his classmates and teachers at a private school.

The last time Diane Ziemba saw her two children alive, they were walking into an unfinished house with Joseph Aulisio. Two days later, the bodies of four-year-old Christopher and eight-year-old Cheryl Ziemba were found in an abandoned strip mine. They had been killed by two blasts from a .12 gauge shotgun fired at close range.

Fifteen-year-old Joseph denied killing the children but admitted being at the scene of the killings. Police also discovered that prior to the killing, Joseph owned a .12 gauge shotgun and ammunition. After the killing, the shotgun and ammunition disappeared, but blood-spattered spent shotgun shells were found beneath Joseph's bed.

Based on this strong circumstantial evidence, Joseph was indicted on two counts of capital murder. At Joseph's trial, a psychologist testified that the fifteen-year-old was learning disabled and had an IQ that was just two points above the borderline mentally retarded range. The psychologist also testified that Joseph was an anxious, insecure, angry, and depressed youth, so alienated from others that "he feels lonely even when he's with other people." Other witnesses told the jury that Joseph had grown up in a chaotic home and had been profoundly affected by his parents' divorce and the earlier death of his infant sister.

When the jury announced its verdict of guilty on both counts, Joseph turned to members of his family in the courtroom, raised a clenched fist, and told them, "It's party time." Following his conviction, Joseph was sentenced to die in the electric chair. In 1987, the Pennsylvania Supreme Court affirmed his convictions but overturned the death sentence and ordered Joseph Aulisio imprisoned for life.

Torran Lee Meier, whose case was described in detail in Chapter 2, helped two friends strangle his mother and then tried four times to kill his younger brother, ultimately tying the boy inside a gasoline-soaked car, setting the car ablaze, and then pushing it over a sixty-foot California cliff.

Evidence presented at Torran's murder trial showed that he had been psychologically abused by his mother for years prior to the killing. Expert testimony from a psychiatrist-neurologist indicated that Torran was a youth with a brain disorder and a significantly impaired ability to cope with stress. The physician testified that Torran demonstrated an extremely rare brain wave abnormality and suffered from brain damage, severe allergies, and frequent headaches, all of which impaired his ability to deal with the accumulating stress created by his mother's abuse. Although this testimony was disputed by experts who testified for the prosecution, the jury accepted Torran's defense that when he killed his mother he was in a state of "diminished capacity" and thus guilty of manslaughter rather than first- or even second-degree murder.

Brenda Spencer's father gave his daughter a semiautomatic rifle for Christmas in 1978. A month later, the petite seventeen-year-old high school senior randomly fired the rifle into a crowded elementary schoolyard across the street from her San Diego home. The school's principal and janitor were both killed as they tried to shield children from the gunfire. Eight children and a police officer were wounded before Brenda stopped shooting. After a six-hour standoff with police, Brenda was captured. When police asked why she fired into the crowded playground, Brenda told them, "I don't like Mondays. Mondays always get me down."

Brenda was charged with first-degree murder. After two court-ordered psychiatric examinations, Brenda, who was described as "a quiet tomboy obsessed with guns, violence, and fantasies of killing police," pleaded not guilty by reason of insanity. Later, however, she changed her plea to guilty and was sentenced to two terms of twenty-five years to life in prison.

On Valentine's Day 1986, Monnie and Edwina Henslee went out to celebrate. They left their two children, four-year-old William and twenty-one-month-old Crysta with a sixteen-year-old babysitter, Robert Ward. When the Henslee's returned to their Oklahoma home later that evening, they walked in to find Robert pointing two guns at them. The couple went across the street to Robert's house and got the boy's father. When his father approached, Robert shot him in the stomach.

The police were called, arrived, and negotiated with Robert for half an hour before storming the house and arresting him. While searching the house, police entered Crysta's bedroom and found the bodies of William and Crysta. Both children had been shot with a .38 caliber pistol. Robert was charged with murder and ordered to undergo psychological evaluations. All the examiners, several psychologists and one psychiatrist, agreed that Robert was mentally ill but found him competent to stand trial.

Certified to stand trial as an adult, Robert Ward pleaded guilty to two counts of murder. Although Robert was sentenced to serve two consecutive life terms in prison, the sentencing judge ordered him committed to a state mental institution until he is found mentally competent to serve his prison sentence.

In 1987, Nicholas Elliott's mother decided to send him to a private Christian academy, where she hoped he would be able to overcome his shyness and learning problems. One of twenty-two blacks in a student body of more than five hundred, Nicholas was frequently taunted by his classmates and exchanged racial slurs with them.

On December 16, 1988, sixteen-year-old Nicholas came to school armed with a semiautomatic pistol and two hundred rounds of ammunition. He entered a classroom in the Virginia Beach school and started shooting. Teachers and students screamed and ran for cover. The shooting stopped abruptly when the gun jammed and Nicholas was disarmed. But when the spray of gunfire was over, one teacher lay dead and another seriously wounded.

Despite evidence that he had the mentality of a twelve- or thirteen-year-old, Nicholas Elliott was charged as an adult. Although expected to plead not guilty by reason of insanity, he ultimately pleaded guilty to murder, attempted murder, and weapons charges. Evidence at sentencing portrayed Nicholas as a learning disabled youth who suffered from a schizoid personality disorder. The psychiatrist who made that diagnosis testified that Nicholas was an isolated "pressure cooker" who was unable to express his feelings and "exploded" after being tormented by his classmates.

Hearing all the evidence, the judge concluded that Nicholas was a "time bomb who went off and could go off again," and that "if that gun hadn't jammed . . . I would be presiding over a mass murderer." For what he called "cold-blooded crimes," the judge sentenced Nicholas to life in prison plus 114 years. The judge then suspended fifty years of the sentence, making Nicholas Elliott eligible for parole in fifteen years.

8

Gang Killings

WHILE RIDING A Los Angeles public transit bus one day
in April 1989, sixteen-year-old Ramon Rios, Jr. was confronted and then shot and killed by two Los Angeles street
gang members as fifteen terrified passengers watched. Most
Los Angeles gangs are loosely affiliated with either of two
larger gang families, the "Bloods" or the "Crips." Each has
it own "color"—the Bloods' color is red and the Crips' is
blue. The two shooters were Bloods. One of them, a fifteen-
year-old, was apprehended. He said they shot Ramon, who
was not a gang member, because he was wearing a blue
Los Angeles Dodgers baseball cap.

Nine-year-old DeAndre Brown, a Los Angeles fourth-
grader, was playing in the sandbox in a small public park
near his home on June 24, 1987. Suddenly DeAndre found
himself caught in the crossfire of a shoot-out between rival
street gangs. One gang fired first, and the other responded
in kind. DeAndre was struck by a stray bullet and died
half an hour later. The next day, police arrested his killer:
a seventeen-year-old gang member.

*   *   *

On April 15, 1989, sixteen-year-old Stephanie Beasley was gunned down while standing on a front porch in Chicago at about 8:00 P.M. Her killers, two gang members ages seventeen and sixteen, had been involved in a gang fight at the same address half an hour earlier. When they returned, they opened fire into a group of people standing on the porch. Stephanie, an innocent bystander, was struck in the head and died before she reached the hospital.

Just a day later, on April 16, 1989, twenty-year-old Luis Bonilla stood in front of Maria Gonzalez' Chicago home and "signaled" to a passing car driven by rival gang members. Street gangs have their own hand signals, which members use to proclaim their loyalties. An hour later, another car drove by Maria's home. Three passengers, all wearing ski masks, opened fire with automatic rapid-fire weapons, including an Uzi submachine gun. Luis and two girls were wounded. Sixteen-year-old Maria was killed. Three gang members, two seventeen-year-olds and a sixteen-year-old, were charged with murder and attempted murder.

At about 8:00 on the evening of November 1, 1989, a car carrying five youths pulled up to a stop sign in downtown Bridgeport, Connecticut. Within seconds, eighty shots rang out from various automatic and semiautomatic weapons wielded by three youths standing on the street corner. The car was hit at least 20 times, one seventeen-year-old passenger was killed, and the other four (ranging in age from fifteen to twenty-two) were wounded.

The next day, police arrested three youths—a fourteen-year-old and two seventeen-year-olds—and charged each with one count of murder and four counts of attempted murder. Police said the ambush with high-powered weapons was linked to drugs and possibly to a turf war between competing drug gangs. They said that one of the alleged gunmen had earlier accused one of the victims of being part of a "drug rip-off."

*   *   *

Major cities, small towns, and suburbs across the country are being terrorized by juvenile gangs, some highly organized and others put together on the spur of the moment. In cities such as Boston, New York, Chicago, Washington, Detroit, and Los Angeles, gang killings, many of which are drug-related, have reached record proportions.

Solid data regarding juvenile gang involvement in homicides are hard to come by. Although juvenile gangs exist in communities of all sizes across America, very little is known about these gangs except for those operating in the largest metropolitan areas. Gangs in these areas have come under greater scrutiny because they are larger, better organized, and more involved in serious crime such as homicide. But even in the largest cities, there is a paucity of gang membership data. For example, while these gangs are often referred to as juvenile or youth gangs, their age make-up is not entirely clear. Some are truly juvenile gangs, others are really young adult gangs, and still others have members ranging from children to middle-aged adults.

Los Angeles is clearly the single area of the United States most heavily infested with juvenile street gangs. At latest count, Los Angeles County has approximately six hundred active street gangs and over 70,000 gang members. In 1987, there were 387 gang-related killings in Los Angeles County. Even that all-time record was broken in 1988, when 452 people died in gang-related killings, and again in 1989, when the number of gang-related homicides topped five hundred. According to the Los Angeles Times, by the end of 1988, gang homicides in the county had "increased 50 percent in three years," and according to a May 1989 report issued by the Los Angeles district attorney, "one out of every three homicides in Los Angeles County is gang-related."

In the city of Los Angeles, the overall homicide rate dropped by 11.7 percent in 1988—a year in which there were 734 homicides, the lowest number in ten years. But the number of gang-related homicides rose from 207 in 1987 to

257 in 1988: a 25.3 percent increase. Thus, in 1988, 37.9 percent of all homicides in the city of Los Angeles were gang-related. Similarly, during the first quarter of 1989, 78 (38.4 percent) of the 203 reported homicides in the city were gang-related.

The majority of people killed in gang-related homicides in Los Angeles are not gang members, but others, including robbery victims and innocent bystanders killed in drive-by shootings aimed at rival gang members. The other victims of these homicides are mainly gang members killed in drive-by shootings or in drug-related turf wars. In some cases, these drive-by shootings are part of the initiation rites for younger boys who want to become gang members.

Law enforcement authorities in Los Angeles blame the increase in gang-related killings on "heightened narcotics trade and increased use of powerful semi-automatic weapons, particularly among members of black street gangs," which have been described by the authorities as "the main distributors of crack throughout the Western United States."

Most gang members in the Los Angeles area are black or Hispanic. It is estimated that of the more than 70,000 gang members in the county, almost two-thirds are Hispanic, nearly a third are black, and a small but growing percentage are white and Asian. Most of these gang members come from impoverished, drug-infested, high crime-rate neighborhoods in Los Angeles, which lack economic and recreational opportunities and have inordinately high dropout rates.

Even outside Los Angeles County, however, gangs flourish in less urban parts of Southern California. In nearby Orange County, for instance, there are known to be at least one hundred street gangs with a membership of about 7,000 youths. The city of Santa Ana alone has sixty gangs with between 5,500 and 6,000 members. Halfway through 1989, the Orange County district attorney had already filed criminal charges against 792 gang members, including thirty charged with murder or attempted murder.

Other cities, including Boston, New York, Chicago, Miami, San Francisco, Milwaukee, Kansas City, Denver, and Seattle, have also experienced recent increases in juvenile gangs and gang homicides. In Boston, where official statistics on gang killings are not reported, there were estimated to be as many as twelve or more gang killings in 1988. In the first quarter of 1989, two people were killed and more than a dozen injured in Boston gang violence.

Although the police have played down the significance of gang activity and involvement in Boston homicides, law enforcement authorities there recently acknowledged that "youth gangs not only exist in Boston but are becoming larger and more violent." Still, according to the Boston Police Department, these gangs are not as large or as well-organized as those in Los Angeles, but are often only small, "loosely organized" groups—"kids from one street getting together and calling themselves by their street name."

As in Los Angeles, gang activity in Boston seems confined largely to the city's poorest neighborhoods—areas where the school dropout rate runs as high as 40 percent. Although there are said to be only half a dozen "major" juvenile gangs in Boston, there is also what authorities have described as a "host of cliques, subsections and 'wannabees,' kids who aspire to be hard-core gang members."

In Chicago, where some 12,000 youths belong to about 125 gangs, drive-by shootings and other youth gang killings, often committed with automatic and semiautomatic firearms, have become commonplace. There, as in Los Angeles, victims include both rival gang members and innocent bystanders caught in the crossfire. In 1988, Chicago recorded its lowest murder rate in twenty years, but gang-related killings increased by 28 percent—rising from forty-seven (6.8 percent) of the 691 homicides in 1987 to sixty (9.1 percent) of the 658 homicides in 1988.

Chicago law enforcement authorities say this increase in gang-related killings is the result of the growing availability of more powerful firearms and the recent closing of inner-city hospitals, which increases the likelihood that victims of gang violence will die from their wounds.

In Chicago, homicides are reported as gang-related only when they can be tied to "organized gang activity," but in Los Angeles "any killing committed by a gang member is classified as gang-related." If Chicago used the Los Angeles definition of "gang-related," the number of gang-related killings there would probably be twice as high. As in Los Angeles, Chicago's youth gangs are not confined to the city proper; they extend into the suburbs as well. At least twenty Chicago suburbs are plagued by juvenile gangs, and some of these towns and cities have experienced gang-related homicides.

In New York City, youth gangs include both highly organized drug gangs and informal bands of youthful marauders who come together solely to attack, rob, rape, and sometimes kill.

New York City drug gangs, whose members range in age from their teens to midtwenties, use violence, including homicide, primarily to further their trafficking in cocaine and crack. It is estimated that there have been as many as 523 drug-related gang killings in the past five years in upper Manhattan alone. The vast majority of these killings involve territorial fights between rival gangs or disputes with drug customers, but a number of innocent bystanders have also been killed. According to police investigators, many drug gang members "demonstrate toughness" by killing in broad daylight on crowded streets, shooting their victims in the head at close range with semiautomatic weapons, and making no effort to avoid being identified.

The other sort of gang violence common in New York City is that committed by "wolf packs" or "posses"—impromptu gatherings of anywhere from a few to several dozen teenage or younger boys who commit *en masse* acts of criminal violence, such as the widely publicized 1989 rape and attempted murder of a woman jogger in New York's Central Park. In many instances, older teens decide to "gather a pack" and pressure younger boys to join them in committing crimes that include larceny, robbery, rape, and homicide. On average, three such incidents occur each day in New York City.

Random, apparently motiveless rampages of the sort committed by these posses and packs have come to be referred to as "wilding"—the word teens used to describe their gang attack on the Central Park jogger. Although the name is new, New York City law enforcement officials say that "wilding" has gone on in the city at least since 1983.

By far, the majority of juvenile gang-related homicides are committed by members of at least loosely organized gangs—established groups that generally have names, "uniforms" or "colors" (distinctive clothing, jackets, caps, etc.), and special signals for distinguishing their members from those of rival gangs.

Occasionally, members of organized juvenile gangs kill in the course of committing other crimes. For example, killings related to drug trafficking are common. For the most part, however, members of organized juvenile gangs seem much more likely to kill for reasons most would regard as senseless; for example, vengeance, protecting the gang's turf, or just for "fun."

Juvenile gang killings related to drug trafficking are generally motivated by greed. These killings are intended to prevent drug operations from being revealed to authorities, eliminate competition, and enforce collection of drug debts. In Detroit, for example, one so-called teenage drug lord recently paid a contract killer to execute one of his competitors. The hired killer broke into the rival drug dealer's home armed with a semiautomatic firearm loaded with armor piercing bullets. After ordering the rival drug dealer and three others to lie on the floor, the paid assassin shot and killed all three.

More recently, in New York City, a fourteen-year-old boy, who had been using and dealing cocaine and other

drugs since he turned thirteen, was convicted of murder
and sentenced to nine years to life in prison. Owed $150
by two customers who couldn't or wouldn't pay, the boy
lured both men to a rooftop in the South Bronx and then
shot and killed them.

Though common, gang-related robberies and rapes, like
robberies and rapes in general, rarely result in murders
or attempted murders. But when they do, the homicidal
behavior is often both senseless and especially heinous.
Consider, for example, the following two cases.

On January 9, 1986, five young gang members grabbed a
twenty-six-year-old woman who was walking down a street
in South Central Los Angeles. The youths, four of whom
were under the age of eighteen, dragged the woman into
an alley, took turns raping and sodomizing her, knocked
her unconscious, threw her into a dumpster, covered her
with a Christmas tree, and then lit both her and the tree
on fire.

The victim—who survived but lost an arm, a leg, and
both breasts and was hospitalized for months—testified that
the last thing she heard before being knocked unconscious
was one of the youths saying, "We gotta kill her. She
knows me." The three oldest youths were convicted of
various crimes, including kidnapping, rape, and attempted
murder, and sentenced to prison for ninety-seven years,
sixty-nine years, and thirty-four years, respectively. Their
two younger accomplices, ages fourteen and fifteen, were
convicted in juvenile court and remanded to the custody of
the California Youth Authority.

On April 9, 1987, three Los Angeles street gang members, two of whom were juveniles, committed two robbery-
killings within the space of two hours. First they accosted a
minister and his wife, who had stopped at a phone booth to
call for help after their church choir bus broke down. The
youths grabbed the woman's purse, knocked her down, and
then robbed, shot, and killed her husband as he stood in the
phone booth. They then drove to a liquor store and bought

beer and cigarettes with the money they had stolen.

Two hours later, the trio returned to the store, approached two men sitting in a car, and demanded money. When the men resisted, one of the youths shot them, killing one and seriously wounding the other. According to police, this second slaying occurred because it was the juvenile perpetrator's "turn to show that he too is a tough guy. He wanted to do a killing."

The vast majority of organized juvenile gang-related killings seem entirely senseless. Most commonly these killings result from the efforts of gang members to injure or kill members of rival gangs. Victims include both gang members and innocent bystanders, many of whom are killed in drive-by shootings. In other cases, innocent bystanders, particularly children, are wounded and killed when caught in the crossfire in shoot-outs between rival gangs.

Juvenile gang members also frequently kill each other, most often to exact revenge or maintain control of territory. A typical vengeance gang killing is the recent stabbing of a seventeen-year-old Santa Monica youth by members of a rival street gang from Venice, California. The youth was beaten, kicked, and fatally stabbed by five gang members (ranging in age from fifteen to twenty-four) as "payback" for an earlier gang attack by Santa Monica gang members on rival gang members from Venice.

In a typical gang killing committed in the course of turf warfare, seventeen-year-old Ralph Hernandez and several fellow gangsters attacked two members of a rival gang. Ralph shot one youth in the head, thigh, and testicles and then beat him with a four-foot-long spiked weapon. The attack and killing occurred after graffiti painted on a building by members of Ralph's gang was crossed out and replaced with the insignia of the victim's gang. According to a probation report filed in the case, this action "was interpreted as a symbolic challenge."

Ralph Hernandez, who was "trying to make a name for himself," apparently accepted that "challenge." Convicted of first-degree murder, he was sentenced to serve thirty-eight years to life in prison.

Although most juvenile gang-related killings are committed by members of organized street gangs, many crimes of violence and at least some homicides are committed by gangs of juveniles formed on the spur of the moment solely for the purpose of committing a single crime or series of crimes. Undoubtedly the best known incident of this kind is the 1989 gang rape and attempted murder of a twenty-eight-year-old investment broker who was jogging in New York City's Central Park.

Accounts of this crime vary widely, but it seems clear that a dozen or more young teenage boys attacked the woman and that as many as eight raped her. One of the youths arrested, a fourteen-year-old who was one of a dozen teenage boys waiting behind trees when the victim ran past, told police: "Someone said, 'grab her.' . . . Somebody hit her . . . . Somebody dragged her into the bushes." The woman was stripped, raped, beaten with fists, a brick and a pipe, and left for dead.

Although the woman survived and made a remarkable recovery from life-threatening injuries, there is no doubt that her assailants thought they had killed her. In a confession shortly after the crime, one teenage suspect told police, "I know who did the murder." Another added, "We thought she was dead."

Although the woman was raped, the attack seemed senseless and not primarily motivated by sexual desire. Interviewed after the crime, another juvenile suspect in the case was asked why the youths committed this crime. His response: "It was something to do. It was fun."

The dozen or so youths involved in the rape and attempted murder were apparently just an accidental subset of a much larger spontaneously organized group—perhaps as many as three dozen youths who had been "wilding" in Central Park that night. Earlier in the evening, boys from this larger group stole a homeless man's sandwich, stoned a taxicab, chased two bicyclists, and attacked a male jogger.

Interestingly, the juvenile "wilders" arrested in the Central Park attack bore little resemblance to the typical members of organized street gangs, who come primarily from impoverished and extremely disadvantaged backgrounds. Most of the Central Park attackers came from working-class or middle-class homes and were described as "children of strict parents" and "good students."

Other cases involving what might be called "wilding" or "wolfpack" mentality have resulted in deaths. For example, when a fight recently broke out among a mob of over one hundred black and Hispanic teenagers in front of a Newark pizzeria, a "good Samaritan" tried to intervene but was attacked by the youths, one of whom beat him to death with a golf club. The seventeen-year-old who wielded the club was convicted of reckless manslaughter.

Not far away, in New York's Spanish Harlem, a man was recently beaten to death by a group of six to eight youths, none with criminal records. After stealing a $20 bill from a bakery, the victim was chased by the group, surrounded, beaten, kicked, and stomped before being arrested by the police and rushed to a hospital. Four of his attackers, including a fourteen-year-old boy, were arrested and charged with manslaughter after the man died four hours later.

More recently, in a rather atypical if not bizarre killing committed by a spontaneously organized juvenile gang, four California teenagers—two fifteen-year-old boys, a nineteen-year-old boy, and a sixteen-year-old girl—attacked their parents with shotguns and baseball bats. Three parents survived gunshot wounds, but a fourth died after her fifteen-year-old son repeatedly beat her in the head with a baseball bat. The girl, who led the gang, allegedly ordered the January 1989 attacks, including the shooting of her own parents.

Although there was some evidence that some of the four youths were involved in Satanism, law enforcement authorities discounted any serious relationship between Satanism and the group's homicidal rampage. According to the prosecutor, none of the four were "normal everyday kids"; all were youths from disturbed families who "found each other and agreed to kill their parents."

Finally, in some instances, juvenile "wolf packs" commit repeated crimes over time, including homicide. For example, in June 1989, six Chicago youths, five of whom where under the age of eighteen, robbed a thirty-four-year-old man on a subway platform. When the man resisted, the teens killed him with his own hunting knife. Chicago police said the group was suspected of committing as many as fifty "strong-arm" robberies on subway platforms and trains in the span of a few months. One officer said the juveniles committed the robberies to get money for drugs and video games.

9

Little Kids Who Kill

IN APRIL 1985, nine-year-old Britt Kellum argued with his eleven-year-old brother and then used a 16-gauge shotgun to kill the older boy. Britt's mother was charged with neglect, and custody of Britt and his surviving brothers was awarded to their father. Finding Britt too young to be held accountable, juvenile authorities ordered him to undergo counseling. After four years in psychotherapy, Britt was charged with shooting his six-year-old brother to death.

According to a Michigan prosecutor, on October 30, 1989, Britt Kellum shot the younger boy with his father's .38 caliber handgun—a gun Britt's father taught him to shoot and left where he could get it. Following this second killing, Britt, who cannot be tried as an adult because of his age, was ordered locked up pending further proceedings. In ordering the thirteen-year-old's detention, a judge noted that Britt's five-year-old brother might be in danger. If adjudicated a delinquent on charges of murder, Britt Kellum could be incarcerated only until age twenty-one.

One afternoon in March 1986, two small boys wandered onto the balcony of a fifth floor Miami Beach apartment while their parents were talking in another room. The five-year-old pushed the three-year-old, who grabbed onto a ledge to keep from falling. The older boy then pried the younger boy's fingers loose, and the three-year-old fell five stories to his death.

The five-year-old readily confessed but told authorities the younger boy wanted to die because his parents abused him. Psychiatrists and attorneys concluded that the five-year-old was actually describing himself and his own parents. Prosecutors decided that the boy should not be prosecuted but committed to a residential treatment center for psychotherapy.

In 1983, a three-year-old New York City boy started a fire in his family's apartment. Although he was placed in long-term psychotherapy, the boy continued to play with matches. In September 1988, at the age of eight, he set another fire while playing with a cigarette lighter in a closet. Three family members escaped the fire unharmed, but his ten-year-old sister was critically injured and his eleven-year-old sister died after suffering burns over half her body. Although police concluded that the eight-year-old was unable "to comprehend the damage a fire can do," the boy was charged with murder.

In July 1981, a twelve-year-old New Mexico girl repeatedly forced an eight-year-old girl underwater in a public swimming pool until the younger child lost consciousness. Five days later, the eight-year-old died from drowning. Although a defense lawyer dismissed the incident as "horseplay" that went too far, the prosecutor argued that the killing was deliberate since the twelve-year-old not only held the younger girl's head underwater but watched a clock while she did it. The twelve-year-old was convicted of second-degree murder and sentenced to spend two years at a state home for girls.

In October 1988, a three-year-old Detroit boy watched as his father beat his mother. The father, who was drunk, laid a gun on a nearby table. The three-year-old grabbed the gun and used it to shoot and kill his father. Initially police could not believe the boy had killed his father, but five witnesses said they saw him do it. Gunpowder residue tests also established that the three-year-old had, in fact, fired the gun.

The boy's mother described the killing as an accident, but the boy told authorities: "I killed him. Now he's dead. If he would have hit my mother, I would have shot him again." Concluding that the boy was unable to form an intent to kill, the prosecutor declined to press criminal charges.

On August 7, 1986, a ten-year-old Los Angeles girl was left at about 12:30 A.M. to babysit the one-year-old daughter of her father's live-in girlfriend. When the father and his girlfriend returned home sometime after 2:00 A.M.—more than an hour and a half after leaving home "to buy milk and diapers"—the baby was not breathing. They rushed the infant to the hospital but she was dead on arrival. A police investigator said the ten-year-old girl "strangled the infant with her bare hands." Convicted of murder in juvenile court, the girl was committed to a children's psychiatric facility for an indeterminate period.

On March 6, 1989, Jessica Carr, a seven-year-old first grader from Pennsylvania, was shot and killed as she rode on the back of a snowmobile. The fatal shot was fired by a nine-year-old boy who said he was playing "hunter" with his father's .35 caliber hunting rifle. The boy, an honor student and Cub Scout, entered his parents' bedroom, took the key to his father's gun cabinet, unlocked the cabinet, removed and loaded the gun, and went outside where Jessica and other children were snowmobiling. After shooting the girl in the back, he removed the spent cartridge, hid it, and then put the gun back and relocked the cabinet.

The boy claimed that he accidentally fired the gun, but law enforcement authorities said the killing was deliberate, perhaps in reaction to the girl's bragging that she was better than the boy at playing Nintendo, the popular video game. A ballistics expert reported that the rifle could not have been discharged accidentally unless struck with a severe blow forcing the hammer to hit the firing pin.

Based on this evidence, and citing the boy's stability, academic achievement, and the deliberate nature of the killing, a judge ordered the boy to stand trial as an adult. If the judge's order stands, the boy will be the youngest person in the United States tried on murder charges in the twentieth century.

The incidence of juvenile homicide varies directly and positively as a function of age. The older children are, the more likely they are to kill. Preteens very rarely kill. Children under ten years of age consistently account for less than 1 percent of all juvenile arrests for murder and non-negligent manslaughter in the United States. Children between the ages of ten and twelve consistently account for only about 1.5 percent of such arrests.

Arrest data, of course, underestimate the true incidence of homicides committed by preteens since many younger children who kill are not arrested but dealt with in some other less formal legal fashion. In fact in most states, the law specifically provides that youngsters under the age of seven are not responsible for their criminal acts, including homicide. Still, even accounting for this arrest bias, it is clear that very few killings are committed by children under the age of thirteen.

Except for sexually related killings, which are almost unheard of in the twelve and under age range, homicides committed by preteens run roughly the same gamut as those committed by teenagers. Homicides committed by preteens include intrafamilial killings, killings committed in the course of other crimes, and senseless killings.

"Look at her face." She doesn't look like a "brutal murderer." She looks like a "little girl who is sweet and affectionate." That's what twelve-year-old Heidi Gasparovich's lawyer told the judge faced with deciding whether or not Heidi was guilty of helping to murder her father.

On February 17, 1986, Matthew Gasparovich, Sr. was shot five times and killed in his Iowa home. Heidi and her fifteen-year-old brother Matthew, Jr., who had previously lived in California with their mother, had been sent to live with their father just two months earlier. According to their mother, she sent the children to their father because they needed stability and because he was a strict disciplinarian.

In charging both youngsters with murder, the prosecutor argued that Heidi and Matthew hatched the plot to kill as part of a plan to get back to California. According to the prosecutor, Heidi held back a bedroom curtain while Matthew pumped five shots into their sleeping father. Immediately following the killing, both youths took off together in their father's car, headed for California, but were picked up by police when the car went off the road into a ditch.

The judge who tried the case agreed with the prosecutor. He found that while Matthew did the actual killing, Heidi "actively participated" and "lent countenance and approval." Heidi and Matthew were both found guilty and committed to state custody until their eighteenth birthdays. Heidi appealed, but the Iowa Supreme Court upheld the trial judge's verdict, concluding that the judge "correctly found that she participated in her father's murder."

Preteens who kill parents most often kill their fathers or stepfathers. As in teenage patricides, spousal or child abuse is often the common denominator. Consider, for example, the three-year-old mentioned earlier who shot and killed his father as the man abused his mother. And recall from Chapter 2 eleven-year-old Mary Bailey who shot and killed her sleeping stepfather at her mother's request. Interviewed after the killing, Mary said, "I was afraid he was going to get up and kill mommy."

Juvenile matricide is quite uncommon. Matricides committed by preteens are even more uncommon; indeed, they are almost unheard of. There are no published clinical reports of preteenage youngsters killing their mothers and almost no such reports in the popular media. The only recently reported case of a preteen killing his mother is that of a twelve-year-old suburban Washington, D.C. boy who shot both his parents with a .22 caliber hunting rifle. The boy's mother was killed and his father was seriously injured.

The boy, a learning disabled junior high school student described by a neighbor as "real quiet" and "real polite," shot his parents on February 24, 1989. The seventh-grader had just been suspended from school for three days for carrying a small knife. After arguing with his mother over the suspension, he fetched one of his father's many rifles from the attic and shot her four times as she stood in the kitchen cooking dinner. A short time later, the boy's father came home from work and found his wife's body on the kitchen floor. Before he could flee, his son shot him, chased him out of the house, and then shot him several more times.

Despite being physically and psychologically abused, eleven-year-old Arva Betts managed to make the fourth grade honor roll in Fort Lauderdale, Florida. Forced to babysit her two younger half-siblings for long hours while her mother worked two jobs to support the family, Arva was depressed and repeatedly told a school social worker she felt like killing herself.

On March 13, 1989, the day before her twelfth birthday, after five months of counseling with the social worker, Arva was babysitting when her two-year-old half-brother Andrew tried to drink bug spray and her fifteen-month-old half-sister Tiffany broke some figurines. Feeling overwhelmed and unable to control the two toddlers, Arva strangled Andrew and choked and hit Tiffany. Andrew was killed and Tiffany suffered permanent brain damage.

After pleading guilty to reduced charges of manslaughter and aggravated child abuse, Arva was sentenced to twelve years probation and ordered to undergo extensive counseling and psychotherapy. The judge, who handed down this sentence, also prohibited further contact between Arva and her mother, saying: "There are three victims in this case. There's Andrew, there's Tiffany and there's Arva."

In April 1986, a four-year-old New York City girl awoke before dawn and found her three-week-old twin brothers asleep in their cribs. She picked up one brother and dropped him to the floor when he scratched her. She picked up the other, and when he squirmed and started to cry, she threw him back into his crib. Hearing the commotion, the girl's parents rushed into the nursery and found both twins dead from fractured skulls.

Preteens who kill within the family are most likely to kill siblings—most often younger siblings, especially infants and toddlers. Most of these killings are impulsive, and many seem almost accidental. Fratricides and sororicides of this sort are nothing new; they are among the earliest juvenile homicides ever reported in the professional and clinical literature. For example, two of the earliest published psychological reports on children who kill each described preteens who killed siblings.

In 1942, Dr. Ralph Patterson described an eleven-year-old boy, with average intelligence, above-average school achievement, and no prior delinquency, who shot and killed his sister "in a quarrel over a few pennies." In 1959, in her now classic article, "Children and Adolescents Who Have Killed," Dr. Lauretta Bender described two cases in which five-year-old boys killed younger siblings. One boy choked his four-week-old sister to death because he was "bothered by her crying." The other impulsively pushed his three-year-old brother out the window. Dr. Bender described both boys as "mentally defective."

More recent psychological reports of young children killing or trying to kill their siblings have emphasized some extremely troubling findings: In many of the cases, the child perpetrator is a disturbed, abused child whose prior efforts to kill or injure a sibling have not been taken seriously.

For example, in "The Small Assassins: Clinical Notes on a Subgroup of Murderous Children," Dr. Kay Tooley described two neglected and abused six-year-olds who tried repeatedly to kill their siblings. "Mary," who was often sexually abused by her mother's boyfriend, set fire to her younger brother and then later tried to pour liquid bleach down her infant half-sister's throat. "Jay," who was frequently beaten by his father, set fire to his sister's dress and later held her head under water in a swimming pool. Dr. Tooley found Mary and Jay's parents "startlingly complacent and unconcerned with the dangerous extremity of their children's behavior."

Drs. William Easson and Richard Steinhilber of the Mayo Clinic described the case of an eight-year-old, who, like Dr. Tooley's "small assassins," made several "murderous assaults" on a younger sibling. The boy first choked his brother until the younger child was "blue in the face." Next he tried to strangle him with a belt. Finally, he was discovered in the act of trying to drown his brother by holding the younger boy's head underwater in a bathtub.

Like the parents of Mary and Jay, this boy's mother and father were also quite unperturbed by these assaults. After learning of the choking incident five days after it occurred, the boy's mother said she felt "It was too late to do or say anything," so she never told the boy's father. After learning of the incident with the belt, the boy's parents did nothing because the father thought the attempted strangling was just "part of growing up." Only after the attempted drowning did these parents seek psychiatric help for their older son.

More recently, Drs. Theodore Pettiman and Leonard Davidman described nine "homicidal school-age" (six to eleven) children, seven of whom either killed or tried to kill one or more of their siblings. Only two of the nine children were living in intact family units; three had been subjected to child abuse; seven were depressed and three were characterized as borderline psychotic; and six had mothers and three had fathers with histories of psychiatric treatment.

*   *   *

James McClure was just twelve years old when, on May 7, 1985, he broke into the home of an eighty-year-old neighbor in San Diego. Armed with a pocketknife and looking for something to steal, James was unexpectedly confronted by the elderly man. Frightened, he pulled the knife from his pocket and stabbed the man once in the heart. Questioned by police, who told him "nobody would be angry with him for telling the truth," James confessed to the burglary and killing. Although his confession was thrown out as improperly induced, James McClure pleaded guilty to a reduced charge of manslaughter and was ordered to remain in the custody of the California Youth Authority until his twenty-fifth birthday.

In Wisconsin, an eleven-year-old girl was found guilty in the fatal 1986 stabbing and bludgeoning death of a nine-year-old neighbor. The killing was triggered by an incident in which the girl took the younger boy's bicycle. Although two other youths—boys ages twelve and four-teen—were also implicated in the killing, witnesses said the eleven-year-old girl led the attack. All three youths were adjudicated delinquents and committed to juvenile facilities.

More recently, five youths ranging in age from twelve to twenty stormed into a California home masked and armed. When one of their would-be robbery victims screamed and startled the young robbers, they shot and killed her. Then all five intruders fled the house empty-handed. Two of the youths—twelve-year-old Quoc Ngo and thirteen-year-old Man Huynh—were apprehended. After confessing, they were convicted of first-degree murder and remanded to a state reformatory to serve indeterminate sentences.

Although preteens often commit crimes, especially theft-related crimes, they very rarely kill while committing these offenses. When they do, the killings are usually commit-ted by groups of youths and seem to serve no rational purpose.

*   *   *

On June 3, 1989, Suzette Franklin left her room at a Connecticut homeless shelter to sterilize baby bottles for her five-week-old twin daughters. Upon leaving the room, she locked the door. While she was gone, two four-year-olds who lived in the same shelter managed to open the locked door, sneak into the room, and bite and beat one of the twins. Minutes later the baby was found lying on the floor, barely breathing. Rushed to the hospital, she died an hour later from severe head injuries. Questioned by police, the four-year-olds denied any intent to hurt the infant. Authorities said they did not expect to file any charges.

On March 25, 1986, a ten-year-old St. Louis boy, Ryan Merrihew, quarreled with an eleven-year-old neighbor girl in her yard. The girl told Ryan to leave. When he refused, she went inside, got her father's .38 caliber revolver, shot and killed Ryan, and then telephoned the police. The girl, described by police as "mature enough to know what she was doing," admitted the killing and was processed legally as a juvenile.

In Columbia, South Carolina, in one two-week stretch in 1987, two thirteen-year-olds were killed by preteens. In the first killing, an eleven-year-old boy beat another boy to death with a baseball bat after the two argued. In the second killing, a twelve-year-old girl argued with a boy and then shot him in the back as he walked out of the grocery store where she was working.

In January 1989, two Missouri brothers, four and six years old, attacked a twenty-month-old girl with a shovel, screwdriver, hammer, and brick because they thought the girl was "ugly" and because they "didn't like her." The four-year-old boy then ran to tell his father and the girl's father, who were playing cards in the kitchen. "She's dead," the boy told them. Both boys had neighborhood reputations for "unruliness," apparently stemming in part from an earlier incident in which the two broke a car window to steal some juice. At the time of the killing, the boys' father was facing charges of child abuse as a result of a broken arm suffered earlier by the four-year-old.

The vast majority of juvenile killings are best classified as senseless. Although some of these killings are committed by youths who are seriously mentally ill, most preteens who commit senseless killings are not psychotic or otherwise seriously disturbed. Instead their homicidal acts seem to reflect a combination of forces, including immaturity, impulsivity, and infantile rage. Moreover, in many of these homicides, there seems to be a clear element of chance or fortuity. To put it another way, in many cases, the young juvenile killer and his or her victim simply happened to be in the wrong place at the wrong time.

When very young children kill, their victims are most often other children, usually children younger than themselves. Such killings, though relatively rare, often follow one of two predictable patterns: a very young child or infant is killed as a result of head trauma or a child is impulsively or "accidentally" killed with a firearm.

The first pattern, illustrated by the Connecticut and Missouri killings described previously, was first documented in 1972 by the Cuyahoga (Ohio) County Coroner, Mr. Lester Adelson, in an article, "The Battering Child," published in the Journal of the American Medical Association.

Dr. Adelson described five killings, all committed by children eight years old or younger. One case involved an intrafamilial killing: the mother of a seven-week-old infant found the baby dead in her crib after leaving her alone with her seven-year-old brother for about ten minutes. The infant's brother—a "loner" and "slow learner" with an IQ in the borderline mentally retarded range told police he "bopped" his baby sister "many times" with the leg of a spinning wheel and bit her because she was crying.

In Dr. Adelson's other four cases, three boys and a girl ranging in age from two to eight years old each killed an infant less than eight months old. All four infants died from trauma to the skull and brain, and none showed signs of previous abuse. One infant was struck and dropped to the floor, a second was thrown to the floor, a third was hit with several metal toys, and the fourth was rolled off a bed, bitten, and hit repeatedly with a shoe.

Dr. Adelson attributed these killings to a combination of forces, including not only the young perpetrators' jealousy, rage, and lack of impulse control, but also their tiny victims' special vulnerabilities, that is, the frailty and fragility of infants' heads. As Dr. Adelson concluded, cranio-cerebral injuries of the type that killed these infants "occur only in this immature age group."

In February 1985, a twelve-year-old was playing in his room with two twelve-year-old visitors. When the boys left the room, heading for a video arcade, one of the visitors grabbed a baseball. When the visitor refused to give the ball back, his twelve-year-old host picked up a semiautomatic rifle and shot him fifteen times. Charged with murder, the young shooter, who had no history of violent behavior, had never been in trouble before, and had never before fired a gun, offered no defense and was sentenced to the California Youth Authority for an indeterminate term not to exceed his twenty-fifth birthday. Asked why the killing occurred, the boy's attorney said, "He was basically taunted into doing it."

On March 2, 1987, twelve-year-old Nathan Ferris, an overweight seventh grade honor student from Missouri, took his father's loaded .45 caliber pistol to school with him in his gym bag. Later that day, Nathan pulled the gun from the bag and threatened his junior high classmates with it. When one classmate teased him about the gun being plastic, Nathan shot and killed the boy and then himself. A week earlier, Nathan, a "loner" who was often teased by his peers, had warned another classmate not to come to school because he intended to "shoot everyone."

* * *

In a letter to the editor of the *Los Angeles Times*, a reader wrote to complain that a recent *Times* story about young children who kill failed to mention one "obvious" fact: "All these children had easy access to guns and ammunition in their own homes." Easy availability of guns in the home is unquestionably a major factor in homicides committed by preteens. Some of these firearm killings are clearly intentional but impulsive. Others are the result of recklessness or negligence. Still others present some mix of intent, recklessness, or negligence in the handling of a dangerous weapon. What all these killings have in common is that they would not have occurred had the young perpetrators not had ready access to guns and ammunition.

Impulsive firearm killings, such as the two just described and the Pennsylvania case noted previously, usually occur when one child becomes involved in an argument or confrontation with another child and reaches for a gun to help settle the dispute. In these killings the perpetrators and victims are generally older children. Clearly unintentional killings with firearms are more often committed by younger children. Typically, the child is playing with a gun, intentionally or unintentionally fires the gun, and kills a playmate or someone else who just happens to be in the line of fire.

Some of these killings take place in the course of child's play: one young player finds a gun and turns it on a peer. For example, in New Jersey on July 7, 1986, a four-year-old and an eight-year-old were playing "Cowboys and Indians." The four-year-old "cowboy" found a loaded handgun beneath his grandmother's couch and then shot and killed the eight-year-old "Indian." More recently, on October 22, 1989, a Los Angeles area twelve-year-old shot and killed a ten-year-old playmate who was staying at the older boy's home while his parents were out of town. After taking a shotgun from his parent's bedroom, the twelve-year-old aimed the gun at his friend's head and pulled back the hammer. The gun went off and the younger boy was shot and killed.

In a similar tragedy, two South Carolina boys, eight and five, climbed into a plumber's truck, opened the glove compartment and found a loaded .38 caliber pistol. The boys took turns playing with the gun for about two hours. Finally the five-year-old boy fired the pistol and shot and killed a five-year-old girl. Although questions were raised about the young shooter's mental health, and there was evidence that he had been aggressive to other children both before and after the killing, the girl's death was ruled an accident.

More recently, in March 1989, a six-year-old boy fatally wounded a taxi driver in the parking lot of a big city hospital. The boy was waving his father's loaded pistol out the window of the family car, when the gun fired and the taxi driver was shot in the head and killed. Questioned by the police, all the boy said was: "I was playing with the gun." The boy's father, who did not realize his son had taken the gun from a front-seat compartment, was charged with negligence.

10

Girls Who Kill

ATTINA MARIE CANNADAY was sixteen years old when she, David Gray, and Dawn Bushart kidnapped Attina's former boyfriend, Ronald Wojcik, and his girlfriend after Attina caught them in bed together. The trio forced the couple into a van at knifepoint and drove them to a secluded area in rural Mississippi. At Attina's suggestion, David raped the woman. Then—depending on whose story is true—either David or Attina forced Ronald Wojcik into the woods and stabbed him nineteen times with a butcher knife.

Attina, who ran away from home at age thirteen, married and divorced at fourteen, and worked as a dancer, barmaid, and prostitute before the killing, was borderline mentally retarded and had a mental age of under ten years. Still, she was convicted of capital murder and sentenced to die.

Delphine Green was just fifteen when she and Stanley Griffen, twenty-one, and Raymond Kelly, twenty-four, robbed and killed a sixty-four-year-old New Jersey man. Prosecutors said Delphine planned the robbery for months and recruited the two men for "muscle." Delphine knew the man, often visited his home, and was aware that he sometimes collected rent money for his landlord.

The trio broke into the home of William Carter, a retired coal miner who suffered from emphysema and needed an oxygen mask to breathe. After stealing $13, a coat, and a television set from Carter's apartment, Delphine and her companions tied the man up, gagged him, and cut the tubes to his oxygen tank as he pleaded, "Please don't hurt me. Please don't kill me." Left for dead, William Carter suffocated while Delphine, Stanley, and Raymond spent the afternoon in a video game parlor.

Raymond Kelly was convicted of murder and sentenced to life in prison. Stanley Griffen pleaded guilty and, in return for testifying against his accomplices, was sentenced to thirty years in prison. Delphine Green blamed her companions for the killing, testifying that she was "too scared" to stop them. A jury found her guilty of robbery, conspiracy, and felony murder. Rejecting pleas for leniency, the judge sentenced Delphine to a prison term of thirty years to life. When Delphine's attorney argued that locking the teenager up with adult offenders would be "cruel and unusual punishment," the judge told him. "The only thing cruel and unusual is the way William Carter died." Delphine Green will be forty-five years old before she can even be considered for parole.

Patricia Cummings was fourteen when she killed fifteen-year-old Robert Clayton. Patricia, a student at a private school for emotionally disturbed girls, had a New Year's Eve party at her Long Island home in New York. According to police, youths at the party were drinking. Police officers said other guests told them Patricia slapped Robert after he berated her for insulting his girlfriend. When Robert told Patricia her slaps didn't hurt, she plunged a steak knife into his chest. Rushed to the hospital, Robert died from the stab wound an hour later.

Prosecuted as an adult, Patricia Cummings pleaded guilty to second-degree murder. As part of the plea bargain, she was sentenced to a term of five years to life in prison.

* * *

Janice Buttrum was fifteen when she married twenty-six-year-old Danny Buttrum. Danny, an escapee from a prison work camp in Georgia, was a violent man who abused Janice throughout their two-year marriage. The marriage ended when, at the age of seventeen, Janice was arrested for the murder of Demetra Parker.

Janice, Danny, and their eleven-month-old daughter were living in a motel room in Georgia. Nineteen-year-old Demetra Parker lived in another room in the same motel. In the early morning hours of September 3, 1980, Demetra was raped, sodomized, and stabbed ninety-seven times in her room at the Country Boy Inn. Autopsy revealed sixty-seven stab wounds to the chest, twenty-four to the neck, several to the spine, and a number of other cuts to the vagina and anus. Both her vagina and rectum were penetrated, and a plastic toothbrush holder was forced into her vagina. Police found a bloody washcloth and soap in the Buttrum's room, but no sign of Janice, Danny, or the baby.

The next day, while driving Demetra's car, Danny and Janice were stopped and arrested in Florida. Both were charged with capital murder. Danny was tried first. He was convicted and sentenced to die, but hanged himself in his jail cell.

Before and after her trial, Janice gave several different accounts of the killing. In one version, Janice said she and Danny went to Demetra's room to scare her, then took turns stabbing her while their infant daughter played with the telephone.

In another statement, Janice told authorities much the same, but added that Danny sat by and masturbated as she stabbed Demetra. In a third statement contained in a letter she wrote to the sheriff, Janice took full responsibility for the crime, saying she killed Demetra and forced Danny to rape her because the nineteen-year-old woman was trying to have sex with Danny. Finally, at her sentencing hearing, Janice testified that Danny forced her to go to Demetra's room, where she waited outside briefly before entering and finding Danny and Demetra having sex; enraged, she stabbed Demetra in the chest.

Janice's trial was delayed several months because she was pregnant with her second child at the time she was arrested. Although her attorney characterized Janice as "an injured child who gallantly and foolishly tried to save someone she loved," the jury convicted her of murder and sentenced her to die in Georgia's electric chair. In late 1989, a federal judge ordered a new sentencing hearing, but prosecutors said they would appeal.

Lorna Ortiz was fifteen when she killed. Lorna and three of her friends, ranging in age from thirteen to eighteen, met in a Chicago pinball parlor and "decided to hitchhike and rob somebody." That somebody was a thirty-two-year-old salesman who picked up the teenage hitchhikers and drove them to a park. According to the thirteen-year-old girl, who testified for the prosecution, the man asked the girls for sex. Lorna agreed to have sex with the man for $10, but then pulled out a gun and robbed him of $17 and his keys while another girl held a knife to his throat. The man then chased the girls, demanding that they return his keys. Lorna responded by shooting him in the forehead from a distance of about four inches.

Women of any age are extremely unlikely to kill. Annually in the United States, roughly 85 to 90 percent of those arrested for murder or non-negligent manslaughter are men or boys. This gender ratio is not only consistent from year to year but holds true for both juvenile and adult killers.

Girls so rarely kill that most of the research on juvenile homicide has looked exclusively at male killers. Most reported studies have excluded girls altogether—often deliberately. For example, in explaining why all forty-five juvenile killers in their sample were boys, one group of researchers said: "Females were excluded from the study because their numbers were so small that their inclusion would have skewed the statistical analysis."

Despite the lack of systematic research on girls who kill, it is clear that girls kill for a variety of reasons. Some girls kill their abusive or neglecting parents or other family members. Some girls who kill are psychologically disturbed. Other girls kill in the course of committing crimes such as robbery or larceny. And still others commit what appear to be senseless killings.

On July 3, 1985, a fifteen-year-old New York girl was babysitting her eight-year-old brother and seven-year-old sister. At about 1:00 in the morning, the teenager argued with her brother over what television program to watch. The argument turned into a fight, and the girl covered the eight-year-old's face with her hands and suffocated him. After the police alleged that the killing was intentional, the prosecutor charged the girl with murder and asked that she be tried as an adult.

On May 25, 1987, fifteen-year-old Andrea Williams, armed with a combat knife, and her eighteen-year-old boyfriend, Mario Garcia, wielding a machete, hacked Andrea's mother to death for trying to end their romance. The New York City couple—both apparently high on drugs—then left the mother's body on the floor in her apartment. For nine days, until they were arrested, Andrea and Mario continued to use the apartment. Both youngsters pleaded guilty to murder charges. Andrea was sentenced to seven years to life in prison, and Mario received a sentence of fifteen years to life.

On July 10, 1989, a fourteen-year-old Chicago mother was trying to watch television. After being interrupted several times by her one-month-old son who would not stop crying, the girl smothered the infant with a disposable diaper. The teenager was charged with murder, but a judge ruled that given her "previously clean record" she would not be tried as an adult.

*   *   *

When girls kill, they rarely kill strangers. In one recent year, for example, while only about 14 percent of male juveniles arrested for murder or non-negligent manslaughter had killed a parent, stepparent or other family member, 44 percent of the female juveniles arrested for these crimes had killed a parent, step-parent, or other family member. Intrafamilial killings committed by girls differ not only in number but also in terms of the involvement of accomplices and the relationship of the killer to the victim.

The vast majority of juveniles who kill family members act alone. In those relatively rare cases in which a juvenile has help in killing a family member, the juvenile perpetrator related to the victim is almost always a girl. In one recent national study, researchers identified twenty-one intrafamilial juvenile homicides committed by more than a single offender. In twenty of these cases, the identified juvenile perpetrator was a girl. Recent examples include the cases of Andrea Williams, mentioned above; Cheryl Pierson, described in Chapter 2; and Karin Aparo, a Connecticut teenager charged with having her boyfriend kill her mother.

In August 1987, nineteen-year-old Dennis Coleman strangled Joyce Aparo with a stocking and then dumped her body near a highway in another state. Joyce Aparo was the mother of Karin Aparo, Dennis' sixteen-year old girlfriend. Dennis pleaded guilty to murder, but said Karin had begged him for a year to kill her mother. At Dennis' sentencing hearing, a psychologist testified that Dennis was Karin's "sexual slave" and was coerced into the killing under the threat that at Karin would drop him. Dennis was sentenced to serve thirty-four years in prison.

Meanwhile, Karin was ordered to stand trial as an adult on a charge of accessory to murder. Her multiple appeals to be tried as a juvenile have been rejected by both the Connecticut and United States Supreme Courts. According to her attorney, her plan is to raise an insanity defense. Karin reportedly suffers from emotional problems stemming from years of physical and psychological abuse inflicted by her late mother.

The major difference in victim-offender relationships between intrafamilial killings committed by girls ad those committed by boys is attributable to one form of intra-familial homicide committed almost exclusively by females: infanticide. Though committed by both men and women of all ages, most infanticides are committed by unwed teen-age mothers—girls trying to hide the fact that they have given birth or avoid the responsibilities of parenthood.

For example, in January 1986, a newborn killed by multi-ple stab wounds was found in a garage, wrapped in a plastic bag. Police searched the Wisconsin home, found a knife believed to be the murder weapon, and arrested a sixteen-year-old girl on a charge of first-degree murder. The girl—whom no one realized was pregnant—gave birth after seven to eight months of pregnancy and killed the baby almost immediately. After being ordered to stand trial as a juvenile, she pleaded guilty to second-degree murder and was sentenced to serve a year in a state detention facility.

In a similar case, a fifteen-year-old tenth-grader gave birth alone on July 10, 1988, cleaned the baby, wrapped him in a towel, put him in a plastic garbage bag, amd then threw the bag down an eleven-foot embankment outside her upstate New York home. The newborn, who was found by a neighbor three hours later, suffered head injuries and was pronounced dead on arrival at a local hospital. According to the girl's aunt, no one in the family knew the girl was pregnant. After the killing, the girl told police she killed the newborn because she feared her mother would be upset if she learned that her daughter had given birth. The girl was charged with second-degree murder.

In a California infanticide case, the teenage perpetrator's motives were different. A fifteen-year-old girl, who had recently emigrated from Mexico, lived with her impov-erished parents and was already the mother of one child. She did not speak English and had dropped out of junior high school at the age of fourteen, when her first child was born. Her parents told her that if she ever became pregnant again she would have to leave home because they could not support another child.

Shortly thereafter, the girl again became pregnant. Nine months later, on October 9, 1987, she gave birth alone in her parents' home, placed the baby in a plastic bag, and threw the bag into a dumpster, where the baby was later found suffocated.

The girl's lawyer said of the girl and her motives: "She is very young and unsophisticated. She sensed she had no options." The girl was charged with murder and pleaded guilty. Despite the prosecutor's arguments for a sentence of up to seven years in prison, the court sentenced her to serve only a year in the Los Angeles County Juvenile Hall.

"You can't feel sorry for Sandy Shaw because she's cute and sixteen." That's what the prosecutor told the jury during his closing argument in the murder trial of the Nevada teenager charged with masterminding the September 29, 1986 robbery and killing of James "Cotton" Kelly. Testifying in her own behalf, Sandy told jurors that she was just fifteen years old when she asked two teenage friends to beat up the twenty-four-year-old Kelly "because he was bugging me." According to Sandy, Kelly kept calling her and asking her to go out with him and to pose for "suggestive photographs."

Other evidence, however, suggested that Sandy lured "Cotton" Kelly into the desert so that she and two other teens could rob him and get money to post bail for Sandy's boyfriend, who was jailed on unrelated charges. Kelly was robbed of $1,400 and shot six times in the neck and head. The killing was eventually dubbed the "show and tell" murder because Sandy Shaw reportedly took several friends out to see Kelly's body before it was discovered several days later by passing horseback riders.

The jury convicted Sandy Shaw of first-degree murder, and she was sentenced to life in prison without hope of parole. Her accomplices, Troy Kell, eighteen, and William Merritt, seventeen, were also charged in Kelly's death. Troy Kell was convicted of murder. William Merritt, who struck a deal with prosecutors and testified against Troy Kell, was allowed to plead guilty to the reduced charge of being an accessory to murder.

One afternoon in May 1987, fifteen-year-old Paula Cooper and three of her classmates skipped school, drank a bottle of cheap wine, and hatched a plot to steal money and a car. Paula and her friends—fourteen-, fifteen-, and sixteen-year-old girls—talked their way into the home of seventy-eight-year-old Ruth Pelke, a Gary, Indiana Bible teacher. Demanding to know where Mrs. Pelke kept her valuables, Paula stabbed the elderly woman thirty-three times with a foot-long butcher knife as Mrs. Pelke recited the Lord's Prayer. Paula and the three other teens then fled with $10 and Mrs. Pelke's ten-year-old Plymouth. After stopping at a McDonald's to throw the knife away, the girls went for a joy ride until they ran out of gas in Chicago.

Paula Cooper pleaded guilty to murder, was sentenced to die, and joined Janice Buttrum as one of the only two female juvenile killers on death row in the United States. In 1989, however, the Indiana Supreme Court commuted Paula's death sentence to sixty years imprisonment.

Women are in the minority not only among homicide perpetrators but also among perpetrators of virtually all crimes. As one authority put it: "Most crime is not committed by human beings in general. It is committed by men." Just as they rarely kill, girls also rarely rob, burglarize, rape, or commit other crimes of the sort that sometimes end in homicide. The vast majority of these crimes are committed by men and boys.

Occasionally girls do kill in the course of committing another crime—usually robbery. When they do, however, they rarely act alone. Instead, girls who kill during the course of committing other crimes almost invariably have accomplices. While homicides of this sort are quite rare, when they do occur they are frequently among the most heinous of all juvenile killings.

In most cases, girls who kill during other crimes have male accomplices. Sandy Shaw's case is one example. Another is the January 1987 killing of a ninety-one-year-old Pennsylvania woman. Three teens—fifteen-year-old Kristin Rice, fourteen-year-old Tamara Liggins, and sixteen-year-old Wayne Mialki—broke into Marcella Chambers' home, robbed her, and left her bound and gagged. The elderly woman was found tied to a chair on her bathroom floor four days later. Although she survived the ordeal, she died a week later.

The three teens were charged with murder, robbery, and burglary. Kristen Rice pleaded guilty and was sentenced to a term of four to twelve years. Wayne Mialki, who claimed that LSD caused his involvement in the crime, was convicted of murder and sentenced to serve between eight and twenty years in prison. The case of Tamara Liggins was handled in juvenile court, where her guilty plea was accepted.

Although girls who kill in the course of other crimes generally have male accomplices, robbery-related killings are increasingly being committed by two or more girls acting together, without male accomplices. Lorna Ortiz's shooting of a computer salesman is one such case. Paula Cooper's killing of Ruth Pelke is another. The case of Shirley Wolf and Cindy Collier, mentioned in Chapter 7, is yet another. Recall that Shirley, fourteen, and Cindy, fifteen, beat, stabbed, and killed an eighty-five-year-old woman before trying to steal her car.

More recently, on August 23, 1988, in a Los Angeles robbery-related slaying, two fifteen-year-old girls and a twenty-year-old woman jumped from a car, confronted a woman walking on the street, and demanded her purse. When Emma Jean Dorris, a twenty-eight-year-old nurse, resisted, one of the fifteen-year-olds pulled a gun from her waistband and shot Ms. Dorris in the face. A Los

Angeles police detective, who investigated the case, said he had "assumed" the killing was committed by a man and was "shocked" to learn that the killer was a girl. According to Los Angeles Police Department officials, however, in recent years girls in that city have become increasingly involved in gang-related killings, both as accomplices to male gang members and on their own.

11

Punishing Kids Who Kill

BY THE TIME he was fifteen years old, Willie Bosket had committed over 2,000 crimes and stabbed twenty-five people. From ages ten to fourteen, Willie was in and out of juvenile detention facilities. When authorities finally released him to a group home, one of his jailers made a prediction: "One of these days Willie is going to kill somebody."

Before too long, Willie Bosket fulfilled that prophesy. Released from reform school at the age of fourteen, Willie ran away and started prowling the New York City subways, searching for drunks to rob. In an eight-day crime spree, he brutally shot and killed two of his robbery victims.

After his arrest, Willie said he had killed "for the experience." Asked how he felt about the killings, Willie told police, "I shot people. That's all. I don't feel nothing." A short time later, Willie boasted that he could have killed a hundred people and still have been locked up only until age twenty-one.

Willie Bosket knew what he was talking about. As New York law stood then, juveniles under the age of sixteen could be tried only in the Family Court and, if found guilty, sent to a state reform school for no more than five years. Willie Bosket was prosecuted in Family Court, found guilty of the two murders, and given the maximum sentence allowed by law: placement in the custody of the New York State Division for Youth for a period of five years.

Willie Bosket was sentenced in 1978—an election year in New York. Democratic Governor Hugh Carey, who stood for re-election, had repeatedly vetoed legislation that would have restored New York's death penalty. As a result, Governor Carey was painted by Republicans as "soft on crime." Public outrage over the Bosket case, fueled by sensational media reports, gave Governor Carey the perfect reason to flex his crime-fighting muscle and show that he could be tough on crime. Who could be opposed to "getting tough" with juvenile killers like Willie Bosket?

Within a month of Willie's sentencing, New York's "Willie Bosket law" was drafted in a matter of days and presented to the legislature in an "extraordinary session" called by the governor. Introduced on July 14, 1978, the governor's proposal encountered virtually no opposition, passed both the state Assembly and Senate by overwhelming majorities, and was signed into law by Governor Carey on July 20, 1978.

New York's "Willie Bosket law," formally known as the Juvenile Offender Law, provides that thirteen-, fourteen-, and fifteen-year-olds charged with murder and those ages fourteen or fifteen charged with other violent felonies (manslaughter, kidnapping, arson, aggravated assault, rape, sodomy, attempted murder, attempted kidnapping, and first- and second-degree burglary) may be tried as adults in criminal court and, if convicted, subjected to lengthy terms of imprisonment. Had Willie Bosket been tried and convicted under the Juvenile Offender Law, he could have been sentenced to serve nine years to life in prison on each murder count.

Although Willie Bosket was never subjected to his namesake law, neither his incarceration nor his criminal career ended with the five years he spent with the Division for

Youth. Despite assaulting two guards and escaping from a state reform school, Willie was released just days after his twenty-first birthday. Within four months, he mugged an elderly blind man, was convicted of attempted robbery, and was sentenced to serve three and a half to seven years in prison.

Since then, Willie Bosket has set fire to his cell seven times, attacked guards nine times, and tried several times to escape. In his own words, "I'm a monster the system created. I'm a monster that's come back to haunt this system." After being declared a "persistent felon," Willie was sentenced to a term of twenty-five years to life in prison. Prison officials say they expect him to spend the rest of his life behind bars.

The case of Willie Bosket is unusual, if not unique, but New York's "Willie Bosket law" is not. By 1978, when the New York law was enacted, every American jurisdiction except New York, Arkansas, Nebraska, and Vermont had similar laws on the books—laws that allowed certain older juveniles to be prosecuted as adults. Today every jurisdiction in the United States allows at least some juveniles to be prosecuted as adults and, if convicted, punished as adult criminals.

To be tried as an adult, a juvenile offender must meet a number of criteria. Although the criteria vary somewhat from state to state, most juveniles tried as adults have allegedly committed serious crimes of personal violence, have at least reached their teens, and have been found to be both dangerous and not amenable to rehabilitation in the juvenile justice system.

Most state laws provide that to be waived for trial in adult criminal court, a juvenile must be charged with one or more specified felonies, generally including murder, manslaughter, rape, kidnapping, armed robbery, arson, sodomy, aggravated assault, and sometimes burglary. Most states also require that juveniles reach a certain age before they can even be considered for trial as adults.

In four states (Connecticut, New York, North Carolina, and Vermont), juveniles are automatically tried as adults once they reach the age of sixteen. In ten other states, juveniles are automatically tried as adults beginning at age seventeen. In all other states and the District of Columbia, juveniles generally must reach at least the age of eighteen before they can be automatically tried as adults.

Unless a juvenile is automatically tried as an adult, he or she must be certified to stand trial as an adult. As Table 11-1 shows, the age at which a juvenile may be certified for trial as an adult varies among the states and even within some states, depending upon what crime is charged. In some states, juveniles charged with murder may be tried as adults at a younger age than those charged with other felonies.

Although several states set no minimum age for prosecuting a juvenile as an adult, most states require that a juvenile be at least fourteen years old to be tried as an adult for a felony other than murder. The same generalization applies to juveniles charged with murder, but as shown in Table 11-1, nearly half the states have no age minimum at all or set the minimum at or below age thirteen.

As a practical matter, even in those states with no minimum age for prosecuting juvenile murder defendants as adults, adult prosecution of very young killers is exceedingly rare if not unheard of. In most states, juveniles under the age of seven are automatically presumed not responsible for their criminal acts, including homicide. Thus, children six years old and younger who kill may not be prosecuted at all, even as juveniles.

Prosecution of older preteen killers in adult court happens, but only rarely. One recent example is the decision of a Pennsylvania judge that a ten-year-old boy who shot and killed a seven-year-old playmate must stand trial as an adult. If the judge's decision stands in that case, the boy would be the youngest person tried for murder in the United States in this century.

In most states, to be tried as an adult, a juvenile must not only meet age and crime requirements but also be found unsuitable for treatment as a juvenile. That decision is generally made by a judge, and judges are given broad discretion in deciding which juveniles should be tried as adults. Still, in virtually all states, judges are directed by statute or case law to take certain factors into account when making that decision.

Like age and crime requirements, these factors vary from state to state, but most state laws include some variation or combination of the factors specified by the United States Supreme Courts in its 1966 landmark decision, *Kent v. United States*.

Morris Kent, a sixteen-year-old on probation for burglary and purse snatching, broke into a Washington, D.C. apartment, stole the occupant's wallet, and then raped her. Three days later he was arrested and confessed to the crime and other similar offenses as well. No hearing was held, no evidence was taken, and no explanation was given when a judge ruled that Morris Kent would be tried as an adult, despite the fact that he was still a juvenile under the law of the District of Columbia.

Indicted on charges of housebreaking, robbery, and rape, Morris pleaded not guilty by reason of insanity. After presenting expert testimony that he suffered from schizophrenia, Morris was acquitted on the rape charge by reason of insanity but found guilty of the other charges and sentenced to serve thirty to ninety years in prison.

Committed to St. Elizabeth's Hospital for psychiatric treatment prior to imprisonment, Morris appealed his conviction, claiming, among other things, that he was wrongfully denied a hearing before being ordered to stand trial as an adult. Six years after the crime, when Morris was twenty-one, his appeal finally reached the United States Supreme Court. By a five to four vote, the Supreme Court agreed with Morris Kent.

Justice Fortas, writing for the majority, said of the decision to try a juvenile as an adult: "[T]here is no place in our system of law for reaching a result of such tremendous

Table 11-1
Minimum Age at Which Juveniles May Be Tried as Adults, by State.

State	Felonies	Murder	State	Felonies	Murder
Alabama	14	14	Montana	16	16
Alaska	None	None	Nebraska	None	None
Arizona	None	None	Nevada	16	None
Arkansas	15	15	New Hampshire	None	None
California	16	16	New Jersey	14	14
Colorado	14	14	New Mexico	16	15
Connecticut	14	14	New York	14	13
Delaware	16	16	North Carolina	14	14
District of Columbia	15	15	North Dakota	16	16
Florida	14	None	Ohio	15	15
Georgia	15	13	Oklahoma	None	None
Hawaii	16	16	Oregon	16	16
Idaho	15	15	Pennsylvania	14	14
Illinois	13	13	Rhode Island	16	16
Indiana	16	10	South Carolina	16	None
Iowa	14	14	South Dakota	10	10
Kansas	14	14	Tennessee	16	15
Kentucky	14	None	Texas	15	15
Louisiana	15	15	Utah	14	14
Maine	None	None	Vermont	10	10
Maryland	15	None	Virginia	15	15
Massachusetts	14	14	Washington	None	None
Michigan	15	15	West Virginia	16	None
Minnesota	14	14	Wisconsin	16	16
Mississippi	13	13	Wyoming	None	None
Missouri	14	14			

consequences without ceremony—without hearing, without effective assistance of counsel, without statement of reasons." In an appendix to the decision, the Court spelled out "the determinative factors" to be considered by judges in deciding whether a juvenile is tried in juvenile court or waived to adult criminal court:

1. The seriousness of the alleged offense to the community and whether the protection of the community requires waiver;
2. Whether the alleged offense was committed in an aggressive, violent, premeditated or willful manner;
3. Whether the alleged offense was against persons . . . greater weight being given to offenses against persons especially if personal injury is involved;
4. The prosecutive merit of the complaint, i.e., whether there is evidence upon which a Grand Jury may be expected to return an indictment . . . ;
5. The desirability of trial and disposition of the entire offense in one court when the juvenile's associates in the alleged offense are adults who will be charged with a crime . . . ;
6. The sophistication and maturity of the juvenile as determined by consideration of his home, environmental situation, emotional attitude and pattern of living;
7. The record and history of the juvenile, including previous contacts with . . . law envorcement agencies, juvenile courts and other jurisdictions, prior periods of probation . . . or prior commitments to juvenile institutions;
8. The prospects for adequate protection of the public and the likelihood of reasonable rehabilitation of the juvenile (if he is found to have committed the alleged offense) by the use of procedures, services and facilities currently available to the Juvenile Court.

* * *

Although courts in most states are directed to consider many, most, or even all of these criteria, certain factors are especially good at predicting which juvenile killers will be tried as adults. For example, Dr. Joel Peter Eigen, a sociologist, studied the cases of all 154 juveniles arrested for homicide in Philadelphia in one year. Seventy-nine of these juveniles (51 percent) had their cases retained for trial in the juvenile court, and the other sixty-five juveniles (49 percent) were waived for trial as adults.

Dr. Eigen found that four factors best predicted that a juvenile homicide defendant would be waived for trial as an adult: (1) a killing that took place during the commission of a felony; (2) the juvenile being seventeen years old at the time of the killing; (3) the juvenile being the principal assailant of the victim as opposed to an accessory; and (4) the juvenile having a prior criminal record.

When none of these four factors was present, only 12 percent of the juvenile homicide defendants were waived to adult court; when one factor was present, 33 percent were waived; when two factors were present, 61 percent were waived; when three factors were present, 83 percent were waived; and when all four factors were present, 100 percent of the juveniles charged with homicide were waived for trial as adults.

Dr. Eigen also found that the single most powerful predictor of waiver to adult court in these homicide cases was whether the juvenile in question was the principal assailant. Even when no other factors were present, 56 percent of the juveniles who actually inflicted a fatal injury were waived for trial in adult criminal court.

In a more recent and wider study of waiver and disposition in juvenile homicide prosecutions, U.S. Justice Department researchers studied 394 cases adjudicated in 1984 and 1985 in Alabama, Arizona, California, Hawaii, Iowa, Maryland, Mississippi, Nebraska, New Jersey, North Dakota, Ohio, Pennsylvania, Tennessee, Utah, and Virginia. Twenty-eight percent of these cases were waived to criminal court, 36 percent resulted in placement of the youth in a juvenile facility, 11 percent resulted in probation, 12 percent of the youths were released by the juvenile court, and 3 percent of the cases involved some "other" unspecified disposition.

Even more recently, Dr. Dewey Cornell and his colleagues reported the legal outcomes of seventy-two juvenile homicide cases in Michigan. Forty-nine of these youths were above age sixteen and thus automatically charged in adult criminal court. Three youths were under age fifteen and so automatically retained for trial in juvenile court. Thus, twenty of the seventy-two youths—all either fifteen or sixteen years old—were eligible to be waived from juvenile to adult court.

Data were available on nineteen of these twenty youngsters; eighteen of those nineteen had their cases waived for trial in adult court. The single waiver-eligible youth who was not ordered tried as an adult was a fifteen-year-old boy who, after being sexually abused by his father, shot and killed both his parents.

The stakes are high when a court decides whether a juvenile murder defendant will be tried as a juvenile or as an adult. Generally a youth tried in juvenile court faces rather limited punishment if found guilty. For the most part, adjudicated juvenile delinquents may not be locked up in prisons. At worst they may be held in secure juvenile detention facilities—some of which closely resemble prisons but house no adult offenders. Moreover, young killers tried as juveniles may be incarcerated, if at all, only until they reach a certain age, which is often eighteen, sometimes twenty-one, and occasionally twenty-five. Juveniles convicted of murder in adult court face the possibility of lengthy prison sentences and even the death penalty. Capital punishment for juveniles who kill is discussed in Chapter 12.

The case of Robert Demeritt, described in Chapter 3, illustrates just how significant the waiver or transfer decision is in a juvenile murder case. In February 1988, just days shy of his seventeenth birthday, Robert and sixteen-year-old Jayson Moore broke into an elderly woman's home, robbed her, and brutally stabbed her to death. Under New Hampshire law, if tried and convicted as juveniles, Robert and Jayson could be locked up only until they reached the age of eighteen. In Robert's case, that was just about a year from the day he was arrested. If tried and convicted as adults, both boys faced prison terms as long as fifty years to life.

Robert Demeritt was a small, immature boy with limited intelligence, learning problems, and a history of being neglected and abused. Even though he had no prior history of violent behavior, neither psychologist who examined him—one for the prosecution and another for the defense— felt Robert could be adequately rehabilitated by the time he turned eighteen. The court decided that both Robert and Jayson Moore, who had a much more extensive criminal record, should be tried as adults.

In a plea bargain, Robert and Jayson both agreed to plead guilty to second-degree murder in exchange for sentences of thirty-eight years to life. The plea bargain was accepted by the prosecutor but rejected by the judge, who said he was prepared to sentence both boys to as long as fifty years to life in prison. Robert and Jayson took their chances, pleaded guilty, and were eventually sentenced to serve forty years to life.

In Robert Demeritt's case, there was little controversy over the decision to try him as an adult despite mitigating factors such as his learning problems and family background. In many cases, however, the decision is much closer and much more hotly contested. The case of Rickey Dale Mathis is one such case and offers a good example of the tremendous discretion courts have in making these decisions.

Rickey, a sixteen-year-old Oregon runaway, was charged with murder and robbery in the death of a forty-year-old man. The man took Rickey to his mountain cabin, got him to undress, and performed oral sex on him. Afterwards, the man tried to persuade Rickey to penetrate him anally. The man sent Rickey from the bedroom to get some lubricating oil. When Rickey returned with the oil, the man was lying naked, face down on the bed. Rickey took a pocketknife from the man's pants pocket, stabbed him repeatedly in the back, and then beat him to death with a frying pan and hammer. After the killing, Rickey took the man's wallet, drove off in his car, and turned himself in to the police a short while later.

Rickey's attorney sought to have him tried as a juvenile and presented a great deal of evidence in support of that request. After hearing the evidence, however, the juvenile court judge ordered Rickey to stand trial as an adult on charges of murder and robbery. The judge explained his decision as follows:

Rickey Dale Mathis is 16 years of age. . . . [The] decedent persuaded Mathis to engage in sexual perversity, in the midst of which Mathis set upon decedent stabbing him a number of times, attempting to beat him with a small hammer, and beating him with a skillet or frying pan, causing decedent's death . . . Mathis has had, from the beginning of formal schooling, a continuing inability to progress in school in . . . a normal manner. His principal problem appears to be an inability to master reading, and perhaps spelling. . . .

Mathis has had many advantages. It appears material needs (with at least reasonable wants) have been more than adequately provided. . . . [H]e is the last of four children in a household wherein the parents and the other three children apparently succeeded easily in the areas he finds troublesome.

Mathis has not previously been referred to juvenile authorities. He has, however, experimented with some drugs, has drank [sic] alcoholics, he smokes, and uses profane and obscene language. He has on numerous occasions been a truant and a school discipline problem. He has been suspended and was transferred from a "progressive" school setting to "a more conventional" school.

He has twice been a runaway, the last time ending in the present charge.

Mathis' problems at schools caused him to be . . . referred for psychiatric help. He received evaluation and treatment by counseling on a weekly basis for about seven or eight months immediately prior to the offense alleged. This psychiatric therapy was given by an experienced doctor. . . . Another psychiatrist, engaged on behalf of Mathis, found him not to be mentally ill; however, found in addition to the aforementioned school problems, that Mathis had a progressive history of temper tantrums, depressions, runaway, truancy, lying, swearing, and resistance to authority.

Paradoxically, Mathis was an active Boy Scout, excelling in achievement and scouting ability. . . . Mathis has been an exemplary inmate during his confinement in detention. . . .

Both psychiatrists who testified estimate that Mathis will need counseling for three or four years. . . . Testimony has been received from Mathis' parents, treating psychiatrist, teachers and other associates. Most of these witnesses favor retention of juvenile court jurisdiction. . . . It is urged on Mathis' behalf that he has not previously been adjudicated delinquent nor received the services available through counseling. His behavior pattern, however, is a familiar one. It seems most unlikely that any lack of prior juvenile court counseling service is of any persuasive significance in view of the extended efforts by schools to assist him, as well as the weekly psychiatric counseling he received over at least a seven month period of time. In this regard, Mathis' reaction to "crisis" (the truth of the charge being assumed) was of a kind and character weighing against retention of juvenile jurisdiction.

Mathis is at the threshold of maturity. He was a juvenile heretofore; he will not be hereafter. He would, if retained in juvenile court, enter the only facility available to him above the average age of other inmates. From the testimony, it is unlikely he would be retained beyond his nineteenth year, or, any more than three years. A longer period for any re-adjustment as well as a subsequent period of continued supervision seems clearly indicated. The public's interest cannot be otherwise reasonably recognized.

To this rationale, the Court of Appeals added another reason for prosecuting Rickey as an adult rather than a juvenile. Though acknowledging that this was "a close case," a majority of judges on the Appeals Court inferred that "the boy carried a springblade knife, and that under the stress of the situation, and desiring to acquire the victim's money, in a cool and calculated manner he proceeded with the assault."

One Court of Appeals judge, who dissented, saw Rickey and his crime in a rather different light:

This case presents the always difficult problem of whether a child should be remanded for trial as an adult. The alleged crime was committed four days after his sixteenth birthday.

[T]his boy, not yet in high school, had never previously been referred to a juvenile court. His school difficulties were not of major dimensions and in the six months prior to the crime charged they had greatly improved, as a result of a change in schools combined with weekly treatment by a fully qualified child psychiatrist. Nothing in his history remotely hints at violent tendencies. . . .

Nothing in this record indicates any prior involvement whatever of a homosexual nature in the boy's life, nor any indication of violence. Like *Cardiel* [a case in which the Oregon Court of Appeals reversed the juvenile court's decision to try a juvenile as an adult], this, too, was clearly "a one time thing" . . . Unlike *Cardiel*, this boy comes from a strong family background. His mother is and has been a school teacher for many years, holding a Master's Degree. His father, a college graduate, is a highly successful engineer and has worked for more than 20 years in a responsible position for a major corporation. . . . Thus unlike *Cardiel,* where the boy was completely emanicipated and had no family strengths, this boy's family offers unusual strengths to aid in his rehabilitation. Here the trial court concluded that because of the viciousness of the crime it was unlikely that this boy could be rehabilitated before he is 21. No trained professional in either the social work, correctional or medical fields expressed such an opinion. Nor did anyone recommend that this boy should be remanded to the adult court or committed to an adult institution, or that either would be in the best interest of the public or of the boy.

From my examination of this record I conclude that the state has failed to establish . . . that it is in the best interests either of the public or of this child that he be remanded to adult court, let alone both of them, as [the law] requires.

12

Killing Kids Who Kill

ON THE MORNING of April 12, 1985, an eleven-year-old girl and her grandmother passed the small four-room home of two elderly sisters in West Memphis, Arkansas. The girl noticed the women's pocketbooks strewn on the lawn. When she and her grandmother started to knock on the front door of the home, a windowpane fell out. Fearing what they might find if they entered, they called the police. The police responded and found three bodies: the two elderly women, seventy-two and seventy-five years old, and their twelve-year-old grandnephew. Each had been stabbed a half dozen times or more with a butcher knife.

Police investigation of the triple murder quickly led to a neighbor who said he saw and talked to a black youth walking through his yard the night before. Officers showed the neighbor a local school yearbook, and he picked out the picture of fifteen-year-old Ronald Ward. Ronald, whose fingerprints were later found all over the victims' house, told police an implausible tale: He had been pushed into the house at knifepoint by a man named "Crazy Ike," who forced him to rape one of the women but let him leave before anyone was killed.

Several months and several stories later, an all-white Arkansas jury convicted Ronald Ward of murder and then, after weighing his fate for just half an hour, sentenced him to die. A few jurors wanted to take Ronald's age into account, but one juror summarized the feelings of the majority: "If he were eight or nine, maybe." In September 1985, fifteen-year-old Ronald Ward became the youngest person on death row in the United States.

In 1976, Kevin Hughes, a fourteen-year-old Philadelphia boy, was placed on three years' probation for raping an eleven-year-old girl at knifepoint. Three years later, on March 1, 1979, just a week before Kevin turned seventeen, police officers and firefighters found the body of a nine-year-old girl in an abandoned building. The girl's body was badly burned and had a partially burned pillow stuffed between the legs. Autopsy revealed that she had been strangled and sexually abused; injuries she suffered were consistent with attempted vaginal penetration and successful anal penetration. Burned into the ceiling above the girl's body was the word "Peanut."

The killing went unsolved for almost ten months until January 1980, when police interviewed a twelve-year-old girl who had just been sexually abused by a stranger. The girl told police that on January 5, 1980, a teenage boy grabbed her from behind, dragged her off the street and into a vacant house, ordered her to undress, forced her to perform oral sex, stomped on her face and tried to choke her. Shown a police photo array, the girl picked out Kevin Hughes as her assailant.

Armed with a search warrant, police went to Kevin's home and found the word "Peanut" burned into the ceiling above his bed. A short time later, Kevin confessed that he lured the nine-year-old girl into the abandoned building as she walked to school. He then told the girl to take her clothes off. She complied, and he undressed and tried to rape her. When he could not complete the sexual act, he strangled her, tried to burn his nickname "Peanut"—into the ceiling above her body, set the girl ablaze, and fled.

Though diagnosed as suffering from a schizoid personality disorder and having an IQ just above the borderline mentally retarded range, Kevin was convicted of first-degree murder, rape, involuntary deviate sexual intercourse, and arson. For what the prosecutor called "the most gruesome, heartless, sickening homicide in the city's history," Kevin Hughes was sentenced to die in the electric chair.

Late at night on February 5, 1981, sixteen-year-old Frederick Lynn and another teenager, Garrett Strong, broke into the home of Marie Smith, an elderly Alabama woman. Armed with a sawed-off shotgun, Frederick went in through a window, held Mrs. Smith at gunpoint and then opened a back door for Garrett. After forcing Mrs. Smith to sit in a chair, Frederick took her wristwatch and demanded to know where she kept her valuables. When Mrs. Smith denied owning anything of value, Frederick ordered Garrett to search the house.

Garrett did as he was told, but returned minutes later with just a ring and a few coins. Frederick told Garrett "That ain't nothin'." He then put down the shotgun and conducted his own fruitless search for valuables. When Frederick returned to the room where the teens were holding Mrs. Smith, she got out of the chair and started for the door. Frederick grabbed her and told her he would kill her if she tried to run again.

Once Frederick got Mrs. Smith back in the chair, he began prodding and cutting her with a knife. Frederick then told Garrett to go into another room and turn up the volume on the television. Garrett turned the television up "as loud as it would go," but not so loud that he could not hear the gunshot that killed Mrs. Smith.

This account of what happened is the one provided by Garrett Strong, who made a deal with the prosecutor, turned state's evidence, pleaded guilty to a reduced charge, testified against Frederick, and received a sentence of thirty years in prison. Frederick Lynn, who was convicted by a jury of capital murder; was sentenced to die in the Alabama electric chair.

Charles Rumbaugh, known as "Chuckie," committed his first burglary at age six and his first robbery at age twelve. In the fifteen years between his thirteenth birthday and his death at the age of twenty-eight, Chuckie spent all but eight months confined in various reform schools, mental hospitals, and prisons. On September 11, 1985, Chuckie Rumbaugh was put to death by lethal injection in a Texas prison after spending ten years on death row.

Chuckie Rumbaugh's execution was the sixteenth in the United States that year and the forty-fifth since 1978, when a Utah firing squad killed Gary Gilmore in the first U.S. execution in almost a decade. Still, Chuckie's execution made history and front-page headlines across the nation. Why? Because Charles Rumbaugh was seventeen years old when he shot and killed a Texas jeweler during a robbery. His execution in 1985 marked the first time in more than two decades that a person was put to death in the United States for a crime committed while he was a juvenile.

Four months after Chuckie Rumbaugh was executed, James Terry Roach was put to death in the South Carolina electric chair. Terry was seventeen years old when he pleaded guilty to charges of rape and murder in the deaths of a fourteen-year-old girl and her seventeen-year-old boyfriend. Shortly before the killings, Terry—a borderline mentally retarded youth—ran away from reform school. He and a sixteen-year-old friend, Ronnie Mahaffey, teamed up with twenty-two-year-old J.C. Shaw, who gave the boys alcohol and drugs.

In October 1977, all three were high on drugs and went driving around in Shaw's car "looking for a girl to rape." What they found was a teenage couple, sitting in a car near a baseball diamond. At Shaw's direction, Terry fired three shots into the seventeen-year-old boy's head. Then all three dragged the fourteen-year-old girl out of the car, threw her to the ground, stripped and gang-raped her. Shaw then drew a circle in the dirt and forced the girl to put her head in the circle. Terry and Ronnie then shot her five times in the head.

Ronnie Mahaffey turned state's evidence to avoid the death penalty. He was sentenced to life in prison in exchange for his testimony against Terry Roach and J.C. Shaw. Shaw was convicted of murder, sentenced to die, and executed in 1985. Terry Roach was also convicted of murder and sentenced to die. He was executed on January 10, 1986.

On May 15, 1986, four months after Terry Roach was electrocuted, Jay Kelly Pinkerton died by lethal injection, administered in a Texas prison. Jay, an apprentice butcher whose crimes were detailed in Chapter 4, was twice sentenced to die. He was first convicted and sentenced for the 1979 killing of an Amarillo, Texas housewife. Jay was seventeen years old at the time he raped, murdered, and then mutilated the woman as her children lay sleeping in another room. It was for this killing that he was executed. His second conviction resulted from a 1980 sex slaying in which Jay, then eighteen years old, raped another Amarillo woman in a furniture store and then stabbed her more than thirty times.

If Chuckie Rumbaugh and Terry Roach had committed their crimes in almost any other country, neither youth would have been executed. The United States is one of the few nations in the world that allows the execution of individuals for crimes committed while they were juveniles. Since 1979, Amnesty International has documented only eight executions of juvenile offenders in the world. Three of these executions—those of Chuckie Rumbaugh, Terry Roach, and Jay Pinkerton—took place in the United States. The remaining five occurred in Pakistan, Bangladesh, Rwanda, and Barbados.

The execution of juvenile criminals in the United States is rare but not new. Some three hundred juveniles have been executed in the United States since 1642, when sixteen-year-old Thomas Graunger was hanged in Plymouth Colony for having sex with a horse and cow. Ten-year-old James Arcene, a Cherokee Indian hanged in Arkansas in 1885 for robbery and murder, was the youngest person ever legally executed in the United States. The youngest offender executed in this country in the twentieth century was Fortune Ferguson, Jr.—a Florida boy put to death in 1927 for raping an eight-year-old girl when he was thirteen.

More than half of those executed for crimes committed while juveniles were seventeen years old at the time of their crimes, and more than 80 percent were sixteen or seventeen years old. A total of 2,106 death sentences were imposed in the United States between 1982 and 1988, but only fifteen were imposed on individuals for crimes committed when they were under the age of seventeen, and only twenty-four were imposed on individuals who were seventeen at the time of their crimes. Currently, thirty juvenile killers—1.37 percent of the total U.S. death row population—are awaiting execution. More than 90 percent of these young death row inmates are males.

Capital punishment of juvenile killers is governed by statute and case law—primarily three recent decisions of the United States Supreme Court.

Thirty-seven states permit capital punishment of convicted murderers. Twelve of these states (California, Colorado, Connecticut, Illinois, Maryland, Nebraska, New Jersey, New Hampshire, New Mexico, Ohio, Oregon, and Tennessee) prohibit capital punishment for crimes committed before the offender turns eighteen. Three others (Georgia, North Carolina, and Texas) forbid execution for crimes committed before the age of seventeen.

Thus, twenty-five states allow the execution of juveniles convicted of murder, and twenty-two of these states (Alabama, Arizona, Arkansas, Delaware, Florida, Idaho, Indiana, Kentucky, Louisiana, Mississippi, Missouri, Montana, Nevada, Oklahoma, Pennsylvania, South Carolina, South Dakota, Utah, Vermont, Virginia, Washington, and

Wyoming) allow the execution of juveniles convicted of murders committed before they were seventeen years old.

In 1982, 1988, and 1989, the United States Supreme Court decided key cases challenging the constitutionality of state laws permitting the execution of individuals for crimes committed while they were juveniles.

In 1982, in *Eddings v. Oklahoma*, the Court was confronted with the case of Monty Lee Eddings, a sixteen-year-old abused runaway who shot an Oklahoma state trooper through the heart with a sawed-off shotgun and then left the officer to bleed to death on the side of the road. Monty pleaded no contest to a charge of first-degree murder. In sentencing Monty to die, the judge acknowledged that the boy's youth was a substantial mitigating factor but refused, as a matter of law, to consider Monty's disturbed family life and emotional problems as mitigating evidence.

Monty Lee Eddings challenged his sentence as a violation of the Eighth Amendment ban on cruel and unusual punishment, but in a five to four decision, the Supreme Court invalidated his death sentence on much narrower grounds. Justice Powell, joined by four other Justices, held that in a capital sentencing proceeding, the sentencing authority may not "refuse to consider, as a matter of law, any relevant mitigating evidence." Youth, Justice Powell concluded, "is itself a relevant mitigating factor of great weight."

In 1988, in *Thompson v. Oklahoma*, the question before the Court was the constitutionality of executing a person for a crime committed while under the age of sixteen. On January 23, 1983, fifteen-year-old William Wayne Thompson left home with three older friends, after telling his girlfriend they were "going to kill Charles" meaning Charles Keene, William's former brother-in-law. Later that night, William and his companions brutally beat, shot, and killed Keene, apparently in retaliation for his prior abuse of William and William's sister.

After the killing, William admitted that he kicked Charles Keene, cut his throat and chest, and shot him in the head.

William was certified to stand trial as an adult, tried and convicted of murder, and sentenced to die.

When William Wayne Thompson's case reached the Supreme Court, four Justices held that execution of a person who was under the age of sixteen at the time of his or her offense constituted cruel and unusual punishment and thus violated the Eighth Amendment. A fifth Justice, Justice O'Connor, concluded that "a national consensus forbidding the execution of any person for a crime committed before the age of sixteen very likely does exist," but she was "reluctant to adopt this conclusion as a matter of constitutional law without better evidence than we now possess." Still, Justice O'Connor provided the necessary fifth vote to invalidate William Wayne Thompson's death sentence, holding that those "below the age of sixteen at the time of their offense may not be executed under the authority of a capital punishment statute that specifies no minimum age at which the commission of a capital crime can lead to the offender's execution."

Justice O'Connor's decision saved William Wayne Thompson's life, but it failed to resolve the controversy over the age at which the death penalty is a constitutionally valid punishment for murder. A year later, in 1989, the Court confronted that question again in two cases decided together, *Stanford v. Kentucky* and *Wilkins v. Missouri*. This time, the question was whether the Eighth Amendment cruel and unusual punishment clause prohibited the execution of individuals for crimes they committed while either sixteen or seventeen years old.

Kevin Stanford and Heath Wilkins, whose cases were alluded to briefly in earlier chapters, were both sentenced to die for their roles in separate homicides. Kevin Stanford, seventeen years and four months old, robbed a Kentucky gas station, repeatedly raped and sodomized the female attendant, and then drove her to a secluded spot and shot her point-blank in the head and face. Kevin later told a jail guard, "I had to shoot her, she lived next door to me and would recognize me."

Pointing to the heinous nature of Kevin's offenses, his extensive history of delinquency, and the failure of the juvenile system to rehabilitate him, the juvenile court judge concluded that Kevin should be tried as an adult. Tried in criminal court, Kevin was convicted of murder, sodomy, robbery, and receiving stolen property, and was sentenced to death on the murder charge and to forty-five years' imprisonment on the other charges.

Heath Wilkins was sixteen years and six months old when he and an accomplice decided to rob a convenience store and kill "whoever was behind the counter" because "a dead person can't talk." While committing just such a robbery, Heath's accomplice held the cashier while Heath repeatedly stabbed her as she begged him not to kill her. After taking cigarettes, liquor, rolling papers, and about $450 in checks and cash, Heath and his accomplice left the clerk to die on the floor.

Emphasizing the viciousness and violence of Heath's crime, the repeated failure of the juvenile justice system to rehabilitate him, the inability of that system to rehabilitate him within the short time left before he outgrew its jurisdiction, Heath's experience, the maturity of his "appearance and habits," and the need to protect the public, the juvenile court judge ordered Heath to stand trial as an adult. Indicted in criminal court, Heath was charged with first-degree murder, armed criminal action, and carrying a concealed weapon.

Heath waived counsel, pleaded guilty to all charges, refused legal representation at sentencing, presented no mitigating evidence, and told the judge he preferred to die rather than spend his life in prison: "One I fear, the other one I don't." After hearing the state's evidence in favor of capital punishment, the judge sentenced Heath to die.

Justice Scalia summarized the arguments Heath Wilkins and Kevin Stanford ultimately presented to the United States Supreme Court:

The thrust of both Wilkins' and Stanford's arguments is that imposition of the death penalty on those who were juveniles when they committed their crimes falls within the Eighth Amendment prohibition against "cruel and unusual punishments." Wilkins would have us define juveniles as individuals sixteen years of age and under; Stanford would draw the line at seventeen.

In response to those arguments, Justice Scalia and four other Justices concluded that there is no national consensus against executing sixteen- and seventeen-year-olds convicted of murder. Thus, by a five to four vote, the Supreme Court affirmed the right of the state to take the lives of Kevin Stanford and Heath Wilkins. In a strongly worded dissent, Justice Brennan and three other Justices pointed to psychological and psychiatric data indicating that juveniles lack the judgment and moral maturity necessary to hold them fully responsible for their crimes. For want of a fifth vote on the Court, Heath Wilkins and Kevin Stanford remain on death row, awaiting their eventual executions.

After the Supreme Court's decisions in *Eddings, Thompson, Stanford, and Wilkins,* it is clear that there is no constitutional barrier to executing juvenile killers who were at least sixteen years old when they committed their capital crimes. Thompson does not preclude imposing a death sentence upon a younger convicted murderer as long as the governing state law explicitly sets a minimum age for capital sentencing. Finally, *Eddings* requires that, whatever the juvenile killer's age, all mitigating evidence including his or her youth be considered by the sentencing authority, whether judge or jury.

Thus, while it is rarely imposed and even more rarely carried out, the death penalty remains a legal option for punishing juveniles who kill.

13

Juvenile Homicide in the 1990s

HOMICIDE, LIKE MOST behavior, is learned. It is a function of both person and circumstance. We are all capable of killing under some circumstances, and none of us kills under all circumstances. Killings occur only when certain people with certain learning experiences find themselves in certain situations.

Juvenile homicide is no exception. Juvenile killers are not born but made. Although there are as many specific recipes for creating juvenile killers as there are juvenile killings, there is also a general recipe for turning kids into killers. Not every case has every ingredient. In fact, we do not know all the ingredients or their precise proportions, but we do know the major ones. Whatever else may go into the making of a kid who kills, virtually all juvenile killers have been significantly influenced in their homicidal behavior by one or more of just a handful of known factors: child abuse, poverty, substance abuse, and access to guns.

The good news is that we know what these factors are and could do something to reduce their prevalence. The bad news is that we are doing very little. Perhaps the worst news is that, as a result, both the annual number and rate of juvenile homicides have been increasing, will continue to increase, and will probably reach record high proportions before the turn of the century.

Seventeen-year-old Heath Wilkins was sentenced to die for robbing and brutally shooting a convenience store clerk as she begged for her life. Abandoned by his mentally ill father when he was three years old, Heath was raised by his drug-abusing mother who often beat him.

Fourteen-year-old Shirley Wolf, with help from fifteen-year-old Cindy Collier, hacked an eighty-five-year-old woman to death with a butcher knife. From the time she was an infant until she turned fourteen, Shirley was sexually abused by her father, uncle, and grandfather. Cindy was beaten and raped repeatedly throughout her childhood.

With help from his older sister, Deborah, sixteen-year-old Richard Jahnke ambushed, shot, and killed his father—a man who had beaten Richard and sexually abused his sister for most of Richard's life.

Robert Lee Moody shot and killed his father after repeatedly seeing him beat Robert's mother. After hearing of the abuse Robert's father inflicted upon his family over the years, a judge publicly denounced the dead man as "the scum of the earth" and sentenced Robert to probation.

The abuse suffered by Heath Wilkins, Shirley Wolf, Cindy Collier, Richard and Deborah Jahnke, and Robert Lee Moody is not uncommon among juveniles who kill—regardless of who they kill. The single most consistent finding in juvenile homicide research is that juveniles who kill have generally witnessed or have been directly victimized by family violence.

The correlation between child abuse and juvenile homicide makes sense. Some children who are abused or witness abuse of loved ones learn to be violent; their abusive parents are powerful, negative role models. Other abused children suffer psychological or physical trauma that leads to the kinds of neurological or psychological problems often associated with juvenile homicidal behavior. Still other abused children kill in direct response to the abuse they suffer—they kill their abusers.

An unknown but probably large amount of child abuse goes unreported. At the same time, however, the majority of reported cases of child abuse are unsubstantiated. An unsubstantiated report does not mean that the reported abuse did not occur; it means only that the authorities, for whatever reasons, were unable to find the kind of substantiating evidence the law requires to justify state intervention. These problems make it difficult to determine just how much child abuse there really is and whether child abuse is, as many claim, not only increasing but reaching epidemic proportions in the United States.

The best, indeed the only, nationwide data available on child abuse are reporting statistics. Despite their obvious limitations, these data make one thing absolutely clear: there has been a tremendous and steady increase in the number of reported cases of child abuse over the past decade. The American Association for Protecting Children (AAPC) surveyed all fifty states, the District of Columbia, and the U.S. Territories and estimated the annual number of child abuse and neglect reports for the years from 1976 through 1987. The AAPC's estimates, derived from these surveys, are shown in Table 13-1.

Although these data do not establish that *substantiated* cases of child abuse are increasing, testimony given before the U.S. Senate Judiciary Committee in May 1989 indicated that there was a 64 percent increase in the number of *confirmed* child abuse cases in the United States between 1980 and 1986. Other data indicate that child abuse is not only increasing in frequency but also in severity. The clearest indicator that child abuse is becoming more violent and more physically damaging is the recent dramatic increase in child abuse fatalities.

Between 1985 and 1987, there was a 25 percent increase nationally in the annual number of children who died as a

Table 13-1
National Estimates of the Number and Rate of Child Abuse and Neglect Reports, 1976-1987

Year	Number of Reports (and percentage change)		Rate per 1,000 Children (and percentage change)	
1976	669,000		10.1	
1977	838,000	(25.26%)	12.8	(22%)
1978	836,000	(-0.24%)	12.9	(0%)
1979	988,000	(18.18%)	15.4	(19%)
1980	1,154,000	(16.80%)	18.1	(17%)
1981	1,225,000	(6.15%)	19.4	(7%)
1982	1,262,000	(3.02%)	20.1	(4%)
1983	1,477,000	(17.04%)	23.6	(17%)
1984	1,727,000	(16.93%)	27.3	(16%)
1985	1,928,000	(11.64%)	30.6	(12%)
1986	2,086,000	(8.20%)	32.8	(7%)
1987	2,178,000	(4.40%)	34.0	(4%)

direct result of child abuse. In 1988, the number of recorded deaths from child abuse reached 1,225—an increase of 5 percent over the national total for 1987. Between 1986 and 1987, child abuse deaths almost tripled in Utah and virtually doubled in Virginia and North Carolina. During fiscal year 1988, Illinois experienced 97 child abuse deaths, an 80 percent increase over fiscal year 1987. In California, 96 children died in 1988 as a result of child abuse, a 15 percent increase over 1987.

Given the correlation between child abuse and juvenile homicide, increases in the incidence or severity of child abuse will undoubtedly be followed by corresponding increases in the number and rate of juvenile homicides. If, as many contend, the United States is experiencing an epidemic of child abuse, this epidemic will undoubtedly affect the incidence of juvenile homicide for years to come.

Fifteen-year-old Ronald Ward, sentenced to die for viciously slaughtering two elderly women and their twelve-year-old grandnephew, was abandoned by his unmarried mother shortly after he was born. She left Ronald with his elderly grandparents, who raised him as well as they could. For fifteen years, Ronald's grandmother and bedridden grandfather supported Ronald and themselves on their meager Social Security benefits.

In California, a fifteen-year-old girl gave birth to and then killed her second illegitimate child shortly after she and her parents emigrated from Mexico. Impoverished and barely able to support themselves, her parents had told her that if she ever had a second child, she would have to leave home and support herself and her children.

In two separate incidents, seventeen-year-old Milton Jones and eighteen-year-old Theodore Simmons—two youngsters from deprived and impoverished inner-city families—robbed and then stabbed to death two Catholic priests, one of whom had befriended, counseled, and fed them.

The link between poverty and crime, including violent crime, is almost universally recognized. It is impossible to say what percentage of juvenile homicides are committed by youngers living in poverty, but it is undoubtedly high—especially for gang killings, killings committed in the course of robberies, and drug-related killings. Economically impoverished youngsters are more likely to become involved in juvenile gangs, commit economically motivated crimes such as robbery, and be exposed to the temptations of the drug trade often flourishing in their disadvantaged and decaying urban neighborhoods.

Not suprisingly, as the number and rate of juvenile homicides in the United States climbed slowly but steadily in the 1980s, there was a corresponding gradual increase in the number of American juveniles living in poverty. Between 1980 and 1987, the most recent year for which national data are available, the number of individuals under the age of eighteen living below the poverty level increased in all but three states (Delaware, New Hampshire, and Virginia) and grew nationally from 11 million to 13 million. In 1980, 17.9

percent of all Americans under the age of eighteen lived in poverty; by 1987 that figure had risen to 20.4 percent.

These numbers, of course, only begin to tell the real story of juvenile poverty in America. In 1987, the U.S. government officially classified a family of four as living in poverty only if their annual income was less than $11,603. Thus, the percentage of children living in what most people would recognize as poverty is much higher than the government's official one-in-five estimate.

Much of the growth in juvenile poverty and its tragic human consequences during the 1980s resulted from the Reagan administration's "war on the poor"—deep and relentless cuts in federal funding for social welfare programs. Given that little if anything has been done (or looks like it will be done) by the new administration to restore these spending cuts, the percentage of American youths living in poverty is bound to grow as we approach the year 2,000, and that increase will most certainly influence the number and rate of juvenile killings in the 1990s.

Desperate to support his $500-a-day crack habit and propelled by what one psychiatrist called a "cocaine-induced psychosis," seventeen-year-old Leslie Torres killed five people and wounded six others in a seven-day armed robbery rampage in New York City.

Seventeen-year-old Ralph Deer, Jr. washed down six "hits" of LSD with three cups of a grain alcohol and Kool-Aid cocktail before killing a convenience store cashier in a robbery that netted him $11.

Fifteen-year-old runaway, John Charles Smith, left New York for Dallas in search of easy money promised by drug dealers. Hired as an enforcer, he committed three drug-related, execution-style killings, expecting to be paid $5,000. Even after being sentenced to eighteen years in prison, he says he still expects to be paid.

Eugene Turley, a sixteen-year-old junior high dropout, also signed on as a drug enforcer. In his debut, he shot a Virginia woman to death with a .357 magnum after she refused to pay a $75 cocaine debt owed to a District of Columbia drug dealer.

Leslie Torres, Ralph Deer, John Charles Smith, and Eugene Turley are just a few of the many juveniles who have committed drug-related murders in recent years. When drug abuse increases, so does homicide, and that correlation holds for both adults and juveniles.

Recent data from New York City provide a striking illustration. In 1985, officials estimated that there were 97,000 drug abusers under the age of seventeen in all of New York State, including New York City. In 1988, the estimated number of drug abusers under seventeen in New York City alone reached an all-time high of 140,000. As juvenile drug abuse was reaching record highs, so were juvenile homicides. In 1988, the number of murders in New York City reached a record annual high of 1,896, and the number of murders committed by juveniles rose from twenty-four in 1987 to fifty-seven in 1988—a 138 percent increase in a single year.

There are no definitive data on the number or percentage of homicides committed by youths under the influence of drugs, but the most recent research suggests that as many as two-thirds of all juvenile killings are committed by youngsters high on drugs. Drugs play a variety of roles in juvenile homicides. Some drugs, such as crack, appear to stimulate violent or irrational behavior. Others seem to create confusion, lower inhibitions, impair judgment, or make youngsters more susceptible to peer influence. But whatever the role played by drugs in facilitating or encouraging juvenile homicide, drug abuse is clearly a factor that often increases the likelihood that a juvenile will kill.

The federal government estimates that casual drug abuse in the United States has decreased over the last five years but that frequent abuse of certain substances—most notably cocaine and its derivative, crack—has significantly increased over the same time period. For example, between 1985 and 1988, federally sponsored household surveys found that the number of weekly cocaine users rose from 647,000 to 862,000 and the number of daily cocaine users rose from 246,000 to 292,000. During the same time period. emergency room visits related to cocaine use jumped from 8,000 to 46,000.

Most of these increases can be attributed to the growing availability and abuse of crack cocaine. As Dr. William Bennett, director of the National Office of Drug Policy, recently explained: "Drug crime is up, drug trafficking is up, drug deaths are up, drug emergencies in our hospitals are up, all since 1985. And much of this can be explained in one word, and that word is 'crack.'"

At the same time, Dr. Frederick Godwin, director of the Alcohol, Drug Abuse, and Mental Health Administration reported another finding from the 1988 survey: "600,000 young people, aged 12 to 17, had used cocaine within the past year, which places them at heavy risk for continued use, addiction, and severe medical consequences as well as the potential social consequences [including] juvenile crime . . ."

Drug abuse affects the number and rate of juvenile homicides not onlyby altering the psychological functioning of juveniles in ways that make them more likely to kill, but also in at least two other less direct ways: Drugs create an environment in which some juveniles have economic incentives to kill; and drug abuse by parents contributes to the likelihood that they will abuse or neglect their children.

Many juvenile killings are drug-related not because the perpetrators are under the influence of drugs when they kill, but because these homocides are committed to make or protect drug profits. In recent years, the sale of cocaine and crack has become a multi-million dollar industry in the United States. The drug trade, though lucrative, is also extremely competitive. As a result, drug dealers now commonly engage in turf wars—battles over the exclusive "right" to sell drugs in a certain geographic area. Sadly, juveniles like John Charles Smith are often among the homicidal front-line "soldiers" in these wars.

Numerous other juvenile homicides have resulted from the economic environment created by the flourishing drug trade. Drug dealers, like most retailers, have to cope with some buyers who cannot or will not pay. Unable to turn to the usual collection channels employed by legitimate business people, drug dealers often turn to cheap, dispensable enforcers like Eugene Turley—kids who are willing to kill, if necessary, to collect a $75 debt. As drug trafficking increases and becomes more competitive, the number of both turf and enforcement killings committed by juveniles will undoubtedly increase.

Finally, drug abuse will likely have its least direct but most insidious, long-lasting, and potentially most powerful effect on juvenile homicide by contributing to the incidence of child abuse and neglect. Parental drug abuse is clearly one of the major causal factors in child abuse—and child abuse victimization is clearly a major causal factor in juvenile homicide.

Although there is debate as to whether child maltreatment is increasing, there can be no doubt that a steadily growing number of cases of child abuse and neglect involve parents who are drug abusers or addicts. In many cases, the abuse begins even before the child is born, as in the growing number of "cocaine babies"—behaviorally impaired children born to cocaine-addicted mothers. In other cases, child maltreatment results less directly but just as clearly from parental drug abuse and addiction as the effects of substance abuse lead parents to neglect, abandon, abuse, or even kill their children. Since child abuse has its most devastating effect on very young children, the full impact of drug-related child abuse on juvenile homicide rates probably will not be seen for some years to come.

A single mother raising two boys in a tough California inner-city neighborhood kept guns and ammunition in her apartment to protect herself and her sons. After finding a gun and some bullets his mother had hidden, the woman's fourteen-year-old son dared a playmate to shoot a truck

driver in the parking lot outside the apartment. The playmate took the dare and shot and killed the driver.

A Chicago youth gestured to a passing carload of teens.
Interpreting his gesture as the hand signal of a rival gang,
the teens returned and opened fire with automatic weapons,
including an Uzi submachine gun. An innocent bystander
was shot and killed.

A nine-year-old Pennsylvania boy, apparently angry at a
seven-year-old girl who beat him at a home video game,
opened his father's locked gun cabinet, removed a rifle and
bullets, and then shot and killed the girl.

In Missouri, a twelve-year-old boy, often teased by his
classmates, took his father's .45 caliber pistol to school.
After using the gun to kill one of his tormentors, he shot
and killed himself.

In what police said may have been a turf war between
competing drug gangs, three Connecticut teenagers used
high-powered semiautomatic rifles to spray a passing car
with eighty rounds of ammunition. Twenty shots hit the
car, killing one youth and wounding four others.

In New Jersey, a four-year-old boy found a loaded handgun under a couch and used it to shoot and kill his eight-
year-old opponent in a game of "Cowboys and Indians."

Most homicides, including killings committed by juveniles,
involve the use of firearms. Juvenile killers use a variety of
firearms in a variety of ways. In some cases, a youngster
finds a parent's rifle, shotgun, or handgun and uses it to
kill a playmate. In others, an abused child shoots and kills
an abusive parent, often with the parent's own gun. In many
cases, a juvenile robber panics and uses a cheap handgun to
kill the robbery victim. Other juvenile killers—like the teenage gang member who shoots into a crowd in a "drive-by"
or the juvenile drug dealer who assassinates a competitor
in a turf war—do their killing with high-powered automatic
and semiautomatic pistols and assault rifles.

What all these juvenile homicides have in common is
their young perpetrators' access to guns. What most have

in common is that they would not have occurred but for the juvenile perpetrator's access to a firearm.

Solid data on gun ownership and accessibility in the United States are hard to come by, and the available data are often disputed or subject to differing interpretations. Still, several points are beyond dispute: millions of guns, ranging from small handguns to assault rifles, are owned by Americans; many of these weapons are either in the hands of or readily accessible to juveniles; and at least some of these weapons are used by juveniles to kill other people.

It is difficult to say with certainty whether gun ownership in the United States is currently increasing, but it is not difficult to conclude that more Americans than ever own guns and that a growing number of American juveniles have easy access to guns. In 1987, the number of guns imported to the United States reached a ten-year peak. The same year, domestic production of guns increased for the first time in five years. Since then, firearm industry sources indicate that both production and sales of guns in the United States have continued to increase.

A 1989 Harris poll found that virtually every other household in the United States has at least one gun. The Federal Bureau of Alcohol, Tobacco, and Firearms recently estimated that some 70 million Americans own approximately 140 million rifles and 60 million handguns, including 2 to 3 million semiautomatic assault weapons. One particular group of Americans known to be increasing in gun ownership is women. A Gallup poll conducted for one of the nation's leading gun manufacturers found a 53 percent increase in female gun owners between 1983 and 1986.

Given the vast and apparently ever-growing number of guns in America today, it is hardly surprising that more and more of these deadly weapons are ending up in the hands of children and adolescents. The problem of juvenile gun possession is seen perhaps most clearly by looking at data from the place where juveniles spend most of their waking hours: public schools. Guns are regularly found in the possession of high school, junior high, and even elementary school students in American cities, large and small. In California, for example, from 1985 to 1989, there was a 43 percent increase in the number of guns confiscated from elementary and junior high students, and a 50 percent increase in the number of guns taken from high school students. In Florida, gun incidents in the public schools increased by 42 percent from 1987 to 1988.

Although the problem is clearly worse in major urban areas, even schools in relatively small cities are finding that growing numbers of students bring guns to school. For example, in one recent academic year, officials in Jacksonville, Florida found thirty-nine guns in the public schools there. Halfway through the next academic year, they had already found forty-five guns in the city's schools. Official concern over guns in schools has become so serious in the past few years that some school systems now use hand-held metal detectors to help keep guns out of the school environment.

Although there are no national data on guns in the schools, the National School Safety Center has reported the results of a nationwide survey of 11,000 students. Extrapolating from the findings of this survey, the Center estimated that in 1987 roughly 135,000 boys carried handguns to school daily while another 270,000 brought handguns to school at least once.

Some of the juvenile gun possession in public schools is clearly attributable to the drug trade, especially the sale of crack, but one recent study found that many juveniles bring guns to school for their own protection. Youths aged nine to seventeen told researchers that they "believe carrying weapons is the only way they can protect themselves" from others with guns.

Another symptom of the increase access juveniles have to guns is the growing number of accidental shootings of children by other children and the government's response to these accidents. Gun accidents are now the fourth leading cause of death among children under the age of fifteen, and roughly half the children who die in these accidents are killed by guns belonging to their own parents.

In the summer of 1989, these grim facts were hammered home to the citizens and lawmakers in at least three states. In Florida, where 60 percent of all households have at least one gun, five children were shot during a two-week period. All five shootings, three of which were fatal, involved young children, and all were committed with guns belonging to one of the children's parents. Similarly, the summer of 1989 witnessed the accidental shooting deaths of four children in Connecticut and two in Virginia.

Lawmakers in all three states responded almost immediately with legislation aimed at making it a crime to leave loaded guns where they are accessible to children. Indeed, in Florida, in the same month the rash of shootings occurred there, the legislature was called into special session and enacted legislation that the governor immediately signed into law. The new law makes gun owners guilty of a felony if their unsecured guns are used by a child to injure or kill someone and guilty of a misdemeanor if they carelessly store a gun and that gun is used by a child in a manner that even threatens others.

Even the National Rifle Association (NRA), which vehemently opposes virtually any legal controls on gun ownership, has acknowledged the growing problem of juvenile access to guns. Recently, the NRA began producing and distributing *My Gun Safety Book*. This coloring book, designed for children in kindergarten and first grade, tells kids that if they find a gun, they should leave it alone, leave the area, and tell an adult.

Ultimately, gun safety laws and educational campaigns may help stem the tide of juvenile access to guns or at least make that access less deadly. For now and the foreseeable future, however, juvenile access to guns is likely to keep growing and thus continue to contribute to the growing problem of juvenile homicide.

Both the annual incidence and rate of juvenile homicide in the United States have shown a steady increase over the past several years. Indeed, in 1988 (the most recent year for which national data are available), the number of juvenile homicide arrests was the highest in nine years and, for the first time, constituted more than 10 percent of the annual total of all homicide arrests.

Any attempt to project the future incidence and rate of juvenile homicide is bound to be speculative, but there are good reasons to predict that the number and rate of juvenile homicides will continue to increase annually and probably reach record high proportions by the turn of the century.

The basic ingredients for an epidemic of juvenile homicide are all present: child abuse thriving and growing in severity if not also incidence; growing numbers of juveniles living in poverty; increasingly serious substance abuse among both juveniles and adults; and expanding juvenile access to guns, including the most deadly high-powered automatic weapons. Finally, the 1990s can be expected to add one other important ingredient to the recipe: a resurgence of the juvenile population.

Recent increases in the annual rate of juvenile homicide in the United States are a function of two factors: annual increases in the number of juvenile homicides and corresponding annual decreases in the number of juveniles in the American population. To put it another way, in recent years, despite a steady decline in the number of juveniles, the number of juvenile homicides has shown a steady increase. Yet according to recent estimates and future projections prepared by the U.S. Census Bureau, the United States is beginning to undergo a demographic shift in which the juvenile population will increase rather than decrease.

Since the number of homicides committed by children under five is negligible, the relevant juvenile population at risk for committing homicide is basically those between the ages of five and seventeen. The Census Bureau estimates that the number of five- to seventeen-year-olds dropped 3.4 percent between 1980 and 1990 but projects that the number of youths in this age group will increase by 7 percent between 1990 and the end of the century.

If Census Bureau projections are correct, even in the unlikely event that the annual rate of juvenile homicide remained entirely stable instead of continuing to increase as it has since 1984, the final decade of the twentieth century would witness roughly a 7 percent increase in the annual number of juvenile killings. But that optimistic projection assumes a very improbable if not impossible scenario. More realistically, if—as expected—American society does little in the 1990s to reverse the abuse, and children's access to guns, the annual rate of juvenile homicide is almost certain to continue to grow over the next ten years. If that proves to be the case, the number of juvenile homicides will expand much faster than the number of juveniles, and the 1990s will witness the highest annual number of juvenile homicides in American history.

Notes

Chapter 1

p. 1. **Craig Price:** "Boy Gets 6 Years for Slayings of 4," *New York Times,* September 26, 1989 at A-22 ("Iron Man"); Brelis, "R.I. City Picks up the Pieces after Savage Killings," September 24, 1989 at 77 ("smoke a bomber" and "Later"); Richard, "Once Quiet Neighborhood Breathes Easier, But Things Will Never Be the Same Again," *Boston Globe,* September 24, 1989 at 77; Ross, "Stiffer Juvenile Law Promised for Next Year," United Press International (hereinafter UPI) b.c. cycle, September 22, 1989; Richard, "Youth Charged in R.I. Slayings," *Boston Globe,* September 19, 1989 at 1.

p. 2. **Dale Whipple:** Abrams, "Defender of the Indefensible," *Los Angeles Times,* June 7, 1989, part 5 at 1; O'Shea, "Teen who Axed Parents Sentenced to 40 Years," UPI, p.m. cycle, June 18, 1985 ("fear of future . . .").

pp. 2-3. **"Johnny":** Kazmin, "Judge Finds Youth Guilty of Murder in Russian Roulette," *Los Angeles Times,* August 31, 1989, part 2 at 8; Padilla, "School Counselors Help Pupils Cope with the Shock of Classmate's Death," *Los Angeles Times,* June 5, 1989, part 2 at 6.

p. 3. **Christmas Day killings:** "Two Teen-agers charged in Queens Slayings," *Buffalo News,* Associated Press (hereinafter AP), December 31, 1989 at A-18, "Three Teens Charged in Random Killing of Pregnant Woman," UPI, b.c. cycle, December 30, 1989 (quoting New York City police detective Lt. Gene Dunbar).

pp. 3-4. **Timothy Dwaine Brown:** "Youth Gets Life: Killed His Brother with a Bat," *Los Angeles Times,* December 12, 1985, part 1 at 25: "Jury Selection Begins in Juvenile's Triple Murder Trial," UPI, a.m. cycle, December 9, 1985 ("Something just snapped . . .").

p. 4. **Frederick Jones:** "Boy Killed at Alleged Drug House," *Chicago Tribune,* November 13, 1989, at 3.

p. 5. **Population:** U.S. Department of Commerce, Bureau of the Census, *Estimates of the Population of the United States by Age, Sex and Race:* 1980-1986 (1987).

p. 5. **Persons arrested:** U.S. Department of Justice, Federal Bureau of Investigation, *Uniform Crime Reports: Crime in the United States* (hereinafter *FBI Uniform Crime Reports*) (1979-1988).

p. 5. **1988 arrests:** *FBI Uniform Crime Reports* (1988).

p. 6. **Homicide rate for younger juveniles:** *FBI Uniform Crime Reports* (1979-1988).

p. 6. **All reported arrests:** *FBI Uniform Crime Reports* (1979- 1988).

p. 6. **Gender differences:** *FBI Uniform Crime Reports* (1979-1988).

p. 7. **Girls' victims:** Rowley, Ewing & Singer, "Juvenile Homicide: The Need for an Interdisciplinary Approach." 5 *Behavioral Sciences & the Law* 1 (1987).

p. 7. **Black and Hispanic population:** U.S. Department of Commerce. Bureau of the Census, *Estimates of the* *population of the United States by Age, Sex and Race:* 1980-1986 (1987).

p. 7. **Black and Hispanic homicide arrests:** *FBI Uniform Crime Reports* (1979-1988).

p. 8. **Characteristics of kids who kill:** Numerous studies have been published since 1943 dealing with the various characteristics of juveniles who kill. Among the studies referred to at various points in this book are the following: Patterson, "Psychiatric Study of Juveniles Involved in Homicide," 13 *Am. J. Orthopsychiatry* 125 (1943); Bender, "Children and Adolescents Who Have Killed," 116 *Am. J. Psychiatry* 303 (1957); Marten, "Adolescent Murderers," 58 *Southern Medical J.* 1217 (1965); Smith, "The Adolescent Murderer: A Psychodynamic Interpretation," 13 *Archives of General Psychiatry* 310 (1965); Hellsten & Katila, "Murder and Other Homicide by Children Under 15 in Finland," 39 *Psychiatric Quarterly* 54 (1965); Scherl & Mack, "A Study of Adolescent Matricide," 5 *J. Am. Academy of Child Psychiatry* 559 (1966); Malmquist, "Premonitory Signs of Homicidal Juvenile Aggression," 128 *Am. J. Psychiatry* 461 (1971); Walsh-Brennan, "Psychopathology of Homicidal Children," 94 Royal Society of Health 274 (1974); Sendi & Blomgren, "A Comparative Study of Predictive Criteria in the Predisposition of Homicidal Adolescents," 132 *Am. J. Psychiatry* 423 (1975); Tanay, "Reactive Parricide," 21 *J. Forensic Sciences* 76 (1976); Sorrells, "Kids Who Kill," 23 *Crime & Delinquency* 312 (1977); Rosner, Wiederlight, Rosner & Wieczorek, "Adolescents Accused of Murder and Manslaughter: A Five Year Descriptive Study," 4 *Bull. Am. Acad. of Psychiatry & Law* 3342 (1978); Russell, "Ingredients of Juvenile Murder," 23 *Int'l. J. of Offender Therapy* 65 (1979); Petti & Davidman, "Homicidal School-Age Children: Cognitive Style and Demographic Features," 12 *Child Psychiatry & Human Development* 82 (1981); Russell,

"Girls Who Kill," 30 *Int'l. J. of Offender Therapy* 171 (1986); Cornell, Benedek & Benedek, "Characteristics of Adolescents Charged with Homicide: Review of 72 Cases," 5 *Behavioral Sciences & the Law* 11 (1987); Cornell, "Causes of Juvenile Homicide," in E. Benedek & D. Cornell (Eds.), *Juvenile Homicide* 3 (1989); C. Ewing, *When Children Kill: The Dynamics of Juvenile Homicide* (Lexington Books, Lexington, Ma.: 1990).

p. 8. **"The behavior [may have been] psychotic":** King, "The Ego and the Integration of Violence in Homicidal Youth," 45 *Am. J. Orthopsychiatry* 134, 135 (1975).

p. 8. **"Personality disorder" Defined:** American Psychiatric Association, *Diagnostic and Statistical Manual of Mental Disorders,* 3rd Ed., Revised (1987).

p. 8. **"Lewis study:** Lewis, Pincus, Bard, Richardson, Prichep, Feldman & Yeager, "Neuropsychiatric, Psychoeducational, and Family Characteristics of 14 Juveniles Condemned to Death in the United States, 145 *Am. J. Psychiatry* 584, 587(1988).

p. 10. **"Triad":** Justice, Justice & Kraft, "Early Warning Signs of Violence: Is a Triad Enough?" 131 *Am. J. Psychiatry* 457 (1974).

p. 11. **Michaels' article:** Michaels, "Enuresis in Murderous Aggressive Children and Adolescents," 5 *Archives of General Psychiatry* 94 (1961).

p. 11. **Cornell study:** Cornell, Benedek & Benedek, "Characteristics of Adolescents Charged with Homicide: Review of 72 Cases," 5 *Behavioral Sciences & the Law* 11, 18-19 (1987).

p. 11. **1984 data:** Rowley, Ewing & Singer, *supra.*

p. 11. **FBI victim-offender data:** Rowley & Ewing & Singer, *supra.*

p. 12. **New York City data:** Zimring, "Youth Homicide in New York: A Preliminary Analysis," 13 *Journal of Legal Studies* 81, 90-91 (1984).

p. 12. **New York state data:** New York State Division of Criminal Justice Services, Office of Justice Systems Analysis, *New York State Homicide* 1987 (1988).

p. 13. **"Obscure motivation":** Stearns, "Murder by Adolescents With Obscure Motivation," 114 *Am. J. Psychiatry* 303-305 (1957).

p. 13. **FBI data:** Rowley, Ewing & Singer, *supra*.

p. 13. **New York City arrest data:** Zimring, *supra*.

Chapter 2

pp. 15-16. **Richard and Deborah Jahnke:** "Jury Gets Case of Boy 16, Who Killed Father," *New York Times*, February 19, 1983 at 41 ("always chickened out"); "Death of Father Freed Family" UPI a.m. cycle, February 28, 1983; Janos, "On a Windswept Wyoming Prairie an Abused Son Kills a Father to Bring Peace to a Family," *Time,* March 7, 1983 at 34; "Jahnke Conviction Upheld," *Denver Post,* December 13, 1984 at 1A and 28A; Myers, "Deborah Jahnke is Set Free," *Denver Post,* December 18, 1984 at 1A; G. Morris, *The Kids Next Door* 148 (1985).

p. 16. **Jory Kidwell:** "Kidwell," UPI b.c. cycle, May 9, 1984: "Kidwell," UPI a.m. cycle, May 16, 1984; "Kidwell," UPI a.m. cycle, May 17, 1984 ("I know he won't beat me . . ."); "Kidwell," UPI b.c. cycle, June 21, 1984.

pp. 16-17. **Robert Moody:** Galante, "Judge Mulls Proper Sentence for Killer of "Scum"; Public is Asked to Provide Suggestions," *National Law Journal*, February 13, 1984 at 9 ("scum of the earth"); "Judge in Patricide

Case Flooded with Sentencing Propositions," UPI a.m. cycle, February 24, 1984 ("I thought God wanted me to do it."); "Judge Asks Public Help in Sentencing," UPI, a.m. cycle, January 28, 1984; "Charges Reduced Against Youth Who Killed Abusive Father," UPI, a.m. cycle, January 24, 1984 ("He'll only come back and kill us").

pp. 17-18. **Cheryl Pierson:** Kleiman, *A Deadly Silence: The Ordeal of Cheryl Pierson* (1988); "Cheryl Pierson Weds Accomplice," *New York Times,* October 10, 1988 at B-4; "Teen Serves Term for Father's Death," *Washington Post,* January 20, 1988 at A-7; "Brutal Treatment, Vicious Deeds: Cheryl Pierson is only one of America's Troubled Parent Killers," *Time,* October 19, 1987 at 68; Holzberg, "A Tale of Suburbia: Bowling, Little League and Sex Abuse," *National Law Journal,* October 5, 1987 at 6; Kleiman, "Girl Says Hiring Father's Killer Seemed "Like A Game" at First," *New York Times,* September 15, 1987 at B1-B2; "Youth Sentenced in Killing Classmate's Abusive Father," UPI p.m. cycle, April 29, 1987 ("cold blooded murderer").

p. 18. **"Best available data":** Rowley, Ewing & Singer, "Juvenile Homicide: The Need for an Interdisciplinary Approach," 5 *Behavioral Sciences & the Law* 1 (1987).

p. 18. **Estimated Incidence of Parricide:** Timmick, "Fatal Means for Children to End Abuse: Parricide Cases Evoke Conflict in Sympathy, Need for Punishment," *Los Angeles Times,* August 31, 1986, Part 2 at 1.

p. 18. **Annual FBI data:** *FBI Uniform Crime Reports* (1988).

p. 19. **Dr. Tanay:** Tanay, "Reactive Parricide," 21 *J. Forensic Sciences* 76 (1976).

p. 19. **Attorney Mones:** Mones, "The Relationship Between Child Abuse and Parricide: An Overview," in E.

Newberger & R. Bourne (Eds.), *Unhappy Families* 31, 36 (1985).

p. 20. **Dr. Sargent:** Sargent, "Children Who Kill—A Family Conspiracy?" 7 *Social Work* 35 (1962).

p. 20. **Dr. Malmquist:** Malmquist, "Premonitory Signs of Homicidal Juvenile Aggression," 128 *Am. J. Psychiatry* 461, 464 (1971).

p. 21. **Mrs. Jahnke:** "Death of Father Freed Family," UPI a.m. cycle, February 28, 1983.

p. 20. **Eric Witte:** "Court Upholds Conviction of Witte in Slaying of Husband," UPI, b.c. cycle, December 9, 1987.

p. 20. **James Brown:** Testimony of Dr. Charles Patrick Ewing, *People v. Barnwell,* Brown and Small (suppression hearing), Erie County (New York) Court, September 4, 1986.

p. 21. **Mary Bailey:** "Wyers," UPI, a.m. cycle, June 23, 1988; "West Virginia News in Brief," UPI, a.m. cycle, June 17, 1988; "Girlshoot," UPI, b.c.cycle, June 26, 1988 ("I told her yes . . .")

p. 22. **Los Angeles boy:** Rainey, "Police Say Boy 15 Just Snapped, Killed Stepfather," *Los Angeles Times,* July 19, 1988, Part 2 at 3.

pp. 22-23. **Torran Lee Meier:** Klunder, "Youth Who Killed His Mother is Sent to CYA," *Los Angeles Times,* December 20, 1986, part 2 at 6; Klunder, "Meier's Brain Isn't Damaged, 2 Doctors Testify," *Los Angeles Times*, May 22, 1986, part 2 at 8; Quinn, "A Death in the Family," *Los Angeles Times,* May 22, 1986, part 2 at 8; Quinn, "A Death in the Family," *Los Angeles Times,* May 18, 1986, part 2 at 10 ("faggot" and "not man enough"); Quinn, "Boy on Trial in Death of Mother has Brain Damage, Doctor Says," *Los Angeles Times,* May 9, 1986, part 2 at 6; Harris,

"Momslay," UPI, a.m. cycle, December 19, 1985 ("a living hell").

pp. 23-24. **Alonzo Williams:** Walsh, "Williams Gets 20 Years to Life," *Rockland Journal-News,* March 16, 1989 at 1; Ferron, "Rockland Jury Hears Evidence in Murder Trial," *New York Times*, January 14, 1989 at 28, col. 6; Walsh, "Attorney Says Teen Accused in Mother's Slaying was Mentally, Sexually Abused by Her," *Rockland Journal-News,* June 15, 1988 at A1, A8.

pp. 24-25. **William Shrubsall:** Basey & Thompson, "Honor Student Charged with Slaying Mother: Police Believe Argument Led to Fatal Beating," *Buffalo News,* June 26, 1988 at A1, A14; Anzalone, " "Legend" Label for Teen Killer Outrages Neighbors," *Buffalo News,* June 26, 1989 at A1, A4; Andriatch, "Psychologist: Teen Showed Grief," *Niagara Gazette,* June 7, 1989 at 1A: Kurilovitch & Burch, "Shrubsall Pleads Guilty," *Niagara Gazette,* June 7, 1989 at 1A, 2A.

p. 25. **Dr. Wertham:** Wertham, *Dark Legend: A Study in Murder* (1941).

pp. 25-26. **Drs. Scherl and Mack:** Scherl & Mack, "A Study of Adolescent Matricide," 5 *J. Am. Academy of Child Psychiatry* 569 (1966).

p. 26. **Wesley Underwood:** "Mother," UPI, a.m. cycle, December 19, 1986 ("loner" and "spoiled . . ."); "More Teens Attacking Parents," UPI, b.c. cycle, September 11, 1986.

p. 26-27. **Colorado boy:** "All We Want is Something to Do." UPI, a.m. cycle, April 22, 1986.

p. 27. **"Bob":** Benedek & Cornell, "Clinical Presentations of Homicidal Adolescents," in E. Benedek & D. Cornell (Eds.), *Juvenile Homicide* 39, 47 (1989).

p. 27. **Crack matricides:** Hamill, "A Crime That Defies Understanding," *Newsday,* February 1, 1989 at 18.

pp. 27-28. **David Brom: "Teen gets Life for Killing 4 in his Family,"** *Chicago Tribune,* October 17, 1989 at C-17; "Jury Spurns Insanity Defense in Ax Killings of 4 in Family," *New York Times,* October 16, 1989 at A-14 ("depressed, psychotic and suffering from evolving multiple personalities"); "Axemurders," UPI, b.c. cycle, October 16, 1989; 'Axemurders,' UPI, b.c. cycle, October 15, 1989; 'Axemurders," UPI, b.c. cycle, October 12, 1989; "Axemurders," UPI, b.c. cycle, October 10, 1989; 'Axemurder," UPI, b.c. cycle, October 2, 1989; "Classmates Testify in Brom Ax Murder Trial," UPI, b.c. cycle, October 11, 1989 ("they won't be around to oppose it").

p. 28. **Ginger Turnmire:** "Teen Girl Sentenced to Life in Parents' Murder," UPI, p.m. cycle, January 30, 1987; "Tennessee News in Brief," UPI, b.c. cycle, January 28, 1987 ("Charles Manson-type person"); "Teen Indicted in Slayings of Parents," UPI, b.c. cycle, September 17, 1986 ("chewed and winked"); "Teenager will be Tried as Adult for Parents' Deaths," UPI, a.m. cycle, September 12, 1986 ("All efforts . . . have failed . . .").

p. 29. **John Justice:** "Justice Sentenced in Slayings," UPI, a.m. cycle, February 20, 1987; Warner, "Jury Agonized Over Justice's State of Mind," *Buffalo News,* November 16, 1986 at 1, A11; "Jury Finds Teen-Ager Guilty of '85 Murder of his Mother," *New York Times,* November 1, 1986 at 14; Warner, "Justice Family Portrait a Troubled One," *Buffalo News,* September 22, 1985 at 1 ("Check 308 Mang . . .").

pp. 29-30. **Sean Stevenson:** "Inmates," UPI, b.c. cycle, May 23, 1988; "Stevenson," UPI, b.c. cycle, May 13, 1987 ("extremely high degree of emotional impairment" and "was and is severely mentally disturbed"); "16-Year Old Faces Death Penalty in Washington State," *Reuters,* a.m. cycle, May 9, 1987; McFarland, "Stevenson Faces

Death Sentence in Triple-Murders," UPI, a.m. cycle, May 9, 1987; "Stevenson Confessions Recalled," UPI, b.c. cycle, April 28, 1987 ("I think I just shot my family . . ."); "Teenager to Stand Trial as Adult for Family Killings," UPI, b.c. cycle, February 4, 1987.

pp. 30-31. **Patrick DeGelleke:** Knudson, "Expert Testifies Youth Killed Parents Because of "Adopted Child Syndrome," *New York Times,* February 18, 1986 at B2 ("erupt into violent, uncontrollable temper tantrums" and "threw Patrick into . . ."); "Boy 15 Convicted of Murder in Deaths of Adoptive Parents," *New York Times,* February 20, 1986 at B-5; "Boy 15 Convicted of Murder in Deaths of Adoptive Parents," *New York Times,* February 20, 1986 at B-5; "Jury Deliberates in Murder Trial of Teen," UPI, a.m. cycle, February 18, 1986 ("straightforward case . . .").

pp. 31-32. **Jose Hernandez:** "Teen Convicted of Killing Family Gets Life Imprisonment," UPI, b.c. cycle, June 6, 1989; "Warrant Issued for Son in Slayings," UPI, p.m. cycle, March 23, 1988.

p. 32. **Brian Britton:** "200 Mourn Three "Rambo" Shooting Victims," *Buffalo News,* March 26, 1989 at A15; "Teen Held in Killings," *Newsday,* March 23, 1989 at 16; "Teen Charged in Killings of Parents, Brother," *Buffalo News,"* March 23, 1989 at A9; Foderaro, "Parents and a Brother Slain by Self-Styled "Rambo", 16" *New York Times,* March 23, 1989.

p. 32. **Colorado girl:** "Exorcise," UPI, b.c. cycle, April 29, 1987.

pp. 32-33. **Michael Smalley:** "West Virginia News in Brief," UPI, a.m. cycle, April 1, 1988; "West Virginia News in Brief," UPI, a.m. cycle, January 25, 1988; "West Virginia News in Brief," UPI, a.m. cycle, October 2, 1987; "Ohio News in Brief," UPI, a.m. cycle, September 29, 1987.

p. 33. **Chicago youth:** O'Connor, "Brother in Slaying Faces Test," *Chicago Tribune,* January 26, 1989 at C-6; "Sixteen Year Old Charged in Brother's Death," *Chicago Tribune,* February 9, 1989 at 3.

Chapter 3

p. 34. **Clinton Bankston:** "Executions Restricted," *Washington Post,* April 22, 1988 at A-10; "Supreme Court Asked to Rule on Death Penalty," UPI, b.c. cycle, April 8, 1988 ("gave the appearance"); "Georgia News Briefs," UPI, b.c. cycle, May 13, 1988; "Bankston Waives Right to Jury Trial," UPI, b.c. cycle, May 12, 1988; "Judge to Decide if Juvenile will be Tried as an Adult," UPI, a.m. cycle, August 18, 1987.

p. 35. **Milton Jones and Theodore Simmons:** "Two Get 50 Year Terms in Murders of Priests in Buffalo Rectories," *New York Times,* November 3, 1988 at B6; "Youths Charged in Killings Had Similar Backgrounds," AP, p.m. cycle, March 11, 1987; "Teenagers held in Deaths of Two Priests in Buffalo," *Los Angeles Times,* March 9, 1987, Part 1 at 2.

pp. 35-36. **Matthew Schrom and Anthony Holtorff:** "Holtorff," UPI, b.c. cycle, May 1, 1989; "Pennies," UPI, b.c. cycle, March 22, 1989; "Schrom," UPI b.c. cycle, April 6, 1988 ("would never have done anything like that on his own" and "everything"); Wilkinson, "Small Town in Disbelief Over Elderly Man's Slaying for Jar of Pennies," AP, a.m. cycle. January 20, 1988 ("in constant trouble").

p. 36. **Robert Demeritt and Jayson Moore:** Testimony of Dr. Charles Patrick Ewing at sentencing hearing, *State v. Demeritt* (New Hampshire, April 14, 1989); Hohler, "Judge Rejects Agreement on Slaying," *Boston Globe,* March 14, 1989 at 17 ("deprived and dark backgrounds" and "dysfunctional families"); "Youths

Charged in Slaying of Elderly N.H. Woman," UPI, b.c. cycle, February 10, 1988.

p. 37. **Austin Addison:** "Youth Gets Maximum Sentence for Slaying over Leather Coat, AP, a.m. cycle, January 16, 1987.

p. 37. **Homicides in the course of robbery:** *FBI Uniform Crime Reports* (1984-1988).

p. 37. **Juvenile homicides in the course of robbery:** Rowley, Ewing & Singer, "Juvenile Homicide: The Need for an Interdisciplinary Approach," 5 *Behavioral Sciences & the Law 3* (1987).

p. 37. **Robberies, burglaries and homicides:** *FBI Uniform Crime Reports* (1984-1988).

p. 38. **James McClure:** "Fourteen Year Old Pleads Guilty to Killing Elderly Neighbor," *Los Angeles Times,* June 25, 1986, part 2 at 2; Schacter, "Potential for Violence Cited: Stiffest Term Possible for Fourteen Year Old Killer," *Los Angeles Times,* August 5, 1986, part 2 at 2.

p. 38. **"Donald":** Benedek & Cornell, "Clinical Presentations of Homicidal Adolescents," in E. Benedek & D. Cornell (Eds.), *Juvenile Homicide* 50 (1989).

p. 38. **Brian Houchin, Joseph Hallock, and Larry Allen:** Shnay, "Three Convicted of Killing Hammond Bank Teller," *Chicago Tribune,* April 19, 1989 at C-1.

p. 39. **14-year-old robs and kills cab driver:** Hellsten & Katila, "Murder and Other Homicide by Children Under 15 in Finland," 39 *Psychiatric Quarterly* 54 (1965).

p. 39. **"Anthony":** *In the Matter of Anthony M,* 63 N.Y. 270, 471 N.E.2d 447, 481N.Y.S.2d 675 (1984).

pp. 39-40. **Terry Losicco and David Hollis:** Evans, "Court in Told Slain Editor was Sexually Assaulted," *New*

York Times, July 16, 1980 at B-2; Putnam, "Youths Sentenced to Life in Death of Editor," AP, p.m. cycle, June 19, 1981.

p. 40. **New Jersey boys:** "Juveniles," UPI, a.m. cycle, January 30, 1987.

pp. 40-41. **Paul Magill:** *Magill v. Dugger,* 824 F.2d 879 (11th Cir. 1987).

p. 41. **Ralph Deer, Jr.:** "Convicted Teen to be Sentenced in Two Weeks in Burgler Slaying," UPI, a.m. cycle, February 6, 1987; "Louisiana News Briefs," UPI, a.m. cycle, February 5, 1987; "Louisiana News Briefs," UPI, a.m. cycle, July 1, 1986.

p. 41. **"During the course of another crime, such as robbery or rape":** Cornell, Benedek & Benedek, "Characteristics of Adolescents Charged with Homicide: Review of 72 Cases," 5 *Behavioral Sciences & the Law* 11 (1987).

pp. 41-42. **Heath Wilkins:** *Stanford v. Kentucky* and *Wilkins v. Missouri,* 57 *U.S. Law Week* 4973 (1989)("both tripping on LSD" and "He is vulnerable . . .");Rosenbaum, "Too Young to Die?" *New York Times Magazine,* March 23, 2989 at 33-35, 58-61.

pp. 42-43. "Teenagers in Front Lines of Dallas Drug Wars," UPI, b.c. cycle, March 27, 1988.

p. 43. **Eugene Turley:** "Youth gets Life in Va. Slaying," *Washington Post,* September 16, 1989 at B-5; "Virginia News Briefs," UPI, b.c. cycle, August 2, 1989; Brown, "Teen Guilty in Va. Murder over a $75 Cocaine Debt," *Washington Post,* August 1, 1989 at B-1.

p. 43. **Michael Boettlin and John Calvaresi:** "Behead," UPI, b.c. cycle, August 16, 1988 ("lots of money and a nice stereo" and "mistakenly tagged along . . ."); "Judge Beheading Trial Jury may be Sequestered," UPI, b.c. cycle, August 2, 1988 ("redrum"); "Second Suspect Sought in Decapitation Slaying," UPI, p.m. cycle, July 30, 1987.

pp. 43-44. **John Morris and Alton Smith:** "State-West," UPI, a.m. cycle, October 27, 1987; "State-West," UPI, a.m. cycle, March 27, 1987; "Sentenced," UPI, a.m. cycle, February 4, 1986; "Five Youths Held in $500 Robbery of Neighbors: Slaying of Trusting Old Couple a Puzzle," *Los Angeles Times* (AP), March 10, 1985, part 1 at 31; "Five," UPI, a.m. cycle, January 25, 1985.

p. 44. **David Hollis ("The only crime was his failure . . ."):** Berlage, "Teenagers get Life for Editor's Murder," UPI, a.m. cycle, June 19, 1981.

pp. 45-46. **Sean Pica:** Kleiman, *A Deadly Silence: The Ordeal of Cheryl Pierson* (1988)(quotes from psychologists and psythiatrists); Holzberg, "A Tale of Suburbia: Bowling, Little League and Sex Abuse," *National Law Journal,* October 5, 1987 at 6; Kleiman, "Girl Says Hiring Father's Killer Seemed "Like A Game" at First," *New York Times,* September 15, 1987 at B1-B2; "Youth Sentenced in Killing Classmate's Abusive Father," UPI p.m. cycle, April 29, 1987 ("cold blooded murderer").

pp. 46-47. **Robert Pearce:** Gorman, "Escondido Teen Admits Guilt in Pearce Killing," *Los Angeles Times,* October 31, 1989 at B-2; "Second Youth Sentenced in Slaying," *Los Angeles Times,* June 9, 1989 part 2 at 5; Bailey, "Teacher Aide to STand Trial in Killing of Husband," *Los Angeles Times,* May 9, 1989, part 2 at 1; Bailey, "Pair say Teacher's Aide Induced Them: 2 Teens Plead Guilty to Contract Murder," *Los Angeles Times,* April 22, 1989, part 2 at 1; Bailey, "Did Divorce Case Turn into Class on Murder? Arrest of Teacher's Aide, 2 Teens, Shocks Quiet Community," *Los Angeles Times,* April 3, 1989, part 2 at 1.

Chapter 4

pp. 48-49. **Jay Kelly Pinkerton:** Schlagenstein, "Two-Time Murderer Executed," UPI, a.m. cycle, May 15, 1986; "Pinkerton," UPI, b.c. cycle, July 12, 1985; *Pinkerton v. State,* 660 S.W.2d. 58(Tex. Crim. App. 1983)("cut open her abdomen . . ." and "He cut her stomach . . ."); "Pinkerton Sentencing Begins Today," UPI, b.c. cycle, May 13, 1982.

pp. 49-50. **Louis Hamlin and Jamie Savage:** Clarke, "Hamlin," UPI, a.m. cycle, May 11, 1982 ("We were walking along and . . ." and "Now you're going to know . . ."); Clarke, "Hamlin," UPI, a.m. cycle, May 12, 1982 ("some girls" and "only to rape them, tie them up and flee"); Clarke, "Rape Victim Relives Crime," UPI, p.m. cycle, May 12, 1982; Clarke, "Hamlin," UPI, a.m. cycle, May 13, 1982; "Memories of a Murder Lingering in Vermont," *New York Times,* July 19, 1982 at A11.

p. 50. **Marko Bey:** "Man Convicted Again for Murder in 1983," *New York Times,* October 19, 1989 at B-9; *State v. Bey,* 548 A. 2d. 846, 112 N.J. 45 (1988)("I got my nut and . . ."); "Jersey Man Held in Slayings of Two Asbury Park Women," *New York Times,* May 9, 1983 at B-8.

p. 51. **Shawn Milne:** "Teen Convicted of Sex Slaying," UPI, b.c. cycle, June 29, 1987; "Jury Deliberations in Sex Slaying to Continue," UPI, a.m. cycle, June 26, 1987; "Teenager Accused of Rape, Murder to be Tried as Juvenile," UPI, a.m. cycle, January 7, 1986 ("voices commanded him to do things").

p. 51. **Matthew Rosenberg:** Hart, "A Relentless Quest to Keep a Killer Jailed," *Boston Globe,* November 15, 1989 at 32; "Kid Killer to Stay Behind Bars," UPI,

b.c. cycle, September 15, 1989; McNeilly, "Deliberations Begin on Freeing Child-Killer," *Boston Globe*,
September 15, 1989 at 23; "Teen Killer will Remain
in Custody," UPI, p.m. cycle, July 3, 1987.

p. 51. **Robert Ressler et. al.:** R. Ressler, A. Burgess &
J. Douglas, *Sexual Homicide* (1987).

p. 52. **Dr. Stearns:** Stearns, "Murder by Adolescents With
Obscure Motivation," 114 *Am. J. Psychiatry* 303
(1957).

p. 53. **1987 juvenile rape and sex crimes:** *FBI Uniform
Crime Report* (1988).

p. 54. **"Steve":** Woods, "Adolescent Violence and Homicide: Ego Disruption and the 6 and 14 Dysrhythmia,"
5 *Archives of General Psychiatry* 528, 529 (1961).

pp. 54-55. **Curtis Cooper:** Barker, "Fifteen Year Old
Chages Plea to Guilty to Strangling Girl, 7, in
Sex Attack," *Los Angeles Times*, November 3, 1989,
part B at 1 ("kid with real problems"); Connelly &
Kazmin, "Slain Newhall Girl's Father Kills Himself at
her Grave," *Los Angeles Times*, July 12, 1989, Metro at
2; Lozano, "Fourteen Year Old Charged with Murder of
Girl," *Los Angeles Times*, March 29, 1989.

p. 55. **"Charlie":** Benedek & Cornell, "Clinical Presentations of Homicidal Adolescents," in E. Benedek &
D. Cornell (Eds.), *Juvenile Homicide* 50 (1989).

pp. 55-56. **"Tom":** Woods, *supra*.

p. 56. **Missouri boy:** "Youth Charged With Murder," UPI,
b.c. cycle, February 26, 1987.

p. 56. **Illinois boy:** "Thirteen Year Old Found Guilty in
Infant's Death," UPI, p.m. cycle, October 29, 1986.

p. 56. **New Mexico boy:** Cassidy & Burks, "Teen-Age Boy
is Charged in Death of 5-Year-Old," *Alburquerque*

Journal, January 6, 1987; Burks, "Teenager to Remain in Custody," *Alburquerque Journal,* January 7, 1987.

p. 56. **Donald Shedrick (Ohio boy):** "Shedrick Gets Life Prison Sentence," UPI, b.c. cycle. July 6, 1989; "Teenager Found Guilty in Motel Murder," UPI, b.c. cycle, July 2, 1989.

p. 57. **Wayne, Billy, and Frankie:** R. Kramer, *At a Tender Age,* 11-20 (1988).

pp. 57-58. **Marcellus Bradford, Omar Saunders, Larry Ollins, and Calvin Ollins:** "Roscetti Attacker Sentenced," UPI, b.c. cycle, September 20, 1988; "Roscetti," UPI, b.c. cycle, July 11, 1988; "Third Suspect Convicted in Roscetti Murder," UPI, b.c. cycle, June 21, 1988; "Slain Student Pleaded for Mercy," UPI, b.c. cycle, June 14, 1988; "Killer of Medical Student Gets Life Term," UPI, p.m. cycle, March 11, 1988 ("evil person," "strange being," "Note that I avoid . . ." and "a betial, barbaric . . ."); "Roscetti," UPI, b.c. cycle, February 11, 1987.

p. 58. **"Willie":** La. Briefs," UPI, a.m. cycle, August 18, 1987; "La.Briefs," UPI. a.m. cycle, March 10, 1987; "Prosecutor to Seek Death Penalty," UPI, a.m. cycle, March 7, 1987.

pp. 59-60. **Clint Dickens and Richard Cooey:** *State v. Cooey,* 46 Ohio St. 20 (1989); Reall, "Dickens gets Life Term for Coed Murders," UPI, a.m. cycle, January 6, 1987; Reall, "Cooey Sentenced to Death for Coed Slayings," UPI, a.m. cycle, December 5, 1986; Reall, "Judge Allows Dickens' Statement in Rape-Slayings Trial," UPI, a.m. cycle, November 24, 1986; "Police Arrest Teenagers in Killing on Expressway," AP, p.m. cycle, September 4, 1986.

pp. 60-61. **David Buchanan:** *Buchanan v. Kentucky,* 107 S. Ct. 2906 (1987).

Chapter 5

pp. 62-63. **Michael and Dennis Ryan:** *State v. Ryan,* 409 N.W.2d 579 (Nebraska 1987)("he thought it was kind of neat . . ." and "strongly and uncritically"); Robbins, "Murder Trial Starts for Survivalist and Son, Both Accused of Torture," *New York Times,* March 11, 1986 at A18.

pp. 63-64. **Rod Matthews:** Murphy, "Thrill Killer, 15, Sentenced to Life Prison Term," *Buffalo News,* March 11, 1988 at 8; "Medicine Made Teenager Kill, His Lawyer Says," *Buffalo News,* March 9, 1988 at 9 ("he wanted to know what it was like to kill somebody"); "Bat Slaying Trial Nearing a Close," UPI, b.c. cycle, March 8, 1988.

p. 64. **Kenneth Kovzelove and Dennis Bencivenga:** McDonnell, "Youth to be Tried as Adult in Killings of Two Migrant Workers," Los Angeles Times, April 28, 1989, part 2 at 1; "Two Reputedly Hunted Targets for Slaying," *Los Angeles Times,* March 31, 1989, part 2 at 3; McDonnell, "Companion Called Triggerman: One Accused of Killing Migrants Denies Guilts," *Los Angeles Times,* March 28, 1989, part 2 at 1.

p. 65. **Steven Lofton and Chris White:** Scott, "Oklahoma News of the Week," UPI, b.c. cycle, May 15, 1987; "Oklahoma News Briefs," UPI, September 12, 1986.

p. 66. **Carolyn Shelton:** Steinberg, "The Year in Review," *Los Angeles Times,* January 1, 1988, part 2 at 8; Puig, "Fourteen Year Old is Sentenced to CYA Term in Sniper Slaying," *Los Angeles Times,* September 9, 1987, part 2 at 6; Kaplan, "Fourteen Year Old Snipers Convicted of Murder," *Los Angeles Times,* July 9, 1987, part 2 at 8; Feuntes, "Mother of Suspected Sniper Kept Guns for Own Safety," *Los Angeles Times,* April 5, 1987 ("I'm a single parent, and this is a bad neighborhood").

p. 67. **Jimmy Iriel and Robert McIlvain:** "Parents Forgive Teenager Convicted of Toddler's Death," AP, p.m. cycle, January 22, 1987.

pp. 67-68. **"Stephen":** *People v. Stephen D. Roe,* 1989 N.Y. LEXIS 666.

p. 68. **Howard Beach incident:** Lin & Hurtado, "Admission in Howard Beach Case: In Appeal, Lawyers Concede a Racial Motive in Attack," *Newsday,* April 11, 1989 at 7 ("racially motivated"); Goldman, "Youth Apologizes, Gets Shortest Term in Racial Death," *Los Angeles Times,* February 12, 1988, part 1 at 4 ("your senseless loss"); McFadden, "A Judge Dismisses Charge of Murder in Queens Attack," *New York Times,* December 30, 1986 at A-1 ("There's some niggers in the pizza parlor—let's go kill them"); McFadden, "Three Youths are Held on Murder Counts in Queens Attack," *New York Times,* December 23, 1986 at A-1 ("Niggers, you don't belong here").

p. 69. **"Dotbusters":** James, "Youths Convicted of Assault in Death of an Indian Man," *New York Times,* April 1, 1989 at 30; Walt, "A New Racism Gets Violent in New Jersey," *Newsday,* April 6, 1988, part II at 4.

p. 69. **Timothy Cargle:** "Karate," UPI, a.m. cycle, December 16, 1987 ("rid the park of bums" and "totally a straight-out attack"); Fuentes, "Boy Gets 18 Years in Fata Park Beating of Transient," *Los Angeles Times,* December 24, 1987, Part 2 at 9, col. 3 Bater, "Police Arrest Teens in Vagrant Beating Death," UPI, a.m. cycle, May 28, 1986.

p. 70. **Massachusetts:** "Two Men Indicted in Lowell Killing," *Boston Globe,* September 30, 1988 at 18; Barnicle,

"To Hang Out—or to Kill," *Boston Globe,* September 22, 1988 at 23.

p. 70. **Florida:** Bater, "Police Arrest Teens in Vagrant Beating Death," UPI, a.m. cycle, May 26, 1986.

pp. 70-71. **Albany, Georgia:** "Two Albany Teenagers Charged in Slaying of Gay Man," UPI, a.m. cycle, September 11, 1987.

p. 71. **Louis Conner:** "Conner," UPI, b.c. cycle, January 21, 1987; "Boy Sentenced to Therapy for Killing Sex Abuser," UPI, b.c. cycle, July 7, 1986; "Sexshoot," UPI, b.c. cycle, April 23, 1986 ("No, Louis"); "Conner," UPI, b.c. cycle, March 20, 1986.

pp. 71-72. **Alvin Goode and William Owens:** "Goode," UPI, a.m. cycle, September 11, 1987 ("Alvin Goode raped him"); "Goode," UPI, a.m. cycle, September 10, 1987.

p. 72. **George Smoot:** "Gaybias," UPI, b.c. cycle, April 28, 1988; Lindsey, "After Trial, Homosexuals Say Justice is Not Blind," *New York Times,* March 21, 1988 at A17; "The State," *Los Angeles Times,* February 26, 1988, part 1 at 2; "Hazing," UPI, b.c. cycle, February 24, 1988; "Hazing Victim Accused of Killing Gay," UPI, a.m. cycle, February 3, 1988.

p. 73. **Dr. Howard Appledorf:** McCall, "The Fateful Odyssey of Three Teenage Runaways May Take Them to Florida's Death Row for Murder," *People,* January 10, 1983 at 67; "Three Arraigned in New York in Ritualistic Florida Slaying," *New York Times,* September 9, 1982 at B8.

p. 74 **Robert Rosenkrantz:** Klunder, "'86 Homicides Reflect Domestic Turmoil," *Los Angeles Times,* January 4, 1987, part 2 at 4; Klein, "Homosexual Gets Prison Term for Killing Youth who Told," *Los Angeles Times,* July 8, 1986, part 2 at 1; "Teenager gets 17 Years to Life Sentence," UPI, a.m. cycle, July 8, 1986.

p. 74. **Detroit crack dealer:** "Boy says He Killed Drug Dealer for Humiliating his Mom," UPI, b.c. cycle, June 9, 1989.

pp. 74-75. **Nichole Eisel and Marsha Urevich:** Goldstein, "Girls in Suicide Pact Test Drug-Free," *Washington Post,* November 29, 1988 at B-3; Schneider, "Family and Friends Mourn Kensington Teenager," *Washington Post,* November 13, 1988 at B-5; Duggan and Goldstein, "In Md., the Shocking Consequences of Two Teens' Pain," *Washington Post,* November 11, 1988 at A-1; Duggan, "Two Teenage Girls Found Shot to Death in Md.," *Washington Post,* November 10, 1988 at A-1.

pp. 75-76. **Christina Ittermann:** Purdum, "Apparent Pact Leads to Death of 18 Year Old," *New York Times,* April 30, 1986 at B-3, Pessin, "Sweethearts," UPI, a.m. cycle, April 29, 1986.

p. 76. **Daniel Yarbrough and Holly Dvorak:** Lucadamo, "Two Teenagers Found Shot to Death," *Chicago Tribune,* November 28, 1988 at C-8; "Teen Shoots Girlfriend, Kills Self," UPI, b.c. cycle, November 28, 1988.

p. 76. **Steven Porell** Alexander, "N.H. Youth Shot Two Dead, Killed Self, Police Say," *Boston Globe,* June 18, 1989 at 37.

Chapter 6

pp. 77-78. **Jim Hardy, Pete Roland, and Ron Clements:** Jones, "Human Sacrifice: "Fun" Killers Now Paying Devil's Dues," *Los Angeles Times,* October 20, 1988, part 1 at 1; Jones, "Satanists' Trail: Dead Pets to Human Sacrifice," *Los Angeles Times,* October 19, 1988, part 1 at 1 ("Why me, you guys?" and "Because it's fun"); Bryson, "Teenager Convicted in Beating Death of Classmate," AP, a.m. cycle, May 5, 1988;

"Murder and Suicide Among Teens Caught Up in Dark World of Satanism," AP, b.c. cycle, Feburary 14, 1988.

pp. 78-79. **Sean Sellers:** Dawkins and Higgins, *Devil Child: A Terrifying True Story of Satanism and Murder* (1989) ("I fucked up . . ."); Green, "A Boy's Love of Satan Ends in Murder, A Death Sentence—and Grisly Memories," *People,* December 1, 1986 at 154; "Sellers," UPI, b.c. cycle, October 14, 1986; "Teen gets Death Penalty," UPI, b.c. cycle, October 2, 1986.

pp. 80-81. **Richard Kasso:** "Suspect in Satanic Cult Murder Found Hanged in Cell," *Reuters,* North American Service, p.m. cycle, July 7, 1984; Hornblower, "Youths' Deaths Tied to Satanic Rige," *Washington Post,* July 9, 1984 at A-1; "Grand Jury to Hear Testimony Beginning Today," AP. p.m. cycle, July 10, 1984.

pp. 81-82. **Scott McKee:** "Skinheads say They'll Organize after Verdicts," UPI, a.m. cycle, June 25, 1988 ("We're standing strong . . ."); "Skinhead," UPI a.m. cycle, June 17, 1988; "Father Discusses "Skinhead" Sons," UPI, b.c. cycle, March 6, 1988 ("change from happy children . . .")

p. 82. **Tim Erickson:** "Erickson," UPI, b.c. cycle, September 28, 1988 ("because of a cult we believed in"); "Youth Found Guilty in Grisly "Vampire" Murder Case," *Reuters,* Library Report, a.m. cycle, September 24, 1988; "Jury Finds Head of Vampire Cult Committed First Degree Murder," UPI, b.c. cycle, September 24, 1988 ("cut his wrist and drink his blood").

pp. 82-83. **Joseph Bradsberry:** "Cult," UPI, b.c. cycle, January 19, 1989; "Cult Slaying Victim Pleaded with Killers, Court Records Show," UPI, b.c. cycle, December 15, 1988.

p. 83. **Lloyd Gamble:** "Shotgun Slaying of Teen Linked to Satanic Worship," *Reuters,"* North European

Service, a.m. cycle, February 21, 1986 ("acting out a satanic sacrifice"); Kahane, *Cults Thats Kill* 183-195 (1988) ("a hood, along black robe . . ." and "step-by-step instructions . . ." and "into Satanism" and "I think this kid crossed over . . .").

p. 84. **George Geider:** "Youth who Stabbed Three gets Probation," *Chicago Tribune,* May 5, 1989 at C-3 ("very close to fatal" and "What concerns me"); Crawford and Sjostrom, "Elmhurst Teen Charged in Stabbings," *Chicago Tribune,* December 9, 1988 at 1-C ("good boy" and "superficial attempt").

p. 85. **"Bob":** Benedek & Cornell, "Clinical Presentations of Homicidal Adolescents," in E. Benedek & D. Cornell (Eds.), *Juvenile Homicide* 39, 47 (1989).

p. 85. **Thomas Sullivan, Jr.:** "Murder and Suicide Among Teens Caught Up in Dark World of Satanism," AP, b.c. cycle, February 14, 1988.

p. 85. **Marsha Urevich and Nicole Eisel:** Goldstein, "Girls in Suicide Pact Test Drug-Free," *Washington Post,* November 29, 1988 at B-3; Schnieder, "Family and Friends Mourn Kensington Teenager," *Washington Post,* November 13, 1988 at B-5; Duggan and Goldstein, "In Md., the Shocking Consequences of Two Teens' Pain," *Washington Post,* November 11, 1988 at A-1; Duggan, "Two Teenage Girls Found Shot to Death in Md.," *Washington Post,* November 10, 1988 at A-1.

p. 86. **David Ventiquattro:** "Sixteen Year Old Sentenced for Murder of His Playmate," *New York Times,* December 5, 1986 at 30; "Sixteen Year Old is Convicted in Fantasy-Game Slaying of Boy, 11," *New York Times,* November 23, 1986 at 47 ("wanted to kill Martin, but not in real life").

p. 86. **National Coalition on Television Violence (NC-TV) and Bothered About Dungeons and Dragons**

("BADD"): "FTC Asked to Require Warnings Before TV Show: Dungeons & Dragons," *Broadcasting*, January 28, 1985 at 88.

p. 87. **Dr. Thomas Radecki:** Maharaj, "Defense Based on Game Hasn't Won Many Juries," *Newsday*, June 16, 1988 at 27.

p. 87. **Ronald Lampasi:** Hicks, "Lampasi gets 25 Years Plus for Shootings," *Los Angeles Times*, October 18, 1985, part 2 at 1 "a result of Lampasi' acting out a game of Dungeons and Dragons"); Hicks "Lampasi Convicted of Shooting Parents," *Los Angeles Times*, June 7, 1985; part 2 at 1; Hicks, "Attorneys Clash in Closing Arguments of Lampasi Murder Trial," *Los Angeles Times*, June 1, 1985, part 2 at 9; Hicks, "Role-Playing may have Played Role in Slaying, DA Says," *Los Angeles Times*, May 9, 1985, part 2 at 1.

p. 88. **Cayce Moore:** "Judge Gives Moore Life Sentence," UPI, a.m. cycle, October 7, 1987; "Jury Recommends Life Sentence for Moore," UPI, September 5, 1987; Rawls, "Youth in Capital Murder Trial Hospitalized for Drug Overdose," AP, a.m. cycle, August 17, 1987 ("bright, popular, all American youths").

p. 88. **Sean Seller:** Dawkins and Higgin, *Devil Child: A Terrifying True Story of Satanism and Murder* (1989).

Chapter 7

pp. 89-91. **Shirley Wolf and Cindy Collier:** Hanauer, "From Bad Girls to Big Cats," UPI, b.c. cycle, August 30, 1989; "Wolf," UPI, b.c. cycle, January 26, 1988; "Girls," UPI, a.m. cycle, October 12, 1983 ("thoroughly comfortable"); "Girls," UPI, a.m. cycle, September 23, 1983 ("We killed an old lady today. It was fun."); "Girls," UPI, a.m. cycle, September 21, 1983; "Murder," UPI, a.m. cycle, July 30, 1983 ("Perfect car . . ."); McCall, "A Grandmother is Murdered, Two Teenage Girls are Convicted—There the Questions Begin," *People*, August 29, 1983 at 63 ("just for fun" and "wanted to do another one" and "the same childhood . . . rotten . . . since I was born").

pp. 91-92. **Anthony Broussard:** Sujo, "Film Shows Anatomy of a Blank Generation," *Reuters*, b.c. cycle, May 31, 1987; "Coast Youth Who Boasted of Killing Girl is Sentenced," *New York Times*, December 5, 1982 at 26 ("as if nothing touched him"); "California Youth Pleads Guilty to Death He Boasted About," *New York Times*, July 21, 1982 at A-12; King, "Jailing Dropped for Reporter in Murder," *New York Times*, April 4, 1982 at 25 ("I raped and murdered this chick").

pp. 92-93. **Leslie Torres:** Clifford, "Five Killings: 60 Years for Addict," *Newsday, April 15, 1989 ("showed utter and total disregard" and "would kill again"); Sullivan, "Addict Guilty in Crack Rampage Killing"* New York Times, February 28, 1989 at B3 ("cocaine-inspired rampage" and "cocaine induced psychosis").

pp. 93-94. **Daniel LaPlante:** Langner, "LaPlante Convicted, gets Life in 3 Killings," *Boston Globe*, October 26, 1988 at Metro-1 ("disorderly and dirty" and "hard core" . . ." and "no parole" and "receive the same sentence . . ."); Wyman, "For a Small Town, the Killings and Trial were Shocking Ordeal," *Boston Globe,* October 26, 1988 at 44; "LaPlante Attorney asks Jury to Consider Insanity," UPI, b.c. cycle, October 19, 1988 ("Whoever was involved in this is totally crazy"); "LaPlante Trial to Begin Monday," UPI, October 10, 1988 ("always a little scary"); Murphy, "Police Capture Youth Accused of Killing Three," AP, p.m. cycle, December 4, 1987.

pp. 94-95. **Patrick DeGelleke:** Knudson, "Expert Testifies Youth Killed Parents Because of "Adopted Child Syndrome," " *New York Times*, February 18, 1986 at B-2; "Boy 15 Convicted of Murder in Deaths of

Adoptive Parents," *New York Times,* February 18, 1986 ("lost touch with reality . . .").

p. 95.   **John Justice:** "Justice Sentenced in Slayings," UPI, a.m. cycle, February 20, 1987.

p. 95.   **"Delusions, hallucinations . . .":** Cornell, "Causes of Juvenile Homicide: A Review of the Literature," in Benedek & Cornell (Eds.), *Juvenile Homicde* 1, 15, (1989).

p. 96.   **"Alan":**   Benedek & Cornell, "Clinical Presentations of Homicidal Adolescents," in E. Benedek & D. Cornell (Eds.). *Juvenile Homicide* 39, 45 (1989).

p. 96.   **Joseph Aulisio:** *Commonwealth v. Aulisio,* 522 A.2d 1075 (Pennsylvania 1987); Robbins, "Death Sentence for Pennsylvania Boy Reflects Country's Mood, Judge Says," *New York Times,* June 14, 1982 at D-10 ("he feels lonely . . ."); "Pennsylvania Teenager is Given Death Sentence," *New York Times,* May 29, 1982 at 6 ("It's party time").

pp. 96-97.   **Torran Lee Meier:** Klunder, "Youth Who Killed His Mother is Sent to CYA," *Los Angeles Times,* December 20, 1986, part 2 at 6; Klunder, "Meier's Brain Isn't Damaged, 2 Doctors Testify," *Los Angeles Times,* May 22, 1986, part 2 at 8; Quinn, "A Death in the Family," *Los Angeles Times,* May 18, 1986, part 2 at 10; Quinn, "Boy on Trial in Death of Mother has Brain Damage, Doctor Says," *Los Angeles Times,* May 9, 1986, part 2 at 6; Harris, "Momslay," UPI, a.m. cycle, December 19, 1985.

p. 97.   **Brenda Spencer:** "Teenager," *Reuters,* a.m. cycle, August 17, 1979 ("I don't like Mondays, Mondays always get me down."); "Spencer," *Reuters,* a.m. cycle, April 4, 1980 ("a quiet tomboy . . ."); Granberry, "Victims of San Diego School Shooting are Forced to Cope Again 10 Years Later," *Los Angeles Times,* January 19, 1989, part 2 at 1, col. 1.

pp. 97-99. **Robert Ward:** "Oklahoma News Briefs," UPI, b.c. cycle, October 14, 1986; "Babysitter," UPI, b.c. cycle, August 8, 1986; "Babysitter," UPI, b.c. cycle, July 21, 1986; "Oklahoma News Briefs," UPI, b.c. cycle, July 2, 1986; "Oklahoma News Briefs," UPI, b.c. cycle, March 29, 1986; "Okla-briefs," UPI, b.c. cycle. March 27, 1986; "Teenage Babysitter Guns Down Toddlers, Police Say," *Reuters*, a.m. cycle, February 16, 1986; "Babysitter," *Reuters*, a.m. cycle, February 16, 1986.

pp. 97-99. **Nicholas Elliott:** Miller, "Elliott not Eligible for Parole for 15 Years," UPI, b.c. cycle, December 13, 1989 ("pressure cooker" and "exploded"); "teen Sentenced to Life in Prison in Virginia Beach Teacher Killing," *Washington Times* AP, December 13, 1989 at B-4; Miller, "Elliott Sentenced for Shootings," UPI, b.c. cycle, December 12, 1989 ("time bomb . . ." and "if that gun hadn't jammed . . ." and "cold blooded"); "Sixteen Year Old Pleads Guilty in School Shooting Rampage," *Chicago Tribune*, November 1, 1989 at M-4; "Teacher Killed by Student in Virginia," *Chicago Tribune*, December 17, 1988 at C-4; "Boy Kills Teacher; Subdued after Gun Jams," *Los Angeles Times* (UPI), December 17, 1988, part 1 at 22.

Chapter 8

p. 101. **Ramon Rios, Jr.:** Reiner, "Slain Over a Baseball Cap," *New York Times*, May 18, 1989 at A-31.

p. 101. **DeAndre Brown:** Quintana, "Teen Gang Member Arrested in Fatal Shooting of Boy in Park, *Los Angeles Times*, June 26, 1987, part 2 at 1.

p. 102. **Stephanie Beasley:** "Girl, 16, Killed in Gang Shooting," *Chicago Tribune*, April 16, 1989 at C-3.

p. 102. **Maria Gonzalez:** Crimmins, "Three Teenagers Arrested in Girl's Death," *Chicago Tribune*, May 4,

1989 at C-12; Blau, "Gang Automatic Weapon Fire Kills Girl, Wounds Three," *Chicago Tribune*," April 19, 1989 at C-6.

p. 102. **Bridgeport:** "Year-Guns-Killings," UPI, b.c. cycle, December 20, 1989; Fecteau, "Teenage Gunmen Arrested in Shootings," UPI, November 2, 1989 ("turf war" and "drug rip-off").

p. 103. **Los Angeles—600 gangs with 70,000 members and 387 gang-related killings:** Hearn, "Gang," *States News Service*, June 29, 1988; "House of Representatives Overwhelmingly Approves Juvenile Justice Bill," *PR Newswire*, June 1, 1988.

p. 103. **1988 gang homicides in Los Angeles:** Overend & Baker, "Total Murders Down Despite Record High in Gang Killings," *Los Angeles Times*, January 10, 1989, part 2 at 1.

p. 103. **1989 gang homicides in Los Angeles:** "Gunfire in L.A.: Life in the Streets," *USA Today*, December 7, 1989 at 6-A.

p. 103. **"Increased 50 percent in three years":** Overend & Baker, *supra*,

p. 103. **"One out of every three homicides in Los Angeles County is gang-related":** Reiner, *supra*.

p. 104. **City of Los Angeles—overall homicide rate 1988 and increase over 1987:** Overend & Baker, *supra*.

p. 104. **Heightened narcotics trade":** Braun & Feldman, "Killings Related to Street Gangs Hit Record in '87," *Los Angeles Times*, January 8, 1988, part 2 at 3.

p. 104. **"The main distributors of crack throughout the Western United States":** Reinhold, "In the Middle of L.A.'s Gang Wars," *New York Times Sunday Magazine*, May 22, 1988 at 30.

p. 104. **Number of Black and Hispanic Los Angeles gang members:** Baker, "Deeply Rooted in L.A.; Chicago Gangs: A History of Violence," *Los Angeles Times,* December 11, 1988, part 1 at 1.

p. 104. **Orange County gangs;** "Orange County Life: Our Gangs," *Los Angeles Times,* August 25, 1989, part 9 at 2.

p. 105. **Boston gang statistics:** Jacobs & Cullen, "Gang Rivalry on the Rise in Boston," *Boston Globe,* March 26, 1989 at Metro-1 ("youth gangs not only exist in Boston but are becoming larger and more violent").

p. 105. **Boston gangs:** Canellos, "Roxbury Activist Calls for Gang "Cease-Fire" " *Boston Globe,* December 19, 1988, at Metro-17 ("loosely organized" and "kids from one street . . .").

p. 105. **40 percent dropout rate—half a dozen major gangs:** Jacobs & Cullen, *supra* ("host of cliques . . .").

p. 105. **Chicago—12,000 youths belong to about 125 gangs:** Hearn, *supra.*

p. 105. **Chicago gang-killings commonplace:** Recktenwald & Blau, "Chicago Bucking National Trend in Big-City Slayings," *Chicago Tribune,* January 8, 1989 at C-1.

p. 105. **1988 Chicago murder rate and gang-related killings:** Recktenwald & Blau, *supra.*

p. 106. **Gang-related defined—Chicago vs. Los Angeles:** Overend, "New LAPD Tally May Cut Gang-Killing Score," *Los Angeles Times,* October 20, 1988.

p. 106. **Chicago suburbs:** Bosc, "Street Gangs No Longer Just a Big City Problem," *U.S. News & World Report,* July 16, 1984 at 108.

p. 106. **New York City—523 drug gang killings:** Raab, "Brutal Drug Gangs Wage War of Terror in Upper

Manhattan," *New York Times,* March 15, 1988 at B-1 ("demonstrate toughness").

p. 106. **New York City—"wolf packs" or "posses":** Pitt, "Wolf Packs or Posses, Gang Violence is Common," *New York Times,* May 9, 1989 at B01.

p. 107. **New York City—three incidents a day:** Ball, "Clockwork Orange Scourge Terrorises the Big Apple," *Sunday Telegraph Limited,* International at 13.

p. 107. **New York City—"wilding" since 1983:** Pitt, *supra.*

p. 107. **Detroit "teenage drug lord":** Horrock & Hundley, "Portrait of a Gun Culture: Schoolyard Killer's Arsenal is not Unique," *Chicago Tribune,* March 19, 1989 at C-1.

pp. 107-108. **New York City 14-year-old:** Raab, "Youths with Brutal Pasts, in a Prison "Without Cruelty," *New York Times,* June 3, 1989 at 29.

p. 108. **South Central Los Angeles:** Stewart, "Gang Member Gets 97 Years for Role in Gang Rape, Burning," *Los Angeles Times,* April 15, 1988, part 2 at 3; "Two Get Prison Terms for Raping, Burning Women," *Los Angles Times,* December 13, 1987, part 2 at 8; "Two Gang Members Convicted in Rape," *Los Angeles Times,* June 26, 1987, part 1 at 2; "Gang Rape Conviction," *Los Angeles Times,* March 25, 1988, part 2 at 2 ("We gotta kill her. She knows me.").

pp. 108-109. **Los Angeles, April 9, 1987:** Pristin, "Teen Gets 32 Years to Life for Murder of Church Elder," *Los Angeles Times,* July 2, 1988, part 2 at 3 ("turn to show that he too is a tough guy. He wanted to do a killing."); Beene, "Trial in Murder of Church Elder to Begin Monday," *Los Angeles Times,* May 21, 1989, part 2 at 1.

p. 109. **Santa Monica "payback":** "Teen Knifed in Gang "Pay- Back" Dies," *Los Angeles Times,* April 7, 1989, part 2 at 2.

pp. 109-110. **Ralph Hernandez:** Puig, "Violent Gang Loses Leaders, Identity," *Los Angeles Times,* December 5, 1987, part 2 at 10.

p. 110. **New York City Central Park gang-rape:** Weiss, "Grab Her," *New York Post,* April 23, 1989 at 5 ("Someone said, "grab her" . . ."); Wolff, "Youths Rape Jogger on Central Park Road," *New York Times,* April 21, 1989 at B-1.

p. 110. **"I know who did the murder":** Kaufman, "Park Suspects: Children of Discipline," *New York Times,* April 26, 1989 at A-1.

p. 110. **"We thought she was dead":** Pearl, Reyes & Phillips, "Rape Suspect: "It was fun"," *New York Post,* April 23, 1989 at 3.

p. 110. **"It was something to do . . ."** Pearl, Reyes & Phillips, *supra.*

p. 111. **New York City "wilders":** Kaufman, *supra* ("children of strict parents" and "good students").

p. 111. **Newark pizzeria:** "Manslaughter," UPI, b.c. cycle, May 2, 1986.

p. 111. **Spanish Harlem bakery:** Kurtz, "Suspect in $20 Theft in N.Y. is Beaten to Death by Crowd," *Washington Post,* March 22, 1988 at A-3.

p. 111. **California teenagers:** Awalt, "Teen Attacks on Parents Puzzle Authorities, "AP.p.m. cycle, January 23, 1989.

p. 112. **Chicago subway killing:** Blau & Fegelman, "Three Charged with Murder in CTA Platform Stabbing," *Chicago Tribune,* June 14, 1989 at C-1.

Chapter 9

p. 113. **Britt Kellum:** "Boy Charged with Killing Second Brother in Four Years," UPI, b.c. cycle, November 2, 1989.

pp. 113-114. **Miami Beach:** Shulins, "Kids Who Kill—I," AP, b.c. cycle, June 29, 1986.

p. 114. **New York City eight year old:** "Boy, 8, Faces Murder Count in Fire," *Buffalo News,* Septemberr 14, 1988 at A-14; "Eight Year Old Charged with Murder," *Newsday,* September 13, 1988 at 7.

p. 114. **New Mexico girl:** "12 Year Old Convicted of Second·Degree Murder," *Christian Science Monitor,*April 8, 1982 at 2.

pp. 114-115. **Detroit boy:** Ball, "Boy, 3, Kills Father Who Beat Mother," *Daily Telegraph,* October 6, 1988 at 3.

p. 115. **Los Angeles Girl:** Luther, "Testing Ordered for Girl who Killed Baby: Sentencing Awaits Sitter, 10, Convicted in Strangulation Case," *Los Angeles Times,* December 14, 1986, part 2 at 14.

p. 115. **Jessica Carr:** DePalma, "Ten Year Old Boy is Charged as Adult in Fatal Shooting of Seven Year Old Gril," *New York Times,* August 26, 1989 at 6; Blake, "Ten Year Old Pleads Innocent in Shooting," *Buffalo News,* August 27, 1989 at A-13.

p. 116. **Children under ten and children ten to twelve years old:** *FBI Uniform Crime Reports* (1985-1989).

p. 116. **Children under seven not responsible:** W. LaFave & A. Scott, *Criminal Law,* 398-400 (1986).

p. 117. **Heidi Gasparovich:** Sonner, "Court Upholds Gasparovich Conviction," UPI, a.m. cycle, April 15, 1987 ("correctly found that she participated . . ."); "Iowa Supreme Court Told Girl Didn't Help Kill Father,"

UPI, a.m. cycle, March 11, 1987; "Teens Sentenced for Killing Their Father," UPI, p.m. cycle, May 29, 1986; Brewer, "Judge Rules Boy, Sister Guilty of Killing Father," UPI, p.m. cycle, May 15, 1986; Brewer, "Juveniles Convicted in Father's Death," UPI, a.m. cycle, May 14, 1986 ("actively participated" and "lent countenance and approval"); Lavia, "Verdict Awaited in Juveniles' Murder Trial," UPI, a.m. cycle, May 6, 1986 ("Look at her face . . .").

p. 117. **Mary Bailey:** "Eleven Year Old Girl to Appear in Juvenile Court on Murder Charges," UPI, p.m. cycle, April 23, 1987.

p. 118. **Suburban Washington, D.C. boy:** Meyer, "In Wheaton, the Shock of a Family Tragedy," *Washington Post,* February 26, 1989 at D-1, D-11; "Mother Dead, Father Wounded; Boy Charged," *Chicago Tribune,* February 26, 1989 at C-26; Hagigh, "Boy, 12, Feared Parents Would Punish Him," *Montgomery Journal,* February 28, 1989 at A-1, A-4; "Twelve Year Old "Real Polite" Boy Guns Down Parents," *Reuters,* a.m. cycle, February 24, 1989.

pp. 118-119. **Arva Betts:** "12 Year Old gets Probation in Half-Brother's Death," UPI, b.c. cycle, October 17, 1989 ("There are three victims . . ."); "Babysitter Indicted in Slaying," *New York Times* (AP), April 7, 1989 at A-13.

p. 119. **Four-year-old New York City girl:** Shulins, *supra.*

p. 119. **Dr. Patterson:** Patterson, "Psychiatric Study of Juveniles Involved in Homicide," 14 *Am. J. Orthopsychiatry* 125 (1943).

p. 119. **Dr. Bender:** Bender, "Children and Adolescents Who Have Killed," 116 *Am. J. Psychiatry* 510, 511 (1959).

p. 120. **Dr. Tooley:** Tooley, "The Small Assassins," 14 *J. Am. Academy of Child Psychiatry* 306 (1975).

p. 120. **Drs. Easson and Steinhilber:** Easson & Steinhilber, "Murderous Aggression by Children and Adolescents," 4 *Archives of General Psychiatry* 27 (1961).

p. 120. **Drs. Petti and Davidman:** Petti & Davidman, "Homicidal School-Age Children: Cognitive Style and Demographic Features," 12 *Child Psychiatry & Human Development* 82 (1981).

p. 121. **James McClure:** Schacter, "Fourteen Year Old Pleads Guilty to Killing Elderly Neighbor," *Los Angeles Times,* June 25, 1986, part 2 at 2.; Schacter, "Potential for Violence Cited: Stiffest Term Possible for Fourteen Year Old Killer," *Los Angeles Times,* August 5, 1986, part 2 at 2.

p. 121. **Wisconsin girl:** "Kidsplay," UPI, a.m. cycle, September 11, 1987; "Kidsplay," UPI, a.m. cycle, September 3, 1987.

p. 121. **California youths:** "Six Teenagers Held in Sun Valley Slaying," *Los Angeles Times,* May 9, 1989, part 2 at 2.

p. 122. **Suzette Franklin:** "Four Year Olds are Suspected in Infant's Death," *Los Angeles Times* (AP), June 11, 1989, part 1 at 13; "Four Year Old Suspects," *Washington Post,* June 10, 1989 at A-8.

p. 122. **Ryan Merrihew:** "Girl Charged with Murdering Ten Year Old," UPI, a.m. cycle, March 26, 1986.

p. 122. **Columbia, South Carolina:** "Prosecutor Wants 12 Year Old Tried as Juvenile," UPI, a.m. cycle, August 29, 1987.

pp. 122-123. **Missouri brothers:** Tackett, "Boys, 4 and 6, Accused of Attacking a Baby," *Chicago Tribune,* January 31, 1989 at C-8.

pp. 123-124. **Dr. Adelson:** Adelson, "The Battering Child," 222 *J. Am. Medical Ass'n* 159, 160 (1972).

p. 124. **Twelve-year-old boy:** Palermo, " "Good Kids" Who Kill: Violent '80s to Blame?" *Los Angeles Times,* March 2, 1986, part 2 at 4.

p. 124. **Nathan Ferris:** "Teasing Victim, 12, Kills Classmate, Then Himself in Schoolroom, *Buffalo News,* March 3, 1987 at D-5.

p. 125. **Letter to the editor:** Ziraldo, "Children Who Kill," *Los Angeles Times,* March 15, 1986, part 2 ay 7, col. 1.

p. 125. **"Cowboys and Indians":** Russo, "Our Tough Gun Laws Are Not Enough," *New York Times,* April 17, 1988, section 12NJ at 32; "Tennessee News in Brief," UPI, b.c. cycle, July 8, 1986.

pp. 125-126. **South Carolina boys:** Rawls, "Investigation of Five Year Old in Fatal Shooting Stirs Controversy," *New York Times,* October 10, 1981 at 8.

p. 126. **Six year old boy:** "Boy, 6, Accidentally Kills Israeli Cabbie," *Los Angeles Times,* March 7, 1989, part 1 at 9("I was playing with the gun"); "Dad Charged in Gun Mishap; Cabbie Killed," *Chicago Tribune,* March 7, 1989 at M-5.

Chapter 10

p. 127. **Attina Marie Cannaday:** *Cannaday v. State,* 455 So.2d. 713 (Miss. 1984).

pp. 127-128. **Delphine Greene:** "Green," UPI, a.m. cycle, December 2, 1983; "Teenager Sentenced to 30 Years in Robbery-Slaying," UPI, a.m. cycle, April 16, 1984 ("The only thing cruel and unusual . . ."); Sampson, "Girl Convicted in $13 Robbery-Murder," UPI, March 15, 1984 ("Please don't hurt me. Please don't kill me.").

p. 128. **Patricia Cummings:** "Stab," UPI, a.m. cycle, September 20, 1983; "Plea," UPI, a.m. cycle, July 19, 1983; "Teen," UPI, a.m. cycle, January 7, 1983; "Party," *Reuters*, January 2, 1984; "Boy Slain at L.I. Party: Police Accuse Girl, 14," *New York Times* (AP), January 2, 1983 at 30.

pp. 129-130. **Janice Buttrum:** *Buttrum v. State*, 293 S.E.2d. 334 (Georgia 1982); "Buttrum," UPI, a.m. cycle, August 31, 1981 ("an injured child . . .").

p. 130. **Lorna Ortiz:** "Thirteen Year Old Witness in Salesman Slaying to Get Protective Custody," AP, p.m. cycle, December 18, 1980; "Salesman," UPI, a.m. cycle, December 17, 1980; "Hopfner," UPI, a.m. cycle, November 10, 1981; "Two Women Acquitted of Murder," AP, p.m. cycle, November 18, 1981; "Teens Sentenced," AP, a.m. cycle, December 21, 1981.

p. 130. **Females unlikely to kill:** *FBI Uniform Crime Reports* (1985-1989).

p. 130. **"Females were excluded . . .":** Rosner, Wiederlight, Rosner & Wieczorek, "Adolescents Accused of Murder and Manslaughter: A Five-Year Descriptive Study," 7 *Bull. Am. Academy of Psychiatry & Law* 342, 345 (1979).

p. 131. **Andrea Williams:** Hamill, "A Crime That Defies Understanding," *Newsday*, February 1, 1989 at 18.

p. 131. **Chicago mother:** "Teen Mom Won't be Tried as an Adult," *Chicago Tribune*, August 16, 1989 at C-3 ("previously clean record"); "Teen Charged in Son's Death," *Chicago Tribune*, June 12, 1989 at C-3.

p. 132. **Girls raely kill strangers:** Rowley, Ewing, & Singer, "Juvenile Homicide: The Need for an Interdisplinary Approach," 5 *Behavioral Sciences and the Law*, 3 (1987).

p. 132. **Vast majority of juveniles kill alone:** Rowley et. al., *supra*.

p. 132. **Dennis Coleman and Karin Aparo:** Yost, "Teen Begged Boyfriend to Kill Her Mother," UPI, a.m. cycle, November 13, 1987.

p. 133. **Wisconsin infanticide:** "Babystab," UPI, a.m. cycle, February 27, 1986.

p. 133. **New York infanticide:** O'Brien, "Teen Held in Death of Newborn Infant Tells Police of Fear," *Buffalo News*, July 12, 1988 at B-1.

pp. 133-134. **California infanticide:** Hicks, "Girl Who Killed Her Baby Gets Year in Juvenile Hall," *Los Angeles Times*, April 13, 1988, part 2 at 14; Reyes, "Release Denied for Girl, 16, Held in Death of Her Baby," *Los Angeles Times*, October 20, 1987, part 2 at 4.

p. 134. **Sandy Shaw:** "Shaw," UPI, a.m. cycle, February 14, 1987 ("You can't feel sorry for Sandy Shaw . . ."); *"Shaw,"* UPI, b.c. cycle, February 13, 1987 ("because he was bugging me").

p. 135. **Paula Cooper:** Cohen, "Teenage Murderer is One of 35 on Death Row who Killed as Children," AP, b.c. cycle, January 18, 1987.

p. 135. **"Most crime is not committed by human beings in general. It is committed by men."** Archer & Lloyd, *Sex and Gender* (1982).

p. 136. **Kristin Rice, Tamara Liggins, and Wayne Mialki:** "Teen," UPI, b.c. cycle, September 27, 1988; "Mialki," UPI, b.c. cycle, June 24, 1988; "Guilty," UPI, b.c. cycle, April 12, 1988; "Around

Western Pennsylvania," UPI, a.m. cycle, November 3, 1987.

p. 136. **Three Los Angeles females:** Renwick, "Police Find Increasing Number of Girls Involved in Gang Crime," *Los Angeles Times* September 22, 1988, part 2 at 3.

Chapter 11

pp. 138-139. **Willie Bosket:** Butterfield, "A Boy Who Killed Coldly is Now a "Prison Monster," " *New York Times,* March 22, 1989 at A-1 ("One of these days Willie is going to kill somebody" and "I shot people. That's all. I don't feel nothing."); Bauder, "New York's Most Notorious Prisoner Keeps System on Edge," *Buffalo News,* July 10, 1988 at H-8 ("for the experience" and "I'm a monster . . .").

p. 139. **1978—Governor Carey and the Juvenile Offender Law:** Singer & Ewing, "Juvenile Justice Reform in New York: The Juvenile Offender Law," 8 *Law & Policy* 463, 468(1986).

p. 141. **Pennsylvania case:** DePalma, "Ten Year Old Boy is Charged as Adult in Fatal Shooting of Seven Year Old Girl," *New York Times,* August 26, 1989 at 6.

pp. 141-142. **Morris Kent:** *Kent v. United States,* 383 U.S. 541 (1966).

p. 145. **Dr. Eigen:** Eigen, "Punishing Youth Homicide Offenders in Philadelphia," 72 *J. Criminal Law & Criminology* 1072 (1981).

p. 145. **U.S. Justice Department study:** H. Synder, T. Finnegan, E. Nimick, M. Sickmund, D. Sullivan & N. Tierney, *Juvenile Court Statistics 1985* 84 (1989).

p. 146. **Dr. Cornell and colleagues:** Cornell, Staresina & Benedek, "Legal Outcomes of Juveniles Charged with Homicide," in E. Benedek & D. Cornell (Eds.), *Juvenile Homicide* 165 (1989).

pp. 146-147. **Robert Demeritt:** Testimony of Dr. Charles Patrick Ewing at sentencing hearing, *State v. Demeritt* (New Hampshire, April 14, 1989); Hohler, "Judge Rejects Agreement on Slaying," *Boston Globe,* March 14, 1989 at 17; "Youths Charged in Slaying of Elderly N.H. Woman," UPI, b.c. cycle, February 10, 1988.

pp. 147-151. **Rickey Dale Mathis:** *State ex. rel. Juvenile Department v. Mathis,* 527 P. 2d 148 (Or.Ap. 1975).

Chapter 12

pp. 152-153. **Ronald Ward:** Siegel, "Death Penalty Debate: How to Treat Youngsters who Murder," *Los Angeles Times,* November 3, 1985, part 1 at 1.

pp. 153-154. **Kevin Hughes:** *Comm. v. Hughes,* 555 A.2d 1264 (Pa. 1989); "Jury Deliberates Life of Death Sentence for Teen who Killed 9-Year- Old," UPI, a.m. cycle, March 24, 1981 ("the most gruesome . . .").

p. 154. **Frederick Lynn and Garrett Strong:** *Ex Parte Frederick Lynn,* 543 So.2d 709 (Ala. Crim. App. 1988)("That ain't nothin'" and "as loud as it would go"); "Death," UPI, a.m. cycle, October 23, 1984.

p. 155. **Charles Rumbaugh:** Roberts & Goodman, "Punishing Youth Murderers," *New York Times,* September 15, 1985, section 4 at 6; "Teenage Killers," *Washington Post,* September 13, 1985 at A-24; Reinhold, "Execution for Juveniles: New Focus on Old Issue," *New York Times,* September 10, 1985 at A-14; Schlangenstein, "Execute," UPI, a.m. cycle, September 10, 1985.

pp. 155-156. **James Terry Roach:** Stengel, "Young Crime, Old Punishment: An Execution Raises the Issue of the Death Penalty for Juveniles," *Time*, January 20, 1986 at 22; "South Carolina Executes Killer; Age Stirs Protest," *New York Times*, January 10, 1986 at 6 ("looking for a girl to rape").

p. 156. **Jay Kelly Pinkerton:** Schlangenstein, "Two-Time Murderer Executed," UPI, a.m. cycle, Mary 15, 1986; "Pinkerton," UPI, b.c. cycle, July 12, 1985; *Pinkerton v. State*, 660 S.W.2d. 58 (Tex. Crim. App. 1983); "Pinkerton Sentencing Begins Today," UPI, b.c. cycle, May 13, 1982.

p. 156. **Amnesty International:** Brief for Amnesty International as *Amicus Curiae, Thompson v. Oklahoma* (1988).

pp. 156-157. **Juveniles executed in the United States:** *Stanford v. Kentucky*, 57 U.S. Law Week 4973, 3976 (1989); NAACP Legal Defense and Educational Fund, Inc., *Death Row U.S.A.* (March 1, 1989); Streib, "Imposing the Death Penalty on Children," in K. Haas & J. Inciardi (Eds.), *Challenging Capital Punishment: Legal and Social Science Approaces* 245, 251 (1988).

p. 158. *Eddings v. Oklahoma*, 455 U.S. 104(1982).

pp. 158-159. *Thompson v. Oklahoma*, 487 U.S. 104 (1988).

pp. 159-161. *Stanford v. Kentucky* and *Wilkins v. Missouri*, 57 U.S. Law Week 4973 (1989).

Chapter 13

p. 163. **Heath Wilkins:** *Wilkins v. Missouri*, 57 U.S. Law Week 4973 (1989); Rosenbaum, "Too Young to Die?" *New York Times Magazine*, March 12, 1989 at 32.

p. 163. **Shirley Wolf and Cindy Collier:** Hanauer, "From Bad Girls to Big Cats," UPI, b.c. cycle, August 30, 1989; "Wolf," UPI, b.c. cycle, January 26, 1988;

"Girls," UPI, a.m. cycle, October 12, 1983; "Girls," UPI, a.m. cycle, September 23, 1983; "Girls," UPI a.m. cycle, September 21, 1983; "Murder," UPI, a.m. cycle, July 30, 1983; McCall, "A Grandmother is Murdered, Two Teenage Girls are Convicted–There the Questions Begin," *People*, August 29, 1983 at 63.

p. 163. **Richard and Deborah Jahnke:** "Jury Gets Case of Boy, 16, Who Killed Father," *New York Times*, February 19, 1983 at 41; "Death of Father Freed Family," UPI a.m. cycle, February 28, 1983; Janos, "On a Windswept Wyoming Prairie an Abused Son Kills a Father to Bring Peace to a Family," *Time*, March 7, 1983 at 34; "Jahnke Conviction Upheld," *Denver Post*, December 13, 1984 at 1A and 28A; Myers, "Deborah Jahnke is Set Free," *Denver Post*, December 18, 1984 at 1A; G. Morris, *The Kids Next Door* 148 (1985).

p. 163. **Robert Moody:** Galante, "Judge Mulls Proper Sentence for Killer of "Scum"; Public is Asked to Provide Suggestions," *National Law Journal*, February 14, 1984 at 9 ("scum of the earth"); "Judge in Patricide Case Flooded with Sentencing Propositions," UPI a.m. cycle, February 24, 1984; "Judge Asks Public Help in Sentencing," UPI, a.m. cycle, January 28, 1984.

p. 164. **AAPC Child Abuse Survey:** American Association for Protecting Children, *Highlights of Official Aggregate Child Neglect and Abuse Reporting* (1987).

p. 164. **U.S. Senate Judiciary Committee (May 1989):** Moody, "Infant," *States News Service*, May 16, 1989.

p. 164. **Child abuse fatalities:** Karwath, "Child Abuse Deaths Highest in Seven Years," *Chicago Tribune*, November 30, 1988 at C-1; Statement of the National Committee for Prevention of Child Abuse, Washington D.C., March 31, 1989; McCune, "Abuse," *States News Service*, March 31, 1989.

p. 165. **Epidemic of child abuse:** Shapiro & Shapiro, "The Epidemic of Child Abuse Turns Deadly: Parents Who Kill Their Kids" *U.S. News & World Reports,* April 11, 1988 at 35; McGraw, "Lawmaker Proposes Tougher Child Abuse Laws," UPI, b.c. cycle, February 14, 1988; "Children," UPI, b.c. cycle, September 29, 1984 (quoting Rep. Jim McNulty regarding Congress' plans for legislation dealing with "an epidemic of child abuse offenses").

pp. 165-166. **Ronald Ward: Siegel, "Death Penalty Debate: How to Treat Youngsters who Murder,"** *Los Angeles Times,* November 3, 1985, part 1 at 1.

p. 166. **Hispanic girl:** Hicks, "girl Who Killed Her Baby Gets Year in Juvenile Hall," *Los Angeles Times,* April 13, 1988, part 2 at 14.; Reyes, "Release Denied for Girl, 16, Held in Death of Her Baby," *Los Angeles Times,* October 20, 1987, part 2 at 4.

p. 166. **Milton Jones and Theodore Simmons:** "Two Get 50 Year Terms in Murders of Priests in Buffalo Rectories," *New York Times,* November 3, 1988 at B6; "Youths Charged in Killings Had Similar Backgrounds," AP, p.m. cycle, March 11, 1987; "Teenagers Held in Deaths of Two Priests in Buffalo," *Los Angeles Times,* March 9, 1987, part 1 at 2.

p. 166. **Poverty and crime:** J. Wilson & R. Herrnstein, *Crime and Human Nature* 472-476 (1985).

pp. 166-167. **Poverty statistics:** Cocco, "Trying to Mend "Safety Net," " *Newsday,* January 20, 1989 at 7A; U.S. Bureau of Census, *Statistical Abstract of the United States* (1987).

p. 167. **Leslie Torres:** Clifford, "Five Killings: 60 Years for Addict," *Newsday,* April 15, 1989; Sullivan, "Addict Guilty in Crack Rampage Killing," *New York Times,* February 28, 1989 at B3 ("cocaine-induced psychosis").

p. 167. **Ralph Deer, Jr.:** "Convicted Teen to be Sentenced in Two Weeks in Bugler Slaying," UPI, a.m. cycle, February 6, 1987.

p. 167. **John Charles Smith:** "Teenagers in Front Lines of Dallas Drug Wars," UPI, b.c. cycle, March 27, 1988.

p. 167. **Eugene Turley:** "Youth gets Life in Va. Slaying," *Washington Post,* September 16, 1989 at B-5; "Virginia News Briefs," UPI, b.c. cycle, August 2, 1989; Brown, "Teen Guilty in Va. Murder over a $75 Cocaine Debt," *Washington Post,* August 1, 1989 at B-1.

p. 168. **New York City data:** Kerr, "Young Crack Addicts Find There's No Help for Them," *New York Times,* May 2, 1988 at B-1; Guttenplan, "Kids Called Losers in NY War on Drugs," *Newsday,* June 16, 1989 at 29.

p. 168. **Two-thirds of all juvenile killings:** Cornell, Benedek & Benedek, "A Typology of Juvenile Homicide Offenders," in E. Benedek & D. Cornell (Eds.). *Juvenile Homicide,* 61, 73 (1989).

pp. 168-169. **Federal government estimates and surveys:** "Test of President's Speech on National Drug Control Strategy," *New York Times,* September 6, 1989 at B-6.

p. 169. **Dr. Bennett:** Statement of Dr. William Bennett, Director, National Drug Control Policy, July 31, 1989, Humphrey Auditorium, Department of Health and Human Services, Washington, D.C.

p. 169. **Dr. Godwin:** Statement of Dr. Frederick Godwin, Administrator, Alcohol, Drug Abuse and Mental Health Administration, July 31, 1989, Humphrey Auditorium, Department of Health and Human Services, Washington, D.C.

p. 169. **Multi-million dollar industry:** Baker & Cohn, "Crack Wars in D.C.," *Newsweek,* Feruary 22, 1988 at 24; "Two New York Teens Arrested in Murder," UPI, b.c. cycle, August 2, 1988; "Teenagers in Front Lines of Dallas Drug Wars," UPI, b.c. cycle, March 27, 1988.

p. 170. **Parental drug abuse and child abuse:** "Drug Abuse and Child Abuse," *Boston Globe,* June 10, 1989.

p. 170. **Cocaine babies:** Besharov, "Let's Give Crack Babies a Way Out of Addict Families," *Newsday* (Ideas), September 3, 1989 at 4.

p. 170. **Single mother:** Fuentes, "Mother of Suspected Sniper Kept Guns for Own Safety," *Los Angeles Times,* April 5, 1987.

p. 171. **Chicago Uzi submachine gun:** Crimmins, "Three Teenagers Arrested in Girl's Death," *Chicago Tribune,* May 4, 1989 at C-12; Blau, "Gang Automatic Weapon Fire Kills Girl, Wounds Three," *Chicago Tribune,* April 18, 1989 at C-6.

p. 171. **Pennsylvania boy:** DePalma, "Ten Year Old Boy is Charged as Adult in Fatal Shooting of Seven Year Old Girl," *New York Times,* August 26, 1989 at 6.

p. 171. **Missouri boy:** "Teasing Victim, 12 Kills Classmate, Then Himself in Schoolroom," *Buffalo News,* March 3, 1987 at D-5.

p. 171. **Connecticut turf war:** "Year-Guns-Killings," UPI, b.c. cycle, December 20, 1989; Fecteau, "Teenage Gunmen Arrested in Shootings," UPI, November 2, 1989.

p. 171. **"Cowboys and Indians":** Russo, "Our Tough Gun Laws Are Not Enough," *New York Times,* April 17, 1988, section 12NJ at 32; "Tennessee News in Brief," UPI, b.c. cycle, July 8, 1986.

p. 172. **Guns in the U.S.:** Golden, "The Arming of America," *Boston Globe* (Sunday Magazine), April 23, 1989 at 16; "Guns," *U.S. News & World Report,* May 8, 1989 at 20.

p. 172. **Harris Poll:** "guns," *U.S. News & World Report,* May 8, 1989 at 20.

p. 172. **Gallup Poll:** Golden, *supra.*

p. 173. **Guns in the schools:** Efron & Sands, "Children's Access to Guns Worries Authorities," *Los Angeles Times,* December 20, 1989, part A at 27; Center to Prevent Handgun Violence, *Facts About Kids and Handguns* (1989); Fulham, "Youths who Carry Guns are Afraid, Panel Finds," *Boston Globe,* October 5, 1988 at 37 ("believe carrying weapons is the only way they can protect themselves"); Perlez, "New York Schools Consider the Use of Metal Detectors," *New York Times,* May 4, 1988 at B-1, col. 4: Malkin, "Florida Schools Screen for Guns," UPI, b.c. cycle, March 7, 1988.

p. 174. **Accidental shootings:** Schmalz, "Children Shooting Children: The Move is on for Gun Control," *New York Times,* June 18, 1989 at 20; Center to Prevent Handgun Violence, *Facts About Kids and Handguns* (1989).

p. 174. **Florida, Connecticut, and Virgina:** Hatch, "Panel is Set to Consider Curbs on Guns," *New York Times,* September 10, 1989, Section 12CN at 1; Miller, "Stallings to Introduce New Gun Legislation," UPI, b.c. cycle, July 31, 1989; Moline, "Governor Signs Bill," UPI b.c. cycle, July 12, 1989; Bearak, "Careless Firearm Storage Could Mean Jail: Five Child Shootings in Week Spur Gun Safety in Florida" *Los Angeles Times,* June 16, 1989, part 1 at 1.

p. 174. **National Rifle Association:** Secter, "Dick and Jane Find a Gun: Critics Quick to Take Aim" *Los Angeles*

Times, December 17, 1988, part 1 at 30, col. 1; Scott, "NRA Book Touts Safety," *Newsday*, February 10, 1989 at 7.

p. 175. **1989 statistics:** *FBI Uniform Crime Reports* (1989).

p. 176. **Resurgence of the juvenile population:** U.S. Bureau of Census, *Statistical Abstract of the United States* (1987).

Index

About the Author

CHARLES PATRICK EWING, a clinical and forensic psychologist and attorney, is Professor of Law and Clinical Associate Professor of Psychology at the State University of New York at Buffalo. After receiving a Ph.D. from Cornell University, he was a postdoctoral fellow at Yale University and received a J.D. from Harvard University. Dr. Ewing is the author of *Crisis Intervention as Psychotherapy* (Oxford University Press, 1978) and *Battered Women Who Kill: Psychological Self-Defense as Legal Justification* (Lexington Books, 1987) and editor of *Psychology, Psychiatry and the Law: A Clinical and Forensic Handbook* (Professional Resource Exchange, 1985). He is also the author or co-author of numerous articles and chapters dealing with psychology and law, psychotherapy, professional ethics, and violent behavior, and serves as co-editor of the journal *Behavioral Sciences and the Law*. A Diplomate in Forensic Psychology (American Board of Professional Psychology), Dr. Ewing has examined many homicide defendants and testified as an expert in numerous murder trials.

Compelling True Crime Thrillers
From Avon Books

BADGE OF BETRAYAL
by Joe Cantlupe and Lisa Petrillo

76009-6/$4.99 US/$5.99 Can

THE BLUEGRASS CONSPIRACY
by Sally Denton   71441-8/$4.95 US/$5.95 Can

A KILLING IN THE FAMILY:
A TRUE STORY OF
LOVE, LIES AND MURDER
by Stephen Singular with Tim and Danielle Hill

76413-X/$4.95 US/$5.95 Can

LOSS OF INNOCENCE:
A TRUE STORY OF JUVENILE MURDER
by Eric J. Adams   75987-X/$4.95 US/$5.95 Can

RUBOUTS: MOB MURDERS IN AMERICA
by Richard Monaco and Lionel Bascom

75938-1/$4.50 US/$5.50 Can